The Body of Knowledge Unique to the Profession of Education

PI LAMBDA THETA is a national honor and professional association for women in education.

Its purposes are to:

RECOGNIZE women of superior scholastic achievement and high potential for professional leadership;

FOSTER creativity and academic excellence at all educational levels;

SUPPORT, EXTEND, and INTERPRET the function of education in a democracy;

DEMONSTRATE the power of competence in the body of knowledge unique to the profession;

STIMULATE, CONDUCT, and UTILIZE research;

ACCEPT RESPONSIBILITY for evaluation and improvement of the profession of teaching;

CONTRIBUTE to the solution of educational, social, and cultural problems of national and international concern;

PROMOTE professional fellowship and co-operation as a means to positive action.

THE BODY OF KNOWLEDGE UNIQUE TO THE PROFESSION OF EDUCATION

A Report of the First Pi Lambda Theta Catena

PI LAMBDA THETA, WASHINGTON, D.C.

COPYRIGHT © 1966 BY PI LAMBDA THETA

No portion of this book is to be reproduced in any way without written permission from the publisher

Library of Congress Card No. 66-21938

Foreword

THIS BOOK is the culmination of an idea which was first expressed in the spring of 1963. It grew out of the concern of the National Board of Pi Lambda Theta for the professional status of education and for the role that a professional association like Pi Lambda Theta should play.

The idea, simply stated, was that there were matters of concern to the profession of education as a whole which merited objective study and discussion by professionally competent people and that the support of such a project was an appropriate undertaking for an association like Pi Lambda Theta.

In August 1963 the Twenty-third Biennial Council of Pi Lambda Theta approved the expenditure of organization funds for what was to be known as the Catena. The Catena was devoted to the studied consideration of the topic "The Body of Knowledge Unique to the Profession of Education." One of the stated purposes of Pi Lambda Theta is "to demonstrate the power of competence in the body of knowledge unique to the profession." This was the origin of the expression which was studied and which is now the title of this volume.

A catena is a chain of related events. There were three distinct stages in the Pi Lambda Theta Catena. The first stage was characterized by study and planning. Several approaches to the topic under consideration were possible. Various approaches were considered through discussions and reading; some of these were tentatively accepted, then rejected. From these deliberations the decision to approach the topic from an interdisciplinary point of view evolved.

The participants for the colloquy—the second stage of the Catena—were selected from people with backgrounds, respectively, in psychology, philosophy, history, anthropology, sociology, and research. Each participant was asked to prepare a position paper devoted to the stated topic. The papers were to be submitted to the National Office of Pi Lambda Theta on a specified date. One month later copies of the papers were to be distributed to all participants. And one month after that the six participants were to meet together to react to the papers and to discuss the topic. At the time of their acceptance the participants were fully informed of the entire schedule. The writing of the position papers and the subsequent vis-à-vis discussions were interrelated parts of a whole. Each was dependent upon the other; neither part could stand alone as the colloquy was conceived.

The invitations which went to the participants were all the same. The letter outlined each of the steps involved but the statement of the problem was a deliberately general one. Each participant was free to approach the topic in his own way; each was entirely free to express his own opinions and conclusions. Pi Lambda Theta had no preconceived theses for which it was seeking intellectual support. The results were a matter of conjecture at the time the invitations were put in the mail. In view of this, it was particularly interesting to note the agreements that were apparent, first in the papers and later during the discussions.

The moderator of the colloquy was selected in the fall of 1964, after all participants had accepted Pi Lambda Theta's invitation and had begun work on their papers. The meeting of the participants for the post-paper discussion was scheduled for the first weekend in March 1965. An interesting sidelight to a discussion interesting in its own right was the fact that when the moderator met the participants on the scheduled date in March, it was the first time that the six (one of the participants was unable to attend the discussion) had ever met. No one of them was personally acquainted with any other.

The final stage of the Catena has involved the dissemination of the results of the colloquy. The contents of the position papers were made available to the members of Pi Lambda Theta through publication in the Summer 1965 issue of *Educational Horizons*. The contents of the discussion, and the implications of the colloquy as seen by the National Board, are published for the first time in this book, the ultimate stage of the first Pi Lambda Theta Catena.

The Catena was conceived as a professional and intellectual study of a topic of both fundamental and extensive concern to the profession. It is in this context that the contents of this book are being published.

JANE M. HILL
Catena Coordinator

Preface

THIS PUBLICATION is a tangible outcome of a colloquy which constituted one in a series of related events in a Catena on the subject "The Body of Knowledge Unique to the Profession of Education." The sponsor of the Catena, Pi Lambda Theta, is a national honor and professional organization of scholastically outstanding women in education. The Catena was conceived in the spirit of professional self-evaluation, and was in no way concerned with defending education as a profession nor with determining whether its body of knowledge is or is not a discipline. The colloquy—a meeting of individuals who by their specialized study and experience have devoted time and thought to the subject in one or more of its various aspects—was the method selected for the intensive consideration of the topic. The purpose of the colloquy was not to pass judgment on existing programs nor even to establish criteria for evaluation of programs of teacher preparation. In short, the purpose of the colloquy was to provide an opportunity for a rigorous and objective examination of the topic. To accomplish this purpose, a procedure was developed to select six scholars representing different disciplines to analyze and study the subject. Dr. M. Virginia Biggy, immediate past president of Pi Lambda Theta, in the Preface to the Summer 1965 issue of *Educational Horizons*, described the contributions and responsibilities of the colloquy participants as threefold: (1) the preparation of a paper of not more than eight thousand words; (2) the reading of papers prepared by other colloquy participants; and (3) participation in a colloquy.

The meeting place selected for the colloquy was Airlie House in Warrenton, Virginia, which is about forty miles from Washington, D. C. This distinctive type of conference center seemed particularly appropriate for the colloquy sessions held March 5-7, 1965. Airlie House, operated by a nonprofit organization known as the Airlie Foundation, is situated in a rural area where the main building and the associated facilities are spaced at various points over 1200 acres of rolling land broken only by the buildings, groupings of lovely old trees, a winding brook, and a small lake. Since it was first established, Airlie House has served many outstanding groups of educators, scientists, government officials, diplomats, and others from all over the world. It provides a comfortable, quiet atmosphere for deliberation and thought. In fact, Airlie House has sometimes been referred to as a "Think Center." Although other groups were also having meetings at the time of the Pi Lambda Theta colloquy sessions, the separation of the several facilities afforded almost complete privacy for each group.

In attempting to select six outstanding scholars to represent different disciplines, the National Board of Pi Lambda Theta solicited ideas and names of suggested participants from its membership and other professional colleagues. Miss Jane M. Hill served as special Board associate with particular responsibility for organizing and summarizing information.

Those who were invited to prepare position papers and to participate in the colloquy follow: (1) Dr. George W. Albee, professor of psychology and chairman of the Department of Psychology at Western Reserve University, Cleveland, Ohio, represented the discipline of psychology. Dr. Albee's interests and experience are not narrowly confined, as evidenced by his appointment as director of the Task Force on Manpower for the Joint Commission on Mental Illness and Health which made a major effort to examine the problems of the nation's mental health needs and resources. (2) Dr. Donald P. Cottrell, professor and dean of the College of Education at The Ohio State University, Columbus, Ohio, reviewed the history and research relative to the study of education for professional purposes. Dean Cottrell combines a background in philosophy of education and higher education with years of successful administration which has involved the bringing together of representatives from a number of disciplines in instructional and research activities. (3) Dr. Allison Davis, professor of education at the University of Chicago, represented the discipline of sociology and prepared a paper on "Cultural Factors in Remediation," but he was not able to participate in the colloquy because of a serious illness in his immediate family. (4) Dr. George Ferree, associate professor of education at the University of Missouri, Columbia, Missouri, was the participant who represented philosophy. His paper and his discussions reflected his special interests in epistemology and

PREFACE

philosophic semantics. (5) Dr. Solon T. Kimball, professor of anthropology and education at Teachers College, Columbia University, was the spokesman for anthropology, particularly social and applied anthropology. His wide background of study and travel, coupled with his keen observation of peoples of different cultures, provided interesting illustrations in the discussions. (6) Dr. Clara P. McMahon, associate professor of education and director of the Division of Education in the Evening College at The Johns Hopkins University, Baltimore, represented the discipline of history. Although Dr. McMahon's background in history was specialized, her major concern in the colloquy was with the history of education.

Participants in the colloquy and each of the members of the National Board received copies of the position papers well in advance of the meeting at Warrenton, Virginia, thus providing ample time for the careful reading and study of the ideas expressed. The colloquy moderator asked members of the National Board to prepare questions they would like to have given special consideration in the colloquy sessions. She also asked the members of the colloquy for suggestions relative to the organization of the sessions in order to make the most productive use of the time available. After reading all the papers and noting the differences and similarities in the points of view expressed, members of the colloquy thought it would be advisable to give each participant the opportunity to clarify or amplify any of the ideas expressed in his paper before the moderator called for questions and opened the meeting for discussion.

Members of the colloquy thought it necessary to consider and accept common definitions of the terms in the topic "The Body of Knowledge Unique to the Profession of Education" in order to proceed with meaningful discussions. For the most part, the definitions accepted were those which appear in the papers prepared by Dr. George Ferree and Dr. George W. Albee.

"The body of knowledge" was the first term to be considered and this was defined as an ordered set of confirmed statements. By confirmed statements, Dr. Ferree meant statements that had been tested and had been found to be true or highly probable. The word "unique" was not so precisely defined. As the colloquy participants began to analyze what knowledge is unique to education, or for that matter, what knowledge is unique to any profession, they concluded that all professions have derived information and knowledge from a number of disciplines. They agreed this was particularly true in the profession of education. "Unique," as they understood the term, meant uniquely formulated to have specific relevance to education. The body of knowledge unique or fundamental to education is probably modest even though there are volumes which have been written about education. Knowledge unique or appropriate to education is a body of knowledge uniquely formulated and applicable to education, a body of knowledge in which the educator has special interest, a body of knowledge which is relevant to education and which, when mastered, would not be held by the average person.

In his paper, Dr. Albee points up some of the problems in determining what constitutes a profession. Most writers in their discussions of this problem consider the characteristics typical of a profession. Because of the element of public welfare which is associated with any profession, a particular profession ordinarily seeks sanction to practice. This is usually called licensing or certification. A profession must also create training centers and accredit programs. Other characteristics of professions commonly mentioned are technical knowledge and privacy. There is much evidence to support the fact that education possesses the first two characteristics mentioned. Education also has some technical knowledge in its own right and has adapted and is continuing to adapt knowledge relevant and applicable to its purposes. Colloquy participants did agree, however, that education probably has less privacy than other professions.

"Education" was defined as a system of organized schooling, such as from preschool or kindergarten through the university, and into postgraduate study or any other system of organized schooling.

In the discussions, which extended over a period of three days, the particular group of scholars who represented the several disciplines agreed that there was a "body of knowledge unique to the profession of education." The colloquy participants thought that every educator should possess and apply knowledge about *maturation, individual differences,* and *motivation.* They agreed, too, that these three elements or areas have direct relevance to learning theory and that knowledge of *learning theory* is basic for those who wish to practice the profession of education. The participants also believed that *measurement* is a part of the fundamental knowledge needed by all educators. Last, but not least, the group determined that knowledge of the conditions for the *transmission of culture* is essential for members of the teaching profession.

Implicit in the statement of the areas delineated by the members of the colloquy is the need for close working relationships with a number of disciplines if the consumers of education are to benefit fully from the content and resources it can offer. Medicine as well as psychology has much to contribute to knowledge about maturation. Anthropology, sociology, and psychology can help educators in understanding individual differences, but education must also contribute basic knowledge about individual differences and motivation. Education has the largest and most fascinating environment in which to study individual differences and motivation, namely, the school. Observations and research in the school environment should result in contributions to learning theory. Here, also, is a rare opportunity to bring different disciplines together in the application of measurement utilizing new devices and techniques appropriate not only for the measurement of pupil behavior and performance but for evaluation of teaching methods and materials as well. Understanding the transmission of culture requires the knowledge and skills represented by the disciplines mentioned in connection with the colloquy, but specialists in other areas, such as communications, can contribute to the understanding of this complex problem, too. The problems of education are not simple; neither is the knowledge unique to the profession of education.

In a rapidly changing world, every profession needs to examine and reexamine its content and practices which may be subject to many influences. Although the principal purpose of the Catena was conceived in the spirit of self-evaluation, the colloquy also provided an opportunity for participants to examine their own disciplines and especially to consider what areas within their disciplines had special relevance or application to education. Although specific areas from different disciplines may be appropriate and applicable to education, educators themselves must determine how to integrate new knowledge.

In conclusion, members of the colloquy did, indeed, think there was a "body of knowledge unique to the profession of education." They thought this body of knowledge was derived from a number of different disciplines. They were keenly aware of the fact that this body of knowledge is dynamic and changing and that it will increase as new knowledge is developed. They agreed that educators need to select, integrate, and organize appropriate knowledge which will make it applicable to education in a manner consistent with educational philosophy, learning theory, and educational objectives, both cognitive and affective. They recognized, too, that education needs to develop knowledge in its own right.

All those who participated in the colloquy found the experience stimulating and valuable. The reproduction of the papers and discussions on "The Body of Knowledge Unique to the Profession of Education" can provide a basis for further examination and stimulating intellectual experiences. The idea of the Catena, which was conceived and developed in 1963, seems now to have been particularly constructive, courageous, and forward-looking as education stands at the threshold of a new era rich with potential. Public interest, new knowledge, and technological advances must be focused on the problems and responsibilities of education.

ALICE H. HAYDEN
Colloquy Moderator

Contents

vii   Preface by Alice H. Hayden

1   The Participants

    I—Position Papers

9   *Philosophy and the Body of Knowledge Unique to the Profession of Education*
    George Ferree

27   *Psychology and the Body of Knowledge Unique to the Profession of Education*
    George W. Albee

45   *The Transmission of Culture*
    Solon T. Kimball

71   *History and the Body of Knowledge Unique to the Profession of Education*
    Clara P. McMahon

89   *The Study of Education for Professional Purposes*
    Donald P. Cottrell

114   *Cultural Factors in Remediation*
    Allison Davis

    II—The Colloquy

137   The Colloquy

    III—Implications of the Colloquy

209   Implications of the Colloquy

219   Pi Lambda Theta National Board

Airlie Foundation, Warrenton, Virginia: The Scene of the Colloquy

The Colloquy Participants

George Ferree

George W. Albee

Solon T. Kimball

Clara P. McMahon

Donald P. Cottrell

Alice H. Hayden

The Participants

GEORGE FERREE (B.A., A.M., and Ed.D. University of Florida) is associate professor of education at the University of Missouri, with his major teaching responsibility in the philosophy of education. His doctoral major was philosophy of education and his minor was philosophy. His dissertation title was *Selected Tools of Analytic Philosophy and Their Application in Education.*

He has served as assistant professor of education at Tufts University, Medford, Massachusetts; and has been a high school English teacher in Florida. He is a member of Phi Delta Kappa and Kappa Delta Pi, and a fellow of the Philosophy of Education Society.

He is much interested in research, particularly in philosophic linguistics and education. He has contributed articles to a number of professional publications.

GEORGE W. ALBEE (A.B. Bethany College, M.S. and Ph.D. University of Pittsburgh) is George Trumbull Ladd distinguished professor of psychology, and chairman of the Department of Psychology at Western Reserve University, Cleveland, Ohio. He went to Western Reserve University eleven years ago but during that period of time he has spent a year on sabbatical leave in Rome and another year on leave of absence during which he was director of the Task Force on Manpower, Joint Commission on Mental Illness and Health, in Cambridge, Massachusetts. As part of this assignment he wrote a book, *Mental Health Manpower Trends,* described by Nicholas Hobbs as one of the three most significant books on mental health of the decade.

He has served as a Fulbright professor at Helsinki University, Finland, where he did lecturing and supervised the research of students in psychology.

During the past five years he has served as a research or advisory consultant for a variety of government and nongovernment agencies.

He is a prolific writer who has contributed many articles to psychological and educational journals. He has served as president of both the Ohio Psychological Association and the Cleveland Psychological Association; currently he is president-elect of the Division of Clinical Psychology, and a member of the Board of Directors of the American Psychological Association.

SOLON T. KIMBALL (B.S. Kansas State University, A.M. and Ph.D. Harvard University) has been professor of anthropology and education at Teachers College, Columbia University, since 1953. From 1948 to 1953 he was chairman of the Department of Sociology and Anthropology at the University of Alabama.

He is coauthor of *Culture and Community, Education and the New America, The Talladega Story,* and *Family and Community in Ireland.* His research in the anthropology of community includes field studies in the west of Ireland, in Massachusetts, Michigan, and Alabama, and among the Navaho Indians of the Southwest.

His interests in education have taken him to Brazil, where he served for a year as UNESCO consultant on community education to the Brazilian Center for Educational Research, and to Peru, where he helped organize a program to assist the Peruvian Ministry of Education in educational development.

CLARA P. McMAHON (A.B. Goucher College; Ph.D. The Johns Hopkins University) is associate professor of education and director of the Division of Education in the Evening College, The Johns Hopkins University, Baltimore, Maryland. Her major field of study has been history of education with graduate work in history, English, and Latin.

She teaches graduate and undergraduate courses in the history of education and directs masters' essays and doctoral dissertations in that field, in addition to the administrative duties involved in directing the part-time programs in education.

She has served as associate professor of education at Hood College, Frederick, Maryland; and has been a junior high school teacher in Maryland. As program officer in the Division of International Education, U.S. Office of Education, she was in charge of planning programs of study and observation of educational programs under the Smith-Mundt and Fulbright Acts. As an educational specialist and writer in

THE PARTICIPANTS

the Federal Civil Defense Administration, she devised and wrote curricular materials on civil defense for use in schools.

She has written a book and a number of articles in the history of education. She recently conducted a study of the "Public Image of Education" as revealed by interviews with bodies of professional, industrial, and political figures in Maryland. She is now engaged in analyzing the biographical accounts of women scholars in history which are included in the *Dictionary of American Scholars, Vol. I*, in order to draw a composite picture of such scholars.

DONALD P. COTTRELL (A.B. Ohio State University, M.A. and Ph.D. Columbia University) is dean of the College of Education of The Ohio State University. He went to Ohio State in 1946 from Teachers College, Columbia University, where he was professor of education.

He has served as visiting professor of education at Stanford University; and he has served in many advisory and consultant positions which have taken him to Germany, Japan, China, the Philippines, Korea, India, and Guam.

He has also served as educational adviser of the International House at New York City; chairman of the board of trustees of Talladega College; president of the National Society of College Teachers of Education; president of the American Association of Colleges for Teacher Education; chairman of the National Commission on Teacher Education and Professional Standards of the National Education Association; and chairman of the Advisory Council of the Associated Organizations for Teachers Education, a federation of professional organizations in education affiliated with the American Association of Colleges for Teacher Education.

He is the author or coauthor of numerous books, articles, and papers. He is particularly interested in teacher education and much of his writing has been on that subject. He is also the author of survey reports dealing with various individual colleges and universities in America, and has been a consultant to numerous schools and groups on organizational, administrative, and teaching problems.

ALLISON DAVIS (A.B. *summa cum laude,* Williams College; A.M. Harvard University; Ph.D. University of Chicago) is professor of education at the University of Chicago and a member of the interdepartmental Committee on Human Development. He has been a member of the faculty there since 1942.

He has been professor of anthropology at Dillard University; a staff member of the Division of Child Development, Commission on Teacher Education, American Council of Education; visiting professor of sociology at the University of Michigan and at Columbia University; visiting professor of psychology at the University of California; and George E. Miller visiting professor at the University of Illinois.

He has delivered the Alexander Inglis Memorial Lecture at Harvard University, the Billings Lecture at Smith College, and the Horace Mann Lecture at the University of Pittsburgh, and has addressed general sessions of the American Association of School Administrators, as well as general sessions of several different state teachers associations. He was a speaker at the "Mid-Century White House Conference on Children and Adolescents."

He is the author or coauthor of eight books, dealing with such topics as the socialization of the child, adolescent psychology, intelligence and culture, culture and status, and the psychology of the child in the middle class. He is also coauthor of the *Davis-Eells Test of General Intelligence*.

He is a member of Phi Beta Kappa and Sigma Xi. In 1959-60 he was a Fellow of the Center for Advanced Study in the Behavioral Sciences of the Ford Foundation.

ALICE H. HAYDEN (B.S. and M.S. Oregon State College, Ph.D. Purdue University, postdoctoral study Boston University) is professor of education and associate director of the Experimental Education Unit of the Mental Retardation and Child Development Center, University of Washington.

She was formerly director of the University of Washington Pilot School for Neurologically Impaired Children, and director of graduate studies in education at the University of Washington. She has held appointments at the Ohio State University and with the Purdue Research Foundation and taught in the public schools in Massachusetts.

She has served on the Research Board and the Publications and Nominating committees of the Association for Supervision and Curriculum Development and on the Research Committee of the Depart-

THE PARTICIPANTS

ment of Audio-Visual Instruction of the National Education Association. She is a member of the Governor's Inter-Agency Subcommittee on Mental Retardation; the Research Advisory Committee, Washington State Department of Public Instruction; the Washington State Teacher Education Committee; and the Washington State Task Force on Educational Services. She is also cochairman of the Washington State Task Force on Manpower and Training in the area of Mental Retardation.

She has written several books and has contributed to professional periodicals and research reports. She has been editor of three-level social studies readers and other books for children. She is a member of the editorial board of the *College of Education Record*.

She has been a national Vice-President of Pi Lambda Theta, chairman of Pi Lambda Theta's Committee on Studies and Awards, a member of the editorial board of the *Pi Lambda Theta Journal,* and faculty adviser of Zeta Chapter of Pi Lambda Theta.

I
THE POSITION PAPERS

Philosophy and the Body of Knowledge Unique to the Profession of Education

George Ferree
University of Missouri

THERE ARE a great many teacher education institutions in the United States today—departments of education, teachers colleges, colleges of education in large universities, and graduate schools of education. Each of these institutions presumably intends to provide prospective teachers—and, in many cases, in-service teachers—with knowledge which will render their educational efforts more intelligent and effective. The theme of this colloquy, as I see it, concerns such knowledge or, rather, that portion of such knowledge which may properly be labeled a body of knowledge. Is there, or can there be, some body of knowledge which teachers ought to master beyond that which they acquire in their general education and in the mastery of the subject matter they wish to teach? If so, what is the character of such knowledge? Is it knowledge unique to the profession of education? Unique in what sense? What logic of organization does it have? How developed is it? What relation does it have to other bodies of knowledge? These are the principal kinds of questions I understand this colloquy to be concerned with and, accordingly, upon which this essay will focus.

WHAT CONSTITUTES A BODY OF KNOWLEDGE?

At the outset the vague and ambiguous expression "body of knowledge" requires some commentary. How is "body of knowledge" to be employed within the context of the topic "The Body of Knowledge Unique to the Profession of Education"? In this essay the expression will be restricted in its signification to the sort of knowledge which is formulated or, at least, is formulable in sentences. In ordinary discourse a body of knowledge is generally regarded as a body of statements, and the present discussion is merely conforming to this usage. Accordingly, whatever other kinds of knowledge there may be and however important such species of knowledge are, they are beyond the province of the present discussion. If, for instance, there is some sort of mystical, intuitive knowledge—say of a realm of being so completely transcendent that we cannot utter an intelligible word about it—then such knowledge cannot be considered here. Indeed, the very character of such knowledge would militate against any discussion, and as Wittgenstein once said: "Whereof one cannot speak, thereof one must be silent."[1]

Moreover, the expression "body of knowledge," as employed here, *excludes* that kind of knowledge which Gilbert Ryle subsumes under the rubric "knowing how" and which he distinguishes from "knowing that."[2] By "knowing how" Ryle intends the sort of knowledge that can be acquired only by performing, in contrast to "knowing that" which signifies knowledge "embodied in linguistic symbols and . . . taught and learned only through linguistic activities—reading, listening, discussion, etc."[3] Ryle's comment upon the education of a surgeon suggests the basic distinction he wishes to make:

> A man knowing little or nothing of medical science could not be a good surgeon, but excellence at surgery is not the same thing as knowledge of medical science; nor is it a simple product of it. The surgeon must indeed have learned from instruction, or by his own inductions and observations, a great number of truths; but he must also have learned by practice a great number of aptitudes.[4]

To ascertain whether a person *knows how* to perform a given activity—say, how to drive a car—we do not simply elicit verbal responses from him, but we observe him in the performance of the activity, driving or at least attempting to drive a car. Drivers license departments ordinarily give both verbal *and* road tests, and however articulate a person may be on the former, the litmus test of his "know

---

[1] This is the famed Proposition Seven of Ludwig Wittgenstein's *Tractatus-Logico-Philosophicus*. The proposition is alluded to in Joergen Jorgenson, *The Development of Logical Empiricism* (Chicago: The University of Chicago Press, 1951), p. 27.

[2] Gilbert Ryle, *The Concept of Mind* (New York: Barnes & Noble, 1949), chap. ii.

[3] It is apparent that B. Othanel Smith is assuming Ryle's distinction in the passage cited here. See Smith's "A Joint Task: The Preparation of a Teacher," *Journal of Teacher Education*, X (June, 1959), p. 194.

[4] Ryle, *op. cit.*, p. 49.

how" is in his driving performance. One can rightly distinguish between *knowing that* if one depresses the clutch of a standard transmission car, he may shift to a higher gear and *knowing how* to shift gears. A person may have acquired the former kind of knowledge and still be lacking in the latter.

The fact that these two kinds of knowledge can be differentiated, of course, does not mean that the one has no bearing upon the other. Indeed, a mastery of *knowledge that* may well be instrumental to *knowing how* or to more effective *knowing how*. Reading a driver training manual, for example—which certainly to some extent provides *knowledge that*—or hearing an experienced teacher of driving talk *about* how to drive may very well help one to learn how to drive or how to be a more effective driver. Bodies of knowledge *about* teaching, similarly, may well lead to more effective teaching on the part of those who master such bodies of knowledge. Assuredly such is our hope in teacher education institutions where we communicate such knowledge. But we do not limit our efforts to promote *knowing how* to teach to the communication of *knowledge that*. Implicit in our required student teaching programs—which many today see as the very heart of teacher education—is a recognition of a *knowing how* over and beyond *knowing that*, of a *knowing how* not attainable simply through the medium of language.

The central point being labored here, then, is that there is a kind of knowledge—a very important kind of knowledge, *knowing how*—incapable of being formulated in language. In teacher education we often seek to foster this knowledge through programs of student teaching. Such *knowing how*, as important as it is, is largely beyond the province of this essay save as *knowledge that* can be demonstrated to be instrumental to it. Primarily, once again, this essay focuses upon the kind of knowledge which can be set forth in sentences.

But although all bodies of knowledge as treated here are regarded as formulable in sentences, it does not follow that all sentences are components of some body of knowledge or another. Many sentences do not convey knowledge; in fact many do not even make knowledge claims. What is it, then, one may ask, that distinguishes those sentences which convey knowledge from those which do not? As a preliminary to answering this question it will be useful to give the term "statement" a technical sense. "Statement" will here be used to signify a sentence affirming that something is the case and, accordingly, a sentence which admits of truth or falsity, as the case may be.[5] In order to know that a sentence is a statement one need not know whether the sentence is true or false but only that it is the sort of sentence to which the terms "truth" or "falsity" apply. Thus the sentence "There are intelligent living beings on Mars" is a statement even though we do not know its truth value. Many sentences, of course, are not of the sort which have truth values and hence are not statements. To cite a simple instance, a proposal like "Let us break bread together" is not a statement. It does not seek to inform; it does not admit of truth or falsity; it is not even probable or improbable—such terms are simply inappropriate.

What is it that distinguishes sentences conveying knowledge from those that do not? On the view of this essay (1) they must be statements, and (2) these statements must have been confirmed as true or, at least, as highly probable. *An ordered set of such statements which treat of the same sorts of questions* is here regarded as a body of knowledge. The stipulation requiring treatment of the same sorts of questions, of course, rules out mere miscellanies of unrelated statements and also provides a means of distinguishing one body of knowledge from another. Insofar as bodies of knowledge can be discriminated from one another, they are discriminable not by the different classes of things which they discuss but by the different sorts of questions which they are concerned to answer.[6] Psychology, sociology, and anthropology all treat of exactly the same class of things—human beings—but presumably the questions which these bodies of knowledge intend to discuss are different. These different questions allow at least some differentiation into different bodies of knowledge.

Thinkers, of course, may agree on the sense of "body of knowledge" here stipulated and still be in considerable disagreement about whether a given set of sentences consitutes a body of knowledge. To begin with, they may be in basic disagreement about whether cer-

[5] See W. V. Quine's *Methods of Logic* (New York: Henry Holt & Company, 1950), p. 1.
[6] R. S. Peters makes this point well in his contribution to *The Discipline of Education,* ed. John Walton and James L. Kuethe (Madison: The University of Wisconsin Press, 1963), p. 17.

PHILOSOPHY AND EDUCATION

tain sentences are statements or not—noteworthy, for example, the sentences characteristic of ethics. Some thinkers vigorously maintain that ethical sentences make no knowledge claim whatever. Thus Hans Reichenbach says:

> The modern analysis of knowledge makes a cognitive ethics impossible: knowledge does not include any normative parts and therefore does not lend itself to an interpretation of ethics. The ethico-cognitive parallelism renders ethics a bad service: if it could be carried through, if virtue were knowledge, ethical rules would be deprived of their imperative character. The two-thousand-year-old plan to establish ethics on a cognitive basis results from a misunderstanding of knowledge, from the erroneous conception that knowledge contains a normative part.
> ....
> Truth is a predicate of statements; but *the linguistic expressions of ethics are not statements*. They are directives. A directive cannot be classified as true or false; these predicates do not apply because directive sentences are of a logical nature different from that of indicative sentences, or statements.[7] (Italics mine.)

Other thinkers argue equally as vigorously *for* a cognitive ethics. John Wild, for example, contends that ethics is a science providing man with *knowledge* of the moral law or the natural law.[8] Ethical sentences, he maintains, admit of truth or falsity, and, indeed, may be confirmed or disconfirmed by an appeal to empirical evidence. In complete contrast to Reichenbach, then, he regards ethical sentences as statements. Clearly among philosophers the issue of which sentences qualify to be called statements is by no means resolved.

Moreover, the notion of "body of knowledge" offered here does not settle the question of techniques for confirming statements and the adequacy of such techniques. Thinkers may agree that a given sentence is a statement and still decidedly disagree about the extent to which the statement has been confirmed as true or probable. For example, a sentence which an intuitionist might feel perfectly happy to call true, a tough-minded empiricist might wish to challenge not because he does not regard it as a statement but for want of what he regards as adequate confirming evidence. The question of what

---

[7] Hans Reichenbach, *The Rise of Scientific Philosophy* (Berkeley and Los Angeles: University of California Press, 1956), pp. 277 and 280.

[8] See Part I of John Wild's *Introduction to Realistic Philosophy* (New York: Harper & Brothers, 1948). Also see Wild's "Education and Human Society: A Realistic View," *Modern Philosophies and Education,* Fifty-fourth Yearbook of the National Society for the Study of Education, Part I (Chicago: The University of Chicago Press, 1955), pp. 18-19 *et passim.*

constitutes adequate evidence, moreover, is one which even thinkers of similar general philosophic orientations sometimes debate—as heated arguments about statistical conclusions assuredly attest.

Despite these difficulties, the signification of "body of knowledge" stipulated here has some strong features to recommend it. First, it brings into sharp relief basic epistemological considerations which any adequate conception of a body of knowledge invariably must face. It does not unnecessarily compound these considerations but rather identifies and clarifies them.

Secondly, although the view of this essay allows thinkers to disagree about whether certain sentences embody knowledge, it nonetheless enables them to find substantial areas of consensus. It permits thinkers as divergent in their epistemological perspectives as Thomists and logical empiricists, for example, to agree, about a considerable number of statements in history, mathematics, and the various sciences. They may not concur about all sentences, but at least they may find agreement on many, and they may pointedly identify the bases of their agreements and disagreements.

Is There a Defensible Notion of a Body of Knowledge Unique to the Profession of Education?

Assuming the sense of "body of knowledge" stipulated above, is there or can there ever be a body of knowledge unique to the profession of education? Do people engaged in the enterprise of education have some special and unique claim on a certain ordered set of confirmed statements? A great deal depends, of course, on the sense of the term "unique" as employed in these questions. On one sense the answer is undoubtedly a straightforward and emphatic "No." If these questions are asking about a body of knowledge *all* the statements of which are logically subsumable *solely* under the rubric of "education," then there is no body of knowledge that qualifies. One cannot imagine a body of knowledge about education that is unique and autonomous in the sense that it contains no statements whatever that could be considered as appropriate to psychology, sociology, anthropology, political science, or any of various other bodies of knowledge. If in order to be unique to the profession of education, a body of knowledge must meet such a stringent requirement, then at present

PHILOSOPHY AND EDUCATION

there is no such body, and, by the very nature of the case, it is questionable whether there ever could be.

If, on the other hand, these questions are inquiring about a body of knowledge the statements of which—regardless of their sources—are uniquely formulated and ordered in a manner that makes their application to educational contexts explicit, then an affirmative answer is in order. The term "education" here, together with its cognates, signifies "the whole enterprise of schooling qua schooling, from the nursery school through the university, or any other system of deliberate and organized schooling."[9] Certainly there are at present some confirmed statements which are pertinent to the enterprise of education, and in the future there may well be a great many more. It would seem appropriate and defensible to regard the set of all such statements formulated and ordered so as to make their pertinence to education explicit as the body of knowledge unique to the profession of education. Thus conceived, the body of knowledge unique to the profession of education would be unique in three related senses: (1) it would be uniquely formulated and ordered so as to be relevant to the concerns of educators qua educators; (2) it would, then, presumably be of unique and special interest to educators because of its relevance to their work; and (3) when mastered by educators, it would give them a unique fund of knowledge not held by people generally.

Do We Now Have a Body of Knowledge Unique to the Profession of Education?

Of course, the question of the extent to which we now have such a body of knowledge still remains. What is the existing state of affairs? What commentary can be made on the "knowledge" which teacher education institutions are currently attempting to transmit?

In all likelihood the answer to these questions, in general formulation, is that the body of knowledge unique to the profession of education at present is relatively modest in scope and character. There is a vast literature on education, to be sure, but much of it

[9] John Walton, "A Discipline of Education," *The Discipline of Education*, ed. John Walton and James L. Kuethe (Madison: The University of Wisconsin Press, 1963), p. 5.

does not measure up to the requirements stipulated above. For example, a considerable part of what sometimes poses or passes for knowledge about education consists of unconfirmed hypotheses and theories, imprecisely formulated common sense observations, hortatory injunctions, speculations, hunches, testimonials, and the like. Perhaps there is an appropriate place in education for some such linguistic expressions, but certainly they are not to be confused—as they now sometimes are—with components of a body of knowledge. The sentences in a body of knowledge, we have stressed, must be statements that are well confirmed.

These sentences, moreover, to be included in the body of knowledge unique to the profession of education, must not be of the sort with which people are generally acquainted, else there is no justification for giving them unique and special treatment. It is not uncommon, however, to hear certain courses in education impugned, not because they fail to convey knowledge but because the knowledge with which they deal is so obvious, so readily understandable, and so generally held that it does not require the kind of elaborate treatment accorded it. Such knowledge does not meet the requirements laid down in this essay for statements to be included in the body of knowledge unique to the profession of education.

Neither do statements which are communicated in the guise of educational discourse but which basically are not relevant to education or which are not formulated in a manner that makes their relevance to education clear. In this regard, courses that purport to relate one of the behavioral sciences to education are a case in point. Altogether too often courses in, say, the psychology of education have turned out to be basically courses in general psychology—and not always good courses at that—with very limited and sometimes quite vague treatments of educational questions. Such courses, despite their educational labels and impressive catalog descriptions, are not communicating what this essay stipulates as a body of knowledge unique to the profession of education. These observations, let it be understood, are by no means intended to suggest that the body of knowledge unique to the profession of education should not at certain points and, indeed, sometimes in considerable detail enunciate statements appropriate to other bodies of knowledge. The point is that such statements should be selected, formulated, and ordered in a manner that at least eventually brings illumination to education. If they are not able to bring such illumination, clearly they should not be included. If they are relevant to educational concerns, their relevance should be established as precisely and as fully as is possible.

If expurgated of extraneous, unwarranted sentences, there is considerable reason for believing that the current body of knowledge unique to the profession of education is not especially expansive. More bluntly put, our professonal knowledge is meager, especially as compared with the fund of knowledge which engineers and physicians now have to give guidance to their practice. If it is proper to analogize education with the practical fields of medicine and engineering, one may well ponder the disparity in the development of the bodies of knowledge appropriate to these fields. Why has education lagged behind, if in fact it has? Several explanations are possible.

For one thing, those who have attempted to conduct educational research, to formulate knowledge of the sort called for in this essay, have sometimes lacked the kind of preparation and perspectives essential to the generation of such knowledge. Researchers in departments and colleges of education, for example, have sometimes lacked depth in the various parent bodies of knowledge related to and essential for success in their inquiries. They have evidenced great familiarity and sensitivity to a wide range of pressing, hard, practical questions about education, but they have not always possessed a sophisticated command of the appropriate bodies of knowledge requisite to answering these questions, or, at least, to formulating research designs that would be instrumental to answers. Is it any wonder that persons bearing what has sometimes amounted to little more than a courtesy title of "psychologist of education" but lacking depth of knowledge in psychology should have been limited in their teaching and research efforts? The psychology of education, to be sure, is concerned with educational questions—indeed, from the viewpoint of this essay *focally* concerned with such questions—but it is nonetheless psychology and demands high-level psychological sophistication. The same observation applies, of course, to any of various other fields of educational inquiry which bear some special relation to a parent body of knowledge—the sociology of education, the history of education, the philosophy of education, and so on. Is it not reasonable to suppose that the present limitations of the body of knowledge unique to the profession of education may be a function, in part, of the sometimes limited acquaintance of educational researchers with the behavioral sciences and with other fields relevant to their inquiries?

Researchers in schools of education, however, are by no means the only ones to answer for deficiencies in the current body of knowledge unique to the profession of education. Scholars in the behavioral sciences and in certain other provinces of knowledge must also be called into question. Far too often they have neglected if not eschewed questions about education even when, in some cases, such questions have been quite appropriate to their spheres of inquiry. Professional historians, as a special instance in point, have given scant attention until quite recently to the history of education. One wonders whether such historians—especially those who strongly urge that the institutions of a given era of history are in some sense functionally interrelated—have forgotten about educational institutions. Has the influence of educational institutions been so minimal in history as not to have warranted any serious treatment? Why has not the history of education received a greater share of historians' concern? One may well maintain that, for one reason or another, historians simply have neglected questions about education—questions quite proper to the scope of their own work.

Even when representatives of various established bodies of knowledge have made some efforts to discuss educational questions, they have oftentimes been so insensitive to the educational scene and its genuine complicated problems that they have failed to relate their knowledge to education in any pertinent and useful way. Not having an intimate and subtle acquaintance with the demands and problems of education, they have been unable to speak sharply and directly to educational questions and, hence, especially insofar as applications are concerned, have frequently resorted to broad generalities. It was in reaction against such generalities, no doubt, that Jerome S. Bruner recently made the following comments:

> I would as soon see an end to the conventional educational psychology course and its assertions about learning—so full of broad vacuities. Let us begin instead with a concrete psychology that occupies itself with wily strategies for learning specific things like mathematics, or geography, or sonnets. You will say that there is not such a subject matter now—and you are right. But one is coming into being. What is critical about this type of psychological effort is that it is an account of learning that remains

married to what is being learned. It recognizes that the principal way in which the human mind proceeds is by the mastery of conceptual tools—the tools that are inherent in the great disciplines of learning. We are not abstractly learning *responses* to *stimuli* (whatever those terms may mean), but learning instead to use such powerful tools as commutativity to do algebra—that it is often stunningly useful to consider that three fives and five threes are an identity, though we can readily see that three igloos with five Eskimos in each is obviously not identical to five igloos with three Eskimos in each—or the equally powerful exploratory device of the metaphor.[10]

Clearly what Bruner is calling for is a kind of educational psychology that in an intimate manner bears upon specific, concrete educational activities. Such a psychology patently demands full acquaintance with and focus upon the multiplicity of tasks in which educators engage, and it is precisely in this respect that much current educational psychology—even that formulated by competent psychologists—is often deficient. A similar commentary undoubtedly is in order about various other efforts to relate some body of knowledge—sociology, economics, political science, and so on—to education.

The simple point is that the generation of many of the statements appropriate to the body of knowledge unique to the profession of education requires high-level interest and sophistication both in education and in some related body or bodies of knowledge. The requirement is twofold and demanding, and insofar as it has not been met, the body of knowledge unique to the profession of education has been impaired.

Thus far we have spoken as if the behavioral sciences and the other bodies of knowledge which appear to have some relevance to education are fairly large and well developed, simply awaiting appropriate application in educational settings. Could it not be, however, that these bodies of knowledge themselves are deficient in certain respects and that the weaknesses of the body of knowledge unique to the profession of education are to some extent a reflection of deficiencies and weaknesses in these "parent" bodies? How developed are the various sciences of man? What sorts of knowledge are they now capable of delivering which are genuinely relevant to the work of the educator?

When an engineer needs knowledge pertinent to the solution of

---

[10] Jerome S. Bruner, "On Teaching Teachers," *Current Issues in Higher Education,* The Proceedings of the Nineteenth Annual National Conference on Higher Education (Washington, D.C.: Association for Higher Education, 1964), p. 98.

his problems, he now has a fairly large reservoir of knowledge to which he can turn. Physics, for example, enables him to predict with considerable precision the elasticity and wearing power of different sorts of materials used in, say, bridge construction. He has great assurance that if he builds a bridge to meet certain specifications it will be able to withstand certain specifiable sorts of treatment—for example, wind velocities of so many miles per hour. To what extent are the behavioral sciences able to provide educators with analagous sorts of knowledge applicable to their tasks? If, for example, an educator is concerned to foster exploratory and inventive dispositions in his students, can learning theory provide him with knowledge that will enable him to achieve his goal? Can he now predict that if he provides his students with certain specifiable experiences, the probability will be high that their behavior will be more inventive and exploratory in character?

Such questions, many informed commentators maintain, are beyond the reach of the social sciences at present. In this vein Ernest Nagel observes:

In no area of social inquiry has a body of general laws been established, comparable with outstanding theories in the natural sciences in scope of explanatory power or in capacity to yield precise and reliable predictions.... Many social scientists are of the opinion, moreover, that the time is not yet ripe even for theories designed to explain systematically only quite limited ranges of social phenomena.... To a considerable extent, the problems investigated in many current centers of empirical social research are admittedly problems of moderate and often unimpressive dimensions.... In short, *the social sciences today possess no wide ranging systems of explanations judged as adequate by a majority of professionally competent students, and they are characterized by serious disagreements on methodological as well as substantive questions.*[11] (Italics mine.)

The statements characteristic of the social sciences, then, if Nagel is to be believed, have considerable limitations at present. One may find support for this conclusion in a recent volume entitled *Human Behavior: An Inventory of Scientific Findings.*[12] The character of the

---

[11] Ernest Nagel, *The Structure of Science* (New York and Burlingame: Harcourt, Brace, and World, 1961), pp. 447-449. Quoted in Israel Scheffler, "Is Education a Discipline?" *The Discipline of Education*, ed. John Walton and James L. Kuethe (Madison: The University of Wisconsin Press, 1963), pp. 60-61.

[12] Bernard Berelson & Gary A. Steiner, *Human Behavior: An Inventory of Scientific Findings* (New York and Burlingame: Harcourt, Brace & World, 1964).

statements assembled in this work—which purports to catalog existent knowledge in the behavioral sciences—assuredly attests to the fact that these sciences do not yet possess the sorts of basic theories and laws characteristic of the physical sciences. It follows, does it not, that the body of knowledge unique to the profession of education, insofar as it is dependent upon these behavioral sciences, is correspondingly lacking.

The danger of these remarks is that they may suggest to some that at present the behavioral and social sciences have virtually *nothing* to say to education. The intended point, however, is not that they have nothing whatever to offer to education but rather that their offerings may not yet be at the level of the widely ranging laws and theories characteristic of the physical sciences. The offerings of the behavioral and social sciences at present are more likely to be at the level of particular statements, generalizations of modest proportions, and, perhaps, at the level of "theories of the middle range," Robert K. Merton's expression for theories "intermediate to routine research hypotheses and an inclusive conceptual system."[13] If such is the case, clearly many of the statements characteristic of the body of knowledge unique to the profession of education will have to be at the same level. It hardly seems reasonable to expect more.

Granted that the knowledge now available in the behavioral and social sciences may have the limitations specified above, one may still inquire about the extent to which appropriate parts of such knowledge as is available have been incorporated into the body of knowledge unique to the profession of education. Has the present body of knowledge unique to the profession of education made use of all the resources available to it, limited though these resources sometimes may be? Or is there existent knowledge which is relevant to educational concerns but which has not been appropriated and formulated so as to make its pertinence to education explicit? These questions, of course, are empirical questions that can be adequately answered only by investigation. One investigator, who has recently been conducting research on the teaching of concepts at the elementary and secondary levels, has concluded that "the knowledge in works on logic, psychology, philosophy of science, etc. have implica-

[13] Roscoe C. Hinkle, Jr. and Gisela J. Hinkle, *The Development of American Sociology* (Garden City, New York: Doubleday & Company, 1954), p. 67.

tions for the teaching of concepts that *are far more extensive than the suggestions found in the tabloid accounts given in works on educational psychology and teaching.*"[14] (Italics mine.) The point is that even now there may very well be considerably more knowledge available than has been appropriated in the service of education. Thus the present limitations of the body of knowledge unique to the profession of education may reflect not only the unavailability of certain sorts of knowledge but also, unhappily, a failure to employ the knowledge that is available. John Walton seems to be making this very point in an ably written essay on "The Discipline of Education." He says that at present the subject matter of education is scattered over a variety of disciplines and that what is presently needful is a "Diaspora in reverse" to gather such knowledge into one place[15] and, we would add, to make the relevance of such knowledge to educational concerns as explicit as possible.

What Plan of Organization Is Appropriate to the Body of Knowledge Unique to the Profession of Education?

The accomplishment of Walton's "Diaspora in reverse" clearly necessitates some plan or plans for ordering the great variety of statements which may qualify for membership in the body of knowledge unique to the profession of education. How shall the diverse statements, coming as they will from sundry sources, be put together? Surely they cannot defensibly be selected willy nilly and be thrown together into a hodgepodge. A scheme or schemes are needful for ordering the statements into some sort of system.

There are at least three general approaches, or some permutation or combination of them, to the organization of the components of the body of knowledge unique to the profession of education. One of these, which certainly is in evidence both in current and in past efforts to provide a body of knowledge for educators, patterns the organization of a given body of educational knowledge after that of some parent body of knowledge to which it is closely related or from which it is derivative. Thus the sociology of education, at least in

---

[14] B. Othanel Smith and Milton Meux, "Research in Teacher Education: Problems, Analysis and Criticism," *An Analysis and Projection of Research in Teacher Education,* ed. Frederick R. Cyphert and Ernest Spaights (Columbus, Ohio: The Ohio State University Research Foundation, 1964), p. 112.

[15] Walton, *op. cit.,* p. 12.

many of its current embodiments, often closely resembles in its organization the way or ways in which sociology proper has been organized. To be sure the sociology of education—at least, ideally—is concerned predominantly and specifically with educational questions, but the rubrics and logical patterns which provide a way of ordering, clarifying, and dealing with these questions frequently are essentially those of sociology proper. Thus if sociology discusses such topics as social control, social roles and statuses, social stratification, group behavior, and so on, then the sociology of education employs similar organizing rubrics, save of course that under them educational questions presumably are given preponderant consideration. Under the topic of "Social Classes and Education," for example, one may encounter discussions of social class influences upon learning, the middle class bias of teachers, the effect of class on school attendance, and the like. The point, then, is not that educational questions are not discussed but rather that on this particular approach they are discussed within the framework of a logical structure typical of sociology proper. The parent body of knowledge provides the key to the organization of its counterpart in the body of knowledge unique to the profession of education, and, incidentally, this of course means that insofar as there are confusions about the logical structure of the parent body of knowledge, there will no doubt be corresponding confusions in its educational counterpart. Presumably the psychology of education, the history of education, the philosophy of education—insofar as it can be called a body of knowledge—and several other bodies of educational knowledge admit of this scheme of organization. The set of all such bodies of knowledge might well be regarded as at least a substantial part of the body of knowledge unique to the profession of education.

A somewhat different approach organizes educational knowledge on the basis of the various behaviors or activities characteristic of the profession of education—such activities as instructing, counseling, disciplining, curriculum planning, administering a school, and so on. This approach seeks to identify the principal sorts of activities in which educators recurrently and characteristically engage and to provide bodies of knowledge dealing directly with and bringing illumination to these activities. The key feature of the approach is that it makes "educational doings" themselves the focal points for organizing knowledge about education. The activities involved in teaching provide a case in point. These activities or behaviors, on David Ryans' scheme, are divisible into five major classes:

1. Motivating-reinforcing teacher behavior
2. Presenting-explaining-demonstrating teacher behavior
3. Organizing-planning-managing teacher behavior
4. Evaluating teacher behavior
5. Counseling-advising teacher behavior[16]

These five categories serve—or, at least, could serve—as a basis for bringing together and coordinating a variety of statements, many of them having a place in other bodies of knowledge with differing sorts of organization. Thus in discussing presenting-explaining-demonstrating teacher behavior, this approach might employ some statements appropriate to the psychology of education, some appropriate to the sociology of education, some appropriate to logic, and so on, but all chosen because of their relevance to presenting-explaining-demonstrating teacher behavior. The point is that the activities approach crosscuts the organization of numerous bodies of knowledge, bringing together statements from a variety of sources as they are pertinent to the educational activities under discussion. Relevance to educational activities, then, is the principal criterion of selection and organization.

Professor B. Othanel Smith offers an interesting variation of the activities approach in his essay on "The Preparation of a Teacher." He specifically raises the question of what knowledge embodied in linguistic symbols ought to be communicated to persons who at the undergraduate level are being prepared to teach.[17] In answer to his own question he suggests that the appropriate sort of knowledge is that which "can be applied to the analysis and interpretation of protocol material,"[18] with "protocol material" signifying "original records of *what teachers do.*"[19] (Italics mine.) Smith's own examples of protocol materials include

first, case descriptions of pupil misconduct; case histories of failing pupils, of pupils suffering from maladjustment, and records of difficulties pupils encounter in learning; second, transcribed recordings of classroom discussion at different grade levels and in

---

[16] David Ryans, "Teacher Behavior Theory and Research: Implications for Teacher Education," *The Journal of Teacher Education,* XIV (September, 1963), p. 275.

[17] B. Othanel Smith, "A Joint Task: The Preparation of a Teacher," p. 194.

[18] *Ibid.,* p. 195.

[19] *Ibid.*

different subjects, of small group discussion among pupils, of teacher-pupil planning sessions, and the like; third, case materials on teacher-parent interviews, on matters of academic freedom, on personal and civic rights of teachers, and case records on participation in school management.[20]

Smith is proposing that the body of pedagogical knowledge appropriate for prospective teachers be selected and ordered in terms of its rather direct relevance to the sorts of educational activities embodied in protocol material. He specifically recognizes that this approach rules out certain sorts of pedagogical knowledge for the undergraduate, but he suggests that what is omitted at the lower levels can perhaps more profitably be considered at advanced professional levels. Presumably at the more advanced levels, moreover, Smith would not necessarily call for the same scheme of organization of knowledge that he suggests for the lower levels. In any case, for the purpose of instructing preservice teachers Smith strongly urges that substantial portions of the body of knowledge unique to the profession of education be ordered around various aspects of the teacher's work as revealed through protocol material.

A third mode of organization makes the desired ends or outcomes of education the principal foci of organization. Bodies of statements organized in this manner, to be sure, discuss educational activities—often extensively—but the activities under discussion are selected and amplified only as they are pertinent to the given outcome or set of outcomes used as organizing foci. This approach, then, calls for straightforward enunciation of the ends or desired outcomes of education and, once again, for selection of confirmed statements from sundry sources as they may be ordered around these ends. Put together in this manner, the various subsets of statements within the body of knowledge unique to the profession of education may be regarded basically as discussions of means for securing ends, with these means-ends relationships made explicit. Typical of this tack in years past were various efforts to discuss education *for* life adjustment. Discussions of creativity, mental health, good citizenship, and the like provide more current instances of the same approach.

Which of these three modes of organization—or perhaps some other scheme—is most desirable? The question is misleading if it intimates that there is some one and only one defensible logic of organization for the body of knowledge unique to the profession of

[20] *Ibid.*

education. Bodies of knowledge may serve multiple purposes, and different purposes may well call for different organizational schemes. It follows that the task of those concerned to organize the body of knowledge unique to the profession of education is not to look for some single, final logical pattern but rather for different patterns commensurate with different purposes. If they are primarily concerned to prepare beginning teachers, they should seek an organizational scheme which lends itself to that task. If, on the other hand, they are concerned primarily with advanced graduate study of education and with research, they should gear the structure of their knowledge to those pursuits—and there is no guarantee at all that the structure appropriate for the one will be especially apt for the other. Indeed, we would speculate to the contrary although it is a matter of speculation in the absence of any extensive and systematic experimentation with different modes of organization. Such experimentation is certainly very much in order at the present time.

The future of the body of knowledge unique to the profession of education is contingent upon the extent to which the challenges posed in this essay are met. Happily there have been some heartening signs of late—not the least of which is the present colloquy—that these challenges are not being ignored. A number of thinkers within the field of education recognize their need for and are seeking to secure depth in the behavioral sciences and other bodies of knowledge pertinent to their educational work. Moreover, many scholars outside of the field of education are showing an increased interest in education and a willingness to engage in conjoint teaching and research enterprises with thinkers in education. Currently, too, there are some serious projects under way to bring new knowledge to bear upon educational questions and to experiment with new ways of organizing knowledge about education.[21] All of these things signalize the possibility of a new era in education. We may well be hopeful that the next several decades will see the emergence of a much more precise, complete, and useful body of knowledge unique to the profession of education.

[21] One of the most noteworthy of these efforts is the Teacher Education and Media Project of the American Association of Colleges for Teacher Education. This project, under the directorship of Herbert F. LaGrone, is a genuine effort to bring new knowledge to bear upon education and to find new ways to organize educational knowledge.

Psychology and the Body of Knowledge Unique to the Profession of Education

George W. Albee
Western Reserve University, Cleveland, Ohio

KNOWLEDGE has been compared, in a pungent simile, to a fish-market where the necessity for constant renewal becomes obvious in a relatively short time when the sources of supply fail.

In our consideration of knowledge unique to the profession of education we must bear in mind the urgent necessity for the constant renewal, reexamination, and reevaluation of our knowledge. There are no absolutes in knowledge which can be captured, delineated, and preserved forever unless our interest is in fossils rather than fresh and creative ideas.

It is my intention to discuss knowledge which the profession of education has found useful with particular attention to theoretical concepts which it shares with psychology.

I am particularly delighted to have this opportunity because for the past several years I have been arguing at every opportunity for a return to the symbiotic relationship between education and psychology which was so evident during the early years of this century. Psychology, in my judgment, made a critical error in its development, about twenty years ago, when it chose to focus a large measure of its applied efforts on psychopathology, in an alliance with medicine and psychiatry, rather than moving in the direction of closer interrelationships with education. Despite this error broad areas of research in psychology, and especially in the area of learning theory, continue to produce knowledge with more immediate usefulness to education than to psychiatry. If I may be permitted to make an hypothesis on this occasion, it is that twenty years from now psychology will have returned to its more proper and nutritious partnership with education and will have obtained a legal separation if not a divorce from psychiatry.

Another area with which I must deal briefly at the outset involves an examination of the characteristics of professions in general. Our subject is concerned with knowledge unique to the profession of education.

Part of the knowledge available to the profession of education is knowledge of the forces which shape and determine the development, content, and growth of all professions. Only recently have professions become self-conscious and self-critical. The present colloquy is an excellent illustration of this development. By examining what is known about the characteristics of all professions we may arrive at insights affecting our own development. Certainly we will be better prepared to avoid violating certain socio-cultural laws which are expressed in the structure of all professions.

Over the years there has evolved a large number of applied disciplines whose existence attests to a number of fairly definite and specific social needs. Professions have a number of identifiable characteristics, and one branch of social philosophy is concerned with the study and description of these characteristics.

There are a number of accounts of the probable first beginnings of the professions. Some social historians see them emerging out of needs in primitive society for the explanation of natural phenomena which gave rise to a class of people who were concerned with discovering, transmitting, and utilizing knowledge about the world. Certainly it is clear that the *first* criterion of any profession is knowledge. A frequently quoted example of how a profession originates is concerned with the ancient Egyptian priest-astronomers. Egyptian priests, keeping constant vigil in their temples, are believed to have taken advantage of their time at night to watch the stars in transit across the heavens. Such observations led to knowledge of seasonal fluctuations. By observing the coincidence of certain juxtaposition of stars with the annual flood of the Nile, powerful knowledge became available to these priest-astronomers. It was then possible for them to make predictions of floods in advance and to have knowledge *of use to the layman but inaccessible to the layman.* It is not important whether this example is literally true, or whether it is a romance, because it emphasizes one of the most important characteristics of any profession.

In recent years a number of people have devoted a great deal of time and study to the description of professions. I will note the contributions of only two, Abraham Flexner, who wrote early in the century, and Ernest Greenwood, a contemporary social theorist.

Flexner, who is largely responsible for the extensive revision and improvement of medical education in the United States during the early part of the twentieth century, also wrote a great deal about his perspective on professions in general. In describing the characteristics of professions, Flexner stressed the *intellectual* nature of professional activities, their *dependence on science and learning,* and the necessary *limitations* in their scope and purpose. He pointed out that any profession, to be dignified by this designation, must have an *intellectual or theoretical* content which sets it apart from occupations whose principal special requirement is a motor skill or technique. As professions grow and develop, they solidify the intellectual content into such a form that it can be taught to neophytes. As a profession becomes self-organized, strong *in-group feelings* among members of the profession develop. A subculture forms with its own *symbols,* values, and norms of behavior. *Control of entry* into the profession is largely vested in the hands of leaders of the group so that neophytes are chosen with care and instructed into the mysteries of the special knowledge of the group.

Greenwood has built his approach to the nature of professions on the work of Flexner and of more recent theorists. He, too, stresses the importance of systematic theory and points out that whenever a group achieves the status of a profession it *moves its instruction to an academic setting.* While neophytes are given special on-the-job training later in their preparation, much of their early instruction is rooted in theory and knowledge which can be taught only in the college or university. The importance of theory is attested to by the constant preoccupation of professionals with *adding to theory* and sharing new theoretical discoveries. This is accomplished by the *publication* of scientific and professional journals, by the frequent *meetings* of members of the group to discuss new discoveries and problems, by the recognized importance of refresher courses, and other means whereby members of the group can be brought up-to-date on the newest theoretical developments. The attitude toward theory is usually critical rather than worshipful, with a constant attempt to improve and refine theory. All of this implies the importance of a longer and *longer curriculum* as part of the training of the neophyte, because members of the group believe that it is important to make sure that all of the details of theory have been made clear to one before allowing him to practice the skill or technique involved in the profession. It is rare for a professional group to acquiesce to outside suggestions that certain courses, or areas of knowledge, be deleted from the training of fledgling members of their group. Therefore, we constantly witness the tendency of professional training programs to become longer and longer.

Another characteristic of professions which differentiates them from other kinds of service occupations is the relative *privacy* and uniqueness of the knowledge and skills of the professional. This means that, in general, members of the public must accept on faith the ability of the professional to perform the service required. Members of the general public, whatever their special competence, have relatively little choice in the nature of the service received from the professional. The belief is accepted on both sides that the layman is unable to appraise or diagnose his own needs and therefore relies on the appraisal or diagnosis of the specialist. In general, the layman comes to the professional with a willingness to put his own welfare in the professional's hands. Because the client does not have the special knowledge necessary to appraise the service rendered, there grows up the belief that *all* professional service is competent, though perhaps some professionals may be more competent than others! The professional in turn, is expected to take an objective attitude toward the layman coming to him for service and certainly must get no personal gratification out of the relationship beyond the satisfaction of providing good service.

One of the difficulties constantly confronting the profession of education is the fact that almost every parent has had many years of instruction in the schools. This makes the school less subject to the mysterious alchemy of the unknown that provides part of the mystique of most other professional activities. Parents are experts on teachers because they have had many relevant educational experiences of their own. These same parents will trust almost any doctor or dentist to do what they will with their children, but they are constantly looking over the teachers' shoulders making suggestions. As a matter of fact, there is no magic in the training programs for doctors and dentists, but the parents do not *know* this. In the days when the schoolmaster together with the town banker and clergyman formed the educated triumvirate of the village he shared in the mystique of private knowledge—teachers had more freedom and more responsibility then because they had more education than parents of their pupils.

Because of the power over human welfare involved in the professional relationship, professional groups always *seek sanction* from the community for their members to practice. This sanction may take the form of legal certification or *licensing* which restricts the right of untrained people to use the name of the profession or to hold themselves as able to perform the services of the profession. Other comparable forms of acceptance are sought from the community. The right to establish *training centers* and to *accredit educational programs* is sought from the community by professional groups in order to prevent unscrupulous or misinformed peoples from establishing shortcut training courses which leave out the theory so essential to professional training. In seeking concessions from the community, the professions generally take it upon themselves to police their own membership in such a way that no question can be raised about the *public-spirited* and *public-protective* nature of their activities. In the process of taking on this police power, professions develop *ethical codes* which are aimed at insuring the availability of competent service to members of the public, irrespective of their ability to pay. Ethical codes are also aimed at making new knowledge immediately available to all members of the group as soon as it has been shown to be valid, but prohibiting the too early dissemination or use of techniques of questionable usefulness. In the course of all of this in-group activity, strong group loyalties develop, a special *technical language* grows up which enables the members to communicate with each other without revealing clearly their meaning to outsiders, and the notion of the "career" which represents a whole life of service in a particular profession is held up as a model useful in recruiting neophytes into the professional culture.

All of these characteristics of professions are true in varying degrees of the profession of education and they set limits to any attempts to change or alter it.

Naturally an examination of the knowledge which is unique to the profession of education must contain a brief academic quibble which holds that no knowledge is truly unique. While knowledge available to members of a profession may not easily be accessible to the general public, this is more a matter of the inability of individuals to master all knowledge because of its breadth and diversity rather than because of its inaccessibility. Anyone with access to a good library can share the knowledge available to mankind in almost any chosen field, but no one can in a lifetime grasp it all.

What are some of the fundamental concepts which the profession of education shares with other scientifically rooted professions?

First of all, we share the fundamental assumption that we live in *a world that is lawful rather than capricious.* The impact of the rise of science over the past three hundred years has changed fundamentally our view of nature and of the world. Scientific rationalism has replaced superstition as the basic set out of which Western man now perceives his universe as ordered and lawful. There are many areas of uncertainty and much unknown terrain to be explored but we share with other professions the conviction that nature will answer our questions if they are properly framed. We possess a basic confidence that we can obtain answers through scientific investigation. John Stuart Mill provided us with a logical armamentarium which has since been supplemented by more complex mathematical tools and statistical design, but our basic approach has continued in a straight line from Mill. Scientific questions now are said to have a half-life in years rather than decades so that any proper question that we may ask may be answered if our society is willing to invest its resources and talents in obtaining the answer.

I emphasize this fundamental assumption of *lawfulness* at the outset because it pervades our entire educational culture and because it is so omnipresent that it is likely to be overlooked. It underlies our emphasis on the importance of research and on our quasi-religious attitude toward the sanctity of data. This scientific orientation also involves us in a dual responsibility—we must crowd our courses with more and more information which scientific investigations have unearthed, clarified, and defined, while at the same time we must prepare our neophytes for the task of discovering new knowledge, by instruction in research methodology.

The lawfulness of nature is no better illustrated in the field of education than in the area of statistics. The wonder, beauty, and mystery of the Gaussian curve may be lost temporarily on our students struggling to master the derivation of formulae, but it is there nonetheless. Sir Francis Galton's discovery of the coefficient of correlation provided a miraculous tool for demonstrating the interrelationship of events or processes. Statistical manipulations have been criticized, often justly, when they have been misapplied, though we need to remember to direct our criticism to the fallible human statistician, where it may be deserved, rather than to question the underlying order in nature.

The need to predict the future derives largely from the human frontal lobes. Unlike any other animal form, Man has the ability to bind time and to look into the future with hope and fear. Statistics provides one of our best techniques for predicting the unknown future from something that is known in the present.

The frontal lobes, long called the silent areas of the brain, absent or rudimentary in lower forms, are both Man's triumph and his psychological burden. They permit him to plan, to lay up stores of wisdom for the use of future generations, and to foresee the future as an extrapolation from the present. At the same time they lead him to develop anxiety over anticipated tragedies and failures, and they allow him to be confronted with the ultimate mystery of personal finiteness. Man struggles desperately to read the future and to prepare for it. Because statistics provides some of the best predictive and descriptive tools available to educators, I emphasize the importance of this subject, both practically and as a comfortable support for the basic human need to predict.

Before proceeding further to delineate concepts which continue to flow out of the basic scientific assumption of a lawful and predictable world, I feel compelled to interpose a second fundamental and counterpuntal assumption which has profound consequences for both education and psychology. This opposing concept holds that the ultimate mysteries of human existence are unfathomable and cannot be solved or decoded by any approach of which man is capable, and especially including the application of his intelligence. Ultimately man comes face to face with the terror of his finiteness and his mind reels when he attempts to comprehend an infinite universe whose origins long preceded his existence and whose destiny he has no significant part in shaping.

An awareness of the limitations of science and of the reach of human intelligence might be called a concept of ultimate *inscrutability* which education must also share with every other discipline that seeks knowledge. The consequences of this concept, which is not always consciously held, certainly are to be found in the tenacious defense of liberal education and in the pervasive notion that to be a specialist is not to be educated. Certainly the inclusion of the humanities in our curricula and the persistent emphasis on the importance of art, literature, poetry, philosophy, music, and drama attest to the strength of the position that science cannot teach us all we need to experience or to know about life.

I have chosen, wherever possible, to indicate areas of knowledge unique to the field of education which were first outlined by a well-known investigator whose classic study is familiar to every professional educator. Many of the original studies have been picked to pieces by the stone chippers who followed and who have seized for careful examination every attention-getting study from which sweeping generalizations and extrapolations are made. One of the strengths of education and psychology is that we have both kinds of people, those who can design pioneering studies which capture everyone's imagination, and also those patient toilers who bring the sharp light of cross-validation and single variable analysis into play as they scrutinize the validity of generalizations.

Closely related to the concept of orderliness and its statistical elaboration is the concept of *individual differences.* Very early in this century psychologists Binet and Simon were invited by a French educational commission to direct their efforts toward developing techniques for the early identification of those children who would not profit from instruction in the French educational system, or who could not proceed at the same rate as the average school child. You are all familiar with the far-reaching results of this early collaboration between education and psychology. The dramatic discovery by Binet that the intelligence of the average child proceeds at a linear rate of growth paralleling the rate of physical growth, and ultimately the development of the concept of the Intelligence Quotient by Stern, has had educational consequences so numerous and detailed as to fill libraries. The fundamental knowledge which I want to separate out here is the concept of individual differences. Not only do children differ from each other in obvious physical characteristics but they also differ from each other in hidden but measureable ways such as the ability to learn, the ability to conceptualize, and the motivation to achieve. Also, there are variances in their patterns of special interest, and their special abilities. Some of these differences are innate and some are acquired. In either case they have profound influences on the educational process. As educators and psychologists we are all too familiar with the dangers of attempting to predict the child's future (and in a kind of self-fulfilling prophesy thereby to *shape* his future) on the basis of insufficient, invalid, or unreliable assays of these individual differences. On the other hand, we must be prepared to defend with vigor and imagination the fact that our psychometric methods, in the hands of well qualified people, are our best available techniques for dealing with the class of problems that Binet originally set out to solve. The present wave of reappraisal of testing programs may achieve a healthy correction in the use of tests and a critical examination of their validity in special circumstances. But the values of testing are so clear and demonstrable that *test theory and methodology* will continue to be among the most important areas of knowledge we have in education and psychology.

The implications of our knowledge of individual differences apply as much to teachers as to pupils. Knowledge of the critical requirements for successful teaching should enable us to improve our selection procedures to select those qualities in our neophytes as to maximize the effectiveness of the teachers. Unfortunately we have not always taken advantage of knowledge already available in this area. Too often self-selection by the prospective teacher has been a more important factor than carefully planned recruitment. Nor have we taken advantage of knowledge available from industrial psychology in our personnel practices with teachers. A clear example here is the research of Frederick Herzberg and his discoveries of the basic factors associated with the motivation to work. He has found, in a wide variety of settings, and in several cultures around the world, that job satisfaction and job dissatisfaction are not on a continuum. The things that make people unhappy about their jobs Herzberg refers to as hygienic factors. That is to say, they relate to the work environment and to the conditions of employment. People are unhappy about such factors as poor working conditions, poor salaries, and poor fringe benefits. But he found that we often make the mistake of thinking that correction of these environmental frustrations will make for happy employees when as a matter of fact this is not true. Improving the hygiene of the environment makes people less unhappy but it does not make them happy. The things that people like about their jobs and the things that are required to make them satisfied are of quite different orders. These factors, which he calls the motivators, involve such things as opportunities for individual achievement, recognition for good work done, and similar factors associated with the satisfaction of creative and meaningful contributions. As educators we need to absorb the lesson of this research and to pay an equal amount of attention to opportunities in education for creativity and individuality, along with our concern with working conditions and salaries.

Another fundamental area of knowledge of great importance to the educator is subsumed under the general term *maturation*. A profound understanding of the wondrous process of development which begins at conception and continues to unfold until death is essential to the educator. The process of maturation places limits on what may be learned and defines the best time for different kinds of learning.

Although the details of our knowledge of the maturational processes fill volumes, the importance of this field of knowledge may be illustrated with one or two examples. One of the important concepts which determines much that is done in education is the concept of *readiness*. From the time of Myrtle McGraw's classic study of Jimmy and Johnny we have continued to refine our knowledge of the factors associated with the readiness to learn and of the effects of practice. Sometimes, it now seems in the light of present knowledge that readiness to learn was more a function of our teaching methods than it was of organismic maturation. For years we have thought that a mental age of something over six years was necessary before the child could learn to read. Recently we have been confronted with children with mental ages of considerably less than six who obviously have learned to read. Current research into what is now called in psychology the *critical period* promises to revise many of our ideas about readiness.

But this current ferment does not in any way invalidate facts established about prerequisite physiological development for a wide variety of educational experiences. Changes in the concept of readiness consistently have been in the direction of lowering the age at which new material is introduced to the child. Naturally, there are limits to this movement down the age scale but they appear to be earlier than once believed possible.

The myelinization of the neurons of the brain is not complete until sometime after birth and the continuing development of the nervous system only gradually makes possible the acquisition of motor skills including locomotion and speech; also, sensory processes leading to differentiated perception in an orderly sequence must await maturational development.

Always we must differentiate between what is true knowledge of maturational processes and what is authoritative opinion. Many of our cherished notions about the critical period for introducing new levels of complexity in our teaching are now being overthrown by radical demonstrations that the young child is capable of more learning than he is credited with being ready to absorb.

If I may venture a second prediction, it would be that within the next two or three decades we will finally be forced to acknowledge that there is nothing sacred about the sixth year as the optimal time to begin formal schooling, and that indeed we have wasted the most valuable years. More and more evidence is being accumulated which indicates that the hungry mind of the child is at its maximum absorption stage much before age six and that some formal education can and should be instituted very early. We have recently heard considerable discussion about the sanctity of the neighborhood school. I suggest that there may be advantages to the neighborhood school if school begins at age one year, but this would be largely for the convenience of the mother. By the time children reach the ripe old age of six, the argument for the neighborhood school may lose its cogency. We may witness the extension of formal education not only through junior college, as is now being proposed widely, but also to earlier and earlier age levels. The recent revival of the discoveries and methods of Maria Montessori fits right into the psychological *zeitgeist* which more and more emphasizes the ability of the very young child to learn things that tradition and authority have judged him incapable of. Yet the average child masters a complex language in three years, and under the right circumstances can master two in this period. Recent creative research at the Mental Development Center of Western Reserve University, by B. Z. Friedlander, has shown that young infants are capable of making differentiated responses to a variety of stimuli for the reward of being able to control lights, tones, and music. Maturation and readiness is an entire area of knowledge that needs exploration, reevaluation, and renewal.

Another thing we know for certain is that the human *motivational structure* occupies a hierarchical pattern. Abraham Maslow has described the hierarchy in detail. Man is a perpetually wanting animal. The most prepotent of his needs usually preoccupies his attention. When one of his strong basic motives is frustrated, it arouses strong emotion and often some kind of aggressive act occurs. Higher order motives cannot operate in the presence of basic frustration. The hungry man is not concerned with artistic success, nor is the frightened child interested in Latin.

All human motivation rests on physiological foundations, but built on this basic physiological structure is a hierarchy of other needs. The organism needs first and foremost to have his basic physiological requirements for food, warmth, and other anabolic requirements satisfied; after these have been satisfied, the *next level* of need is for *safety*. The organism constantly searches for safety and security, perhaps as a result of the experience of helplessness in infancy, when it was necessary to depend entirely on others for existence itself. Safety involves the need for an orderly world to quiet fears of the unknown. The world must be reasonably predictable for the child to feel safe. At the next higher level are needs for *love* and *affection*. It is a very human motive to want to belong to someone, to a family, to a group, to be accepted as a person, to be appreciated and loved.

At the next higher level is the need for *self-esteem*. A very powerful force in motivating human behavior is the need to be approved and liked by others. Most people strive to achieve goals which are socially approved and rewarding. This is a very powerful motivation in human affairs.

Finally, at the highest motivational level is what might be called the need for *self-actualization*. Here are all the relatively free patterns of behavior through which it is possible for an individual to express himself, where one can be what he is able to be to the limit of his ability and in as creative and meaningful ways as possible.

It is the job of the teacher to maximize the opportunities available to children at these highest levels of motivation. But when the basic needs of children, or of teachers for that matter, are frustrated, learning cannot occur.

We need to realize clearly that children's basic needs for sustenance, for safety, and for love and affection must be taken care of outside the school before they can begin to share the social and educational goals that most of us take for granted.

While the teacher cannot be all things to all pupils, each has a responsibility to use all the influence he possesses in shaping a society where no child goes hungry, where no child is terrified of his environment, and where no child lives without the support of affectionate people in his daily environment.

A great deal of nonsense has been written about various *techniques* for accelerating or enriching the learning experiences of deprived children, without taking into account the basic psychological fact that the human motivational system is hierarchical and that higher order motives cannot operate in the presence of severe frustration at the more basic levels.

Our schools pay a great deal of attention to preparing pupils for later learning by seeing to it that their basic tool skills are developed. We teach reading, writing, and arithmetic very early so that these skills may be used in subsequent learning. But it is also the responsibility of the schools to make clear to the power structure of our society that even more important prerequisites are necessary before learning can proceed. Those social forces which interfere with the satisfaction of the child's fundamental human needs are just as severe in their interference with later learning as poor reading skill. As educators we must be concerned with the social forces which prevent effective teaching and learning.

It is in the area of learning theory that some of the most fundamental knowledge unique to the field of education is to be found. Indeed practically every validated concept here has great relevance; but I have chosen only three examples from a much longer list of significant concepts merely to illustrate the variety of available knowledge. Learning is usually defined as any change in performance which is a consequence of experience; it has direction, and satisfies the motivating conditions of the individual. This is what education is all about. It seeks to change and improve the performance, or the repertoire of potential performance, of individuals through planned and controlled experiences. The educational experience certainly has direction; and if it is to be effective, it must satisfy motives in the pupils and students involved.

The first concept I would stress from learning theory is the empirically derived observation that an organism must *learn how to learn*. As Harlow has shown, an organism exhibits improvement in his attention, readiness, sophistication, and alertness to the fact that a solution is possible, following repeated opportunities to discover correct solutions to problems. The principle is equally valid for monkeys in a puzzle box or for children in a schoolroom. For *learning* to reach its maximum effectiveness, it is necessary (1) that the organism have a long preschool history of problem-solving experiences and (2) that diversification of such experiences be continued throughout the educational program.

One of the most important components of the process of *learning to learn* is the *use of language to acquire language*. We rarely pause to reflect on the central importance of language development to the educational process. As Leonard Carmichael put it, "Teaching of the ability to use language correctly and with grace is probably as general a 'training of the mind' as it is possible to carry out," and "in a most important sense, the development of language in an individual is the growth of the human mind in that person."

A related second area of knowledge derived from the field of learning is the ancient topic of *transfer of training*.

The classic studies of Thorndike and his peers early in this century, and of the endless subsequent research on the subject, have delineated fairly sharply the areas of significant and insignificant transfer. We no longer teach certain subjects in order to "strengthen the mind" nor do we expect any appreciable direct transfer from the study of geometry to the ability to reason in general. On the other hand, we know with certainty that practice of one skill may frequently facilitate learning of a similar skill. For example, students who are taught geometry in a way which emphasizes critical analysis may show marked improvement in other reasoning problems. The complexities of the transfer problem are beyond the scope of the present paper but a detailed knowledge exists and is certainly relevant to a professional educator.

A third classic area in the general field of learning theory, which has an unbroken history of research renewal, is a knowledge of the effects of *praise* and *reproof* or, in more current terminology, reward and punishment or positive and negative reinforcement. Everyone knows Hurlock's classic study on this subject. Again the details of this field are so complex as to make any brief summarization dangerous, but it can be stated with some assurance that positive reinforcement is *essential* for the acquisition of learning and punishment is *ineffective* in eliminating unwanted elements of behavior. Satisfiers strengthen connections, to use Thorndike's language, and annoyers fail to weaken the connections they follow. Countless studies have shown that withholding reinforcement of any kind tends to extinguish behavior more effectively than punishing it, and that rewarding competing responses which are desirable is likewise effective. Related to this whole area of knowledge is the complex detail of conditioning, both the classical and instrumental paradigms. By and large emotional and involuntary reactions are acquired through the Pavlovian form of stimulus contiguity, while voluntary, usually skeletal, responses are acquired through operant methods.

The very rapid recent discoveries of applications of operant technology which have grown from the work of Skinner have produced a technology developing so rapidly that it may change and shape the whole direction of future growth in the field of education. In its very simplest form the experimenter decides in advance which responses he wants to strengthen out of the broad repertoire of emitted behavior. When the response, or a first approximation of it, appears, he delivers an immediate reward; under conditions of more and more restricted reinforcement, for sharpened versions of the response, he obtains the desired behavior. The technology is so powerful that pigeons can very rapidly be taught to play the piano, monkeys can be taught to read a radar scope and to control the flights of spacecraft, and four-year-olds can be taught to type on an electric typewriter, and also learn to read while becoming expert typists.

Certain simple principles can be distilled from the complexity of research going on in the area. The learning process benefits enormously from immediate feedback of information on success, and it benefits from situations controlled in such a way that chances of failing are minimized. Present rapid expansion of teaching techniques of automated instruction based on these principles may turn out to be only the simple beginnings of a revolution comparable to that which followed the development of the internal combustion engine. So many of both over-enthusiastic and over-critical judgments have been made about the teaching machine that it is difficult to arrive at a calm evaluation of its place in the field of education. While I firmly believe that the teacher will continue to be the most important element in the educational process, the field of education must understand and guide the fantastic potential of the automated instructional devices.

I must return again to the statement made at the outset. Fundamental concepts and knowledge in education are not absolute but rather must be adapted to the cultural context as society evolves. There are many conceptual models which might be chosen to illustrate this point. In the field of psychopathology there is a powerful concept usually referred to as the "cultural relativity hypothesis" which suggests that behavior deemed abnormal in our culture might be acceptable in other societies while behavior which other societies consider deviant might be acceptable to us. While the strict interpretation of this hypothesis is no longer held, it served a definite purpose in educating the professional culture to the fact that all behavior and, indeed, all institutions must be understood in the context of the socioculture order in which they occur.

David Riesman has given us one of the most useful conceptual models for understanding people in different kinds of societies and his schema is important for the profession of education to understand in fitting itself into the society which supports and nurtures us.

Briefly, Riesman has suggested that people in evolving societies change from being tradition-directed, to being inner-directed, to being other-directed. In the tradition-directed society the population tends to be decentralized and dispersed. There is a tremendous emphasis on ritual and religion, and a close dependency upon the mighty natural cycles of nature. Education is rudimentry, partly because the stability of the society makes mobility difficult and the need for education very modest and partly because there is relatively little leisure time available for formal instruction.

When certain changes occur, such as the accumulation of capital, and as industrialization of the society begins to build up momentum, the movement of young people from the farms and villages to the industrial cities makes necessary broad changes in the educational institutions. Now each child must be equipped with an individual conscience to carry with him as he leaves the control of the family farm or small village. There is a tremendous incentive to acquire basic educational achievements by the individual in order to further his chances for finding his fortune in the society now assuming widespread change and widespread opportunity. Educational institutions change from a religious to a secular control and the voracious demands by industry for technically trained people in a multiplicity of fields bring pressure on education to emphasize the practical. When the productive machine has been built and when the outpouring of goods of all kinds reaches the point where it is easy to produce more than enough manufactured goods for any level of consumption, the individual pattern changes to become other-directed. Now consumption has replaced achievement as the central theme for large numbers of people. Once again the institutions of society must change to fit the culture. Now a relatively modest output of technicians can minister to the productive machine and education becomes an institution whose primary functions are to keep young people off the labor market for as long as possible. In the absence of large demands for industrial manpower there is strong pressure to keep young people in school through high school and even through college. As a consequence the educator is confronted with new problems which frustrate and baffle him. Classes are too large, buildings are antiquated, and methods are inappropriate. Pupils are no longer retained because of their interest and ability to learn but because of social pressures.

This capsule examination of the relationship between the needs of the economy and the institution of education can only hint at the profound interrelationship between the level of development of society and education. Certainly the profession of education must see itself clearly in its relationship to society, in order that it resist demands which are inappropriate, and in order that it contribute most usefully to a reciprocal influencing of the direction of the human enterprise.

I am painfully aware that much of what I have said is not new. Every elementary course in educational psychology deals with such concepts as maturation, motivation, learning, and measurement. And yet, on reflection, this must in itself be evidence that knowledge of these fields is fundamental to the profession of education. Your intimate familiarity with the subject areas I have delineated might be regarded as evidence of the validity of the selection of these topics as fundamental to the field.

The Transmission of Culture
Solon T. Kimball[1]
Teachers College—Columbia University

IF THERE IS any aspect of human knowledge which is uniquely distinctive of education, and which can be claimed as the major prerogative of professional educators, it is to be found in the conditions and processes associated with the transmission of culture.

Ordinarily when we speak of education we have in mind the formally organized enterprise through which the teaching of subject matter and skills is accomplished. Presumably the purpose of this activity is to prepare the young to take their place in the society of adults. But the achievement of physical maturity, the acquisition of knowledge and skills, the development of moral judgment, and the learning of patterns of acceptable behavior are not restricted to the period of institutionalized and formal instruction. Infancy and early childhood furnish crucial experiences for the formation of the emotional and cognitive patterns that the individual will carry into later life. In fact we can hardly expect to understand the consequences of directed teaching unless we know the personal and cultural antecedents which the child brings with him into the classroom.

We are very far from knowing what can and must be known about these early years, in part because we have not known how to proceed. Study of the psychological aspects of child development has been helpful, but much of our energy has been directed toward accumulating those static data which tests and measurements render. This is not the stuff which reveals to us the intricate interdependencies between individual and environment. They do not lend themselves to a statement of the processes which explain growth and

[1] I wish to acknowledge the helpful comments of Dr. Arthur I. Gates, and of Dr. Fred Eggan and Dorothy Eggan, to whom I turned for a critical reading of this manuscript.

change. Furthermore, those who are wedded to their use are trapped in an intellectual procedure which seeks orderliness through the categorization of the atomistic bits and pieces which they have gathered. There is the temptation to label the results obtained as nonsense since the reality they portray is not that of the world they examine but of the operations which they represent.

Before we attempt to specify the ingredients necessary for a more rewarding approach to this problem, let us make certain that the objective toward which we are moving is clearly understood. If it is our concern to isolate that which is unique to education, then we must extend our perspective to include more than is contained within the limits of formal education. In particular we must view formal education as a special aspect of the socialization of the individual. Furthermore, we cannot say that subject matter, or that any one subject, exemplifies that to which we should pay special attention because knowledge is not in itself inherently related to the manner in which it is learned. We can similarly eliminate the acquisition of skills as the main point of emphasis, for although skills can be taught, and their acquisition implies learning, these are only part of what the individual acquires in his movement toward adulthood. In essence, what we have been rejecting is a concern with the *consequences* of learning, the results of influences, direct and indirect, which shape the individual in his progression from birth onward. Instead, what we propose is that that which is unique to education is knowledge of the conditions which affect the transmission of culture.

When we come to enumerate what should be subsumed within this area, we must include the relationship between teacher and learner; the cultural tradition and social environment within which learning occurs; the organic and psychic capacities of the individual to be modified through experience; and the dynamics of the learning process itself. Although we must examine each of these aspects in some detail we can clarify and place in better perspective the ensuing discussion if at this moment we make brief reference to current learning theory.

The individual has been the focus of almost all of those who have been concerned with learning. This bias is understandable if we view it as stemming from a major theme of Western culture. It is exemplified by the attention given to the great and little in religion, history, and literature and to our interest in explaining their behavior. Traditionally, we have turned to such inner qualities as spirit, wisdom, character, or ambition to give us the key to the forces which have shaped their lives. These explanations are usually of two kinds. On the one hand, they seek a source of external energy such as God or Society for the locus of inspiration, and, on the other, they have turned to an innate force such as the instincts which create a property acquiring economic man as postulated by Adam Smith or the libido-driven patients and disciples of Freud.

In some cultures men are moved by acquisitive desires or by the need for love; but as explanations of pan-human behavior, these suffer from many inadequacies. Some portion of our willingness to accept such schemes can be attributed to our too easy acceptance of motivation as explanatory of the direction which individual human behavior seemingly exhibits. In fact, we would be wiser to treat motivation as a psychological artifact than as a basic human variable. We might with equal cogency argue for the primacy of "guilt" or of "anxiety" or of "fear." These are terms which refer to recognizable emotional states, but we should not confuse the stimuli which evoke behavior and the behavior itself. Which is the motivant?

Those who seek for inner-state explanations of behavior implicitly assume a concreteness in the subject of their inquiry. If something can be treated as an entity, then its qualities or attributes can be made explicit through dissection; and presumably the mechanisms which control its functioning can be made explicit. Unfortunately for those who follow this course, neither "spirits" nor "instinct" nor "id" nor any of the other postulations lend themselves to the kind of examination applied to substances. My objection, however, does not deny that under certain circumstances it is useful to speak of the needs of the organism, or that the designation of emotional states may have utility, or that cerebration is necessary for comprehension and insight. My objection is of a more fundamental kind. It is that the focus upon the individual has led to an inadequate statement of the problem and that, in consequence, the results of analysis have given us only partial, if not inadequate, answers.

In their search for the mechanisms which explain human behavior and learning, the psychological empiricists have made a great contribution in dispelling some of the metaphysical confusions. If we start with the simple pleasure-pain formulation offered by Jeremy Bentham over a century and a half ago, we can trace to the present the genetic links of a long intellectual and theoretical tradition. Its basic formulation is of utmost simplicity, the famous stimulus-cue-response. The focus is clearly upon the individual, but in its pure form it dispels any necessity to rely upon an ineffable "force," and it takes account of variables external to the individual. Among those we associate with advances in this field are Pavlov, Thorndike, Watson, and Skinner. But pleasure-pain, conditioned reflex, tension reduction, need-fulfillment, or reinforcement are still variations within the more general stimulus-response theory and the question at hand is whether or not this theory is sufficiently inclusive to cover the range of empirical evidence with which we must contend.

The problem is an intricate and difficult one because if its solution depends upon unraveling the intricacies of the human neural system, it is far from certain that we can ever arrive at anything more than an approximate solution. The less complex brains and sensory apparatuses of dogs, rats, and pigeons are better subjects for experimentation, but the transferability to humans of the results obtained is always open to doubt.

There is a second and even more valid reason for doubt, however. If we divide behavior into that which reflects the responses based on conditioning and which we call "training" as one category, and classify behavior which is based upon the arrangement of experience in new combinations and which we label "cognition" as another category, then it becomes clearer why stimulus-response as an inclusive formula seems inadequate. As a simple example which distinguishes between the two, we can take the case of the student who learns by rote the answers to set questions. Irrespective of the complexity of either questions or answers, this type of learning falls within the category of training and offers no essential difference from the patterned behavior which a Pavlov instills in his dogs or a Skinner in his pigeons. However, if a student learns how to utilize experience to frame questions the answers to which express relationships, then we can say that the intellectual process has broken free of the limitations imposed by set responses to specific stimuli and exemplifies cognition.

The experimental problems formulated by Pavlov or Skinner represent cognitive behavior; and no matter how elaborate or inten-

TRANSMISSION OF CULTURE

sive the training they give their animals, the latter can never create an experimental situation in which their erstwhile experimenters become the subjects. This does not deny the importance of training in the development of an orderly intellect. But the neural complexity of man's cortex permits the synthesis of experience into new combinations. Furthermore, immediate stimulus to cerebral activity may be apparent, and set stimuli may yield variable responses. Indeed, this may be what those who write of creative thinking have in mind. It is the process of cognition.

The distinction between behavior based on training and that based on cognition is a useful one, but it still leaves some tough questions unasked and unanswered. As yet, we have hardly touched upon the problem of the response as a function of the stimuli. I prefer to phrase the problem differently although the intent can remain the same. Of what relevance is the relation between an individual and his environment to the learning process? In this formulation the emphasis is directed to relationship and process, and the individual and environment are seen as variables. Specifically, both of the latter are seen as undergoing continuous change of greater or lesser magnitude; hence the consequences of the interdependency between them continuously vary.

This formulation is one which avoids the trap of assigning fixed attributes or qualities to an individual and the danger of accepting an enumeration of these as expressing either process or relationship. Furthermore, I believe that the relationship between the individual and his environment is the crucial problem if we are to understand the transmission of culture as a function of conditions. Among other things, this formulation recognizes the cultural system as one aspect of the environment.

But there is much more that needs to be examined, and the remainder of this paper will address itself to the task at hand. In the development of the argument we shall range widely over several disciplines for our facts. Physical anthropology will help us to understand the relationship between the individual as an organic being and the culture milieu. We will then turn to some of the findings in the field of culture and personality, and to the problem of cultural perspective. Next, we shall seek an example in the socialization of the child to exemplify the operation of cultural patterning. This, then, brings us to an analysis of the mechanisms of culture and their relation to learning. Finally, we shall attempt a synthesis of the evidence to provide a new formulation of the processes of the transmission of culture.

Man as a Culture Creating Animal

Among the characteristics which distinguishes man from other forms of animal life is his capacity for culture. But we hold a quite erroneous perspective if we separate for analysis and description the physical attributes of *Homo sapiens* and consider them as developing according to biological processes quite apart from the influence of culture. If we did so, we would then attribute to the human organism the inevitable capacity to achieve full physical maturity outside of the environmental influence which human society provides. The evidence does not support any such assumption. Instead, we are forced to accept, in the spheres of both phylogeny and ontogeny, an intricate arrangement of intermeshing influences between the physical and cultural aspects of man. Each helped to shape the other, and the point in time a million or more years ago when this process began can be justifiably called "The Human Revolution."[2]

It is not our purpose, nor is it necessary, to recount in detail the inferred effects of man's tool-making-and-using pattern of skills, his social groupings, or the appearance of articulate speech with its system of abstract symbols. What we do need to understand, however, is that man represents a unique form of animal life in the creation of a nonphysical, that is, cultural, environment which, in turn, affected the selective process that led to the appearance of modern man.

There are, however, several much commented upon consequences of this evolutionary sequence which need to be mentioned. The human infant at birth, and for a considerable time thereafter, is incapable of survival outside of an environment which provides him with nurture. This dependency of the young upon its mother, or other adults, which is not necessarily restricted to man, is necessary because of its physical immaturity. One consequence of the prolonged dependency is that the individual in his progression toward maturity is subject to an intense and continuous period of learning. Thus the ex-

[2] Charles F. Hockett and Robert Ascher, "The Human Revolution," *Current Anthropology*, V, No. 3 (1964) 135-147.

tended period of dependency may be seen as a function of the immense amount of learning which must be acquired in the context of the minimally developed physiological processes which accompany the individual at birth.

The fact that infants do progress from an original immature condition to full cultural and physical maturity is significant. From this fact we can infer that given the conditions of a cultural environment and of the stage of physical and neural development at birth, the infant does possess the capacities for responding to this environment. Furthermore, the fact that this process is successfully achieved in all known varieties of culture establishes that any existent cultural environment is adequate for the human infant.

We must also decide, however, whether or not mere physical nurture, that is, an environment lacking culture, is sufficient for the human infant to achieve full humanity. The evidence upon which we can reach a conclusion is provided from many sources, but the most dramatic instances are those of feral man. Reports of other children who have lived virtually isolated from human contact substantiate the overwhelming importance of the environment in the shaping of the human infant.[3]

The conclusion to which this evidence leads us is that the achievement of full humanity is not an inevitable attribute of the human infant. Minimal physical nurture can ensure the survival of the individual, but other patterned behavior is essentially a function of the environment. When this evidence is joined with that which studies of child development have provided, we feel secure in accepting the almost infinite impressionability of the human neural system, an impressionability the development of which is itself a function of the environment. If this is the case, then how, we might ask, is it possible to understand the processes of learning or the development of the child if we focus our attention upon the subject, and not upon the influences which shape him? Such a procedure ignores the dynamic interplay between subject and his cultural environment and minimizes or even excludes variability within the environment as a significant factor.

When we come to seek an explanation for the failure to take cul-

[3] Kingsley Davis, *Human Society* (New York: The Macmillan Co., 1949), pp. 204-208.

ture into account as a significant variable there are several reasons which come quickly to mind. Most of those who have been doing research in this area have been trained in psychology and are generally unconversant with culture theory. The minimum advantage which flows from acquaintance with anthropological materials is that, through comparison of findings in several cultures, the danger of assuming a universal application is reduced.

Cross-cultural comparisons, however, can be a trap for the unsophisticated. The assumption that apparently similar culture traits or patterns are identical ignores the possibly divergent meaning which each carries in its original context. Some anthropologists are now attempting to overcome this hazard by developing more comprehensive models which are based upon cognitive comparisons in which they utilize linguistic and relational analysis.[4,5] Their approach has not yet been sufficiently tested, however, to judge if it solves difficulties in comparative analysis.

The most relevant contribution thus far has come from those studies in which psychological theory has been combined with the methods of ethnology in the field of culture and personality. The several studies by Mead, Bateson, Linton, Hallowell, Whiting, Hsu, Honigmann, and others have focused attention upon child training practices as a mechanism for the transmission of culture. Although these studies provide great insights into the variability in the patterning of emotions as a function of cultural differences, very little effort has been made thus far either to describe the cognitive environment within which child training operates, or to ascertain how cognitive patterns are acquired or expressed in the child. Until this deficiency has been corrected, it will remain impossible to construct an adequate theoretical model of learning in its relation to culture.[6] Nevertheless, anthropological studies have confirmed the validity of one enormously valuable principle through clarifying the origin and variability of *perspective* and in demonstrating how the cultural perspective provides the screen through which experience is filtered and interpreted.

[4] A. Kimball Romney and Ray Goodwin D'Andrade (eds.), "Transcultural Studies in Cognition," *American Anthropology*, LXVI, No. 3, Part II (1964).

[5] Anthony Wallace, "Culture and Cognition," *Science* CXXXV (1962), 351-357.

[6] Solon T. Kimball, "Communication Modalities as a Function of Social Relationships," *Transactions of the New York Academy of Sciences*, XXV², No. 4 (1963), 459-468.

In its most comprehensive sense, the perspective system is synonymous with world view. This is the system of thought and feeling which explains the operation of the universe. It makes meaningful to man such natural phenomena as the seasonal rhythms of nature, earth, and heaven, and the origin and destiny of life. It provides the rationale for explaining success, failure, and tragedy. It identifies things and their attributes and expresses relationships between them through categorization. In essence, the world view provides the orderly system through which the aspects of experience are identified and interpreted.

Everyday experience easily confirms the point. Where the sheep rancher views the wolf as a predator, the conservationist sees him as one element in a harmonious balance of nature. Where we rely upon knowledge of the physiology of the body for diagnosing and treating illness, the Navaho sees illness as an active intrusion into the body of a spirit; and the removal of the spirit is accomplished through ritual means.

Even within the realms of science, world view may inhibit or advance the understanding of the processes of nature. One of the more dramatic instances is that of the great scientific naturalist, Louis Agassiz, who refused to accept the implications of his own evidence, and that of others, which supported the concept of evolution.[7] Agassiz believed in a Divine Intelligence which through acts of special creation populated the earth with life forms that were immutable and fixed. From time to time this Divinity caused catastrophes which wiped out all life but in a succeeding epoch brought forth new life forms that were divergent from the preceding period. From this *a priori* conception it was unnecessary and, in fact, impossible to accept any phylogenetic connection between earlier and later species as they were revealed through the succession of geologic strata. Agassiz believed that in his discovery and classification of species he was fashioning the pattern of a great divinely inspired cosmic plan. He even utilized his theory of an Ice Age to support his view of divinely inspired catastrophes.

It seems unnecessary to adduce further examples to establish the point. As a part of each culture is a system of identifying and inter-

[7] Edward Lurie, *Louis Agassiz: A Life in Science* (Chicago: University of Chicago Press, 1960).

preting the things and events which constitute experience. In fact without the culturally induced perspective, experience is meaningless. Furthermore, we may posit that each such system operates within a framework of logical consistency and that it is possible to extract from the behavior of individuals those rules which explain categorization.

Perspective or world view, then, is more than the specific content of culture. It also contains the unstated premises which order thought and feeling. For those who would attempt to make these explicit, the problem they face is to develop those techniques which expose the structural logic of the culture they examine. Some of those who are working in the symbolic analysis of language, as did Whorf, are attempting to do just this. Their results will eventually be of great assistance in examining the transmission of culture, but in the meantime we must explore the problem with such knowledge as we possess.

Understanding of perspective and its variability does have direct relevance, however, for our central problem. It alerts us to the fact that we cannot understand the process of learning by a mere recounting of the sequence of stimuli which the individual receives in passing through infancy to adulthood. Stimuli cannot be viewed as bits and pieces which somehow add up to a whole. They come to the subject from a cultural environment in which the perspective has already colored their meaning, and somehow they are received by the subject in the same manner. Otherwise we could not speak of cultural transmission at all, and an individual would present an idiosyncratic personality. Observation readily establishes that this is not the case, but until we know more about the relation of neural and cultural patterning, we cannot know how one may mirror the other. This should not deter us from seeking the consequence of this process as it is manifested in the behavior of the individual, nor from examining the pattern of the culture which has been embedded in a physical base.

Cultural Patterning and Learning

It would seem that this is an appropriate time to examine what we mean by the patterning of culture and its relation to the socialization of the child. It will be remembered that considerable attention was given to the overwhelming importance of the environment in developing those capacities which make possible the physical, psychic, and cultural maturation of the child. It should also be remembered that variations in environment are reflected in the child's development. This being so, it would seem completely logical that examining the cultural environment itself could make explicit the learning process. This is, of course, what we must do because we must not rule out the possibility that the subject patterns his processes of learning from the influences exerted by those around him.

Although this proposal does not contradict our normal assumption that the infant is already prepared at birth to receive and organize stimuli, it does assert that the pattern of the organization of experience is a variable and is external to the infant in origin. What we insist on is that all the evidence support the view that we cannot look to any innate neural tendency to fashion the impact of the cultural environment in a given direction. The restrictions imposed by the neural system upon the newly arrived, cultureless creature are minimal and give to the infant the capacity to cope with sensory experience of a limited kind only. The higher nervous centers are not yet organized; in fact, they are not fully developed. Only in mythology do we find godlike creatures, not humans, springing fully developed from their progenitors.

In humans, a determinate period must elapse before the child can respond to stimuli on other than a physical basis. Such a proposal does not deny, however, that all the stimuli flowing to the infant from its mother or other persons, as well as the type of physical environment provided for it, are not highly charged with cultural significance. The methods and rhythms of handling, suckling, cleaning, and comforting have been shown in study after study to be culturally variable and presumably significant in personality formation. (This latter supposition would be on much sounder ground if we knew what would happen if we transferred the child to a culturally different environment immediately preceding the appearance of the sense of self.)

The point I wish to make is that child-rearing practices impose upon the infant the necessity of adjusting to a particular set of stimuli and, by implication, to the distinctive cultural patterning which they represent. Specifically, the infant must learn how to learn, an argument advanced by Gregory Bateson some time ago. This line of reasoning adds further support to those who have protested the validity of intelligence tests on the grounds that they are culturally biased, although in this instance the objection is advanced from a different basis. We would argue that the learning process, once acquired, varies from one culture to another, and in each instance organizes experiences differently.

Our understanding of the relation between culture, the mode of its transmission, and learning can be enriched and deepened if we turn now to empirical evidence provided by a study which is relevant to our focus. Most such research has been primarily concerned with the affective aspects of child rearing, and the failure to look at cognitive processes represents a real deficiency. With this limitation in mind, I have chosen a study of the Hopi Indians by Dorothy Eggan for illustrative purposes.[8] Her immediate concern is with "the emotional commitment involved in the socialization process." She contends that the Hopi were experts in the use of *affect* in their educational system, and that the results continued to be effective throughout the life span of the individual as a "reconditioning factor." She also argues that the internalized code of right behavior served as an effective social control for a society which lacked institutionalized means of individual restraint and punishment, and also added stability to the personality structure and to the society.

There are many aspects of Hopi life which need to be known if we are to understand the particular form in which their culture has been cast. We should know that the semi-desert environment in which they live imposes a precarious balance upon their ability to gain a livelihood through agriculture and some livestock grazing. The little villages in which they cluster atop the high mesas probably originally provided some protection against enemies, but also permitted them a better position from which to exploit the meager resources of their habitat. They are grouped in maternal clans which regulate the obligations of their members and provide rules of residence and descent. They possess an elaborate calendar of religious observances; the participation in ceremonies is practically obligatory.

---

[8] Dorothy Eggan, "Instruction and Affect in Hopi Cultural Continuity," in George Spindler (ed.), *Education and Culture* (New York: Holt, Rinehart, and Winston, 1963) pp. 321-350.

When their children come to puberty, they are subject to initiation rites. Although this quick summary barely touches the richness and complexity of the cultural life, particularly that related to cosmology, it hopefully contributes some sense of the situation.

The emotional commitment of the Hopi is contained in the concept of the "good heart." It means a heart at peace with itself and one's fellows. There is no worry, unhappiness, envy, malice, nor any other disturbing emotion in a good heart. In this state, cooperation, whether in the extended household or in the fields and ceremonies, is selfless and easy. Unfortunately, such a conception of a good heart is also impossible of attainment.[9] But the Hopis also recognized the "bad heart—Kahopi," and when an individual was in this state he was threatened by imminent retribution manifested in illness or death, or other misfortune. But he might also cause harm to others and even to the group as a whole. One who was not in a proper state of "grace" when ceremonies were performed and prayers offered might prevent rain and cause the crops to fail. For those who attempted to achieve or maintain the "good heart" the *burden* was enormous, not alone an individual one, but affecting the welfare of the universe since they believed that the Hopi way of life had been bestowed when the world began, and only as it was perpetuated could the world continue.

The duality of good and evil, and the sense of burden gain further significance when we add to them the concept of the "wall of Hopiness." We can think of it as a bounded area within which Hopiness prevails and expresses the separation of inside and outside. The tight relationships which bind a kin group might also be conceptualized as the wall which separates one clan from another. It reflects the sharp sense of identity which has been built on a commonalty of origin, residence, and way of life. It would seem that we would be justified in viewing this cultural centripetality as a force of great potency and in harmony with the other concepts.

The origin and meaning of these concepts must be sought in the environment provided by the family, and in participation in religious practices. In the maternally organized household, usually including more than one generation, the infant learns to make distinctions among those who are his caretakers, distinctions which include the

[9] *Ibid.*, p. 338.

terms, obligations, and feelings toward those who are in one's kin group, toward the outperson or stranger, and also toward oneself as a reciprocally participating member of a group.

Implicit within these learned distinctions, feelings, and behavior are the categories, stated and unstated, which the cultural system provides. These include the dichotomy contained within sexual separation, ordination expressed in generations, the polar duality of good and evil, the inside-outside division based on the distinction of the right and familiar versus the strange and uncertain, the categories by which things and qualities are arranged, and a way of perceiving time, space, and process. These distinctions and arrangements constitute the cognitive pattern. They provide the logical framework upon which world view rests, and when combined with the affective overtones which accompanied their acquisition, they provide the perspective within which all experience is seen and interpreted.

It would still be useful, however, to look at some of the devices which shape the child in the image of Hopi culture. Eggan emphasizes that the effect of the teaching effort was to inculcate in the child a sense of interdependence. Even the act of weaning which in many societies is a beginning step in creating independence for the infant, among the Hopi led to a different consequence. Her apt statement follows:

> He [the Hopi infant] was in no way *forced to find satisfactions within himself;* rather these were provided for him, if possible, by his household or clan group. His weaning, then, was from the breast only, and as he was being weaned from the biological mother he was at the same time in a situation which increased his emotional orientation toward the intimate in-group of the extended family which was consistent with the interests of Hopi social structure. Thus, considering weaning in its wider implications, a Hopi was never 'weaned'; it was not intended that he should be. For these numerous caretakers contributed greatly to a small Hopi's faith in his intimate world and conversely without question to a feeling of strangeness and *emotional insecurity* as adults in any world outside of this emotional sphere.[10]

It is quite clear that the instruction was deliberate and persistent. That which was relevant to kinship behavior was learned within the context of the event through patient and unceasing explanation and admonition until by the time the Hopi was an adult his "kinship reaction patterns were so deeply ingrained in his thinking and feeling,

[10] *Ibid.,* p. 329.

and in his workaday life, that they were as much a part of him as sleeping and eating." But any occasion could be utilized for the recitation of stories, adventures, journeys, or other experience which could illuminate for the child ". . . what it meant to be a good Hopi from a wide variety of determined teachers who had very definite and *mutually consistent* ideas of what a good Hopi is."

But the base upon which all instruction could be effective had been laid in the earliest years. The simplest acts were responded to from the polar reference of the Hopi definition of the "good heart." Offenders soon learned that their acts would evoke the condemning term "Kahopi" and serious offenses brought forth a stern isolation, the most severe of penalties in a world which rewarded interdependence. The desire to want to learn and to observe right behavior was further reinforced by the use of fear. Children were told that their misdeeds might attract the evil spirits who either harm them or take them away. Thus, in these and other ways an emotional base was laid from which all acts, theirs and those of others, could be judged against the ideal of the "good heart." What we must remember, however, is that irrespective of the physiology of the human neural and glandular systems, their response to each stimulus, to each item of experience, was the consequence of a patterned learning that had its origin in culture.

That which is learned in childhood, however, nowhere completes the education that must be given if the cultural heritage is to be transmitted. In one sense childhood should be viewed as the period of preparation for the important knowledge that is still to come. Among those peoples who practice formal initiation ceremonies, usually at the time of puberty, we have the opportunity to observe the dramatic fashion in which the new learning is conveyed.

The analysis by Hart[11] of the differences between prepubertal and postpubertal education has helped enormously to clarify some of the problems related to learning and the transmission of culture. He argues that in most primitive societies the educational vehicle and its purposes in those two periods are clearly distinct. Education in the prepubertal period is provided primarily by one's intimates—the

[11] C. W. M. Hart, "Contrasts Between Prepubertal and Postpubertal Education," in George Spindler (ed.), *Education and Culture* (New York: Holt, Rinehart, and Winston, 1963) pp. 400-425.

members of his family and the associates of his place of residence. He notes the variations, the wide latitude in practices, and even laxness in the insistence that learning occurs at a given time or place or under the supervision of designated personnel. It is true, of course, that a basic commonality exists within and between cultures in the practices observed by the nurturant group in bringing the infant to increasing stages of physical independence and in the training of bodily functions, but this constitutes only a small portion of the skills and knowledge that is learned from peers and adults.

Postpubertal education is an entirely different matter. Among those peoples who observe formal initiation ceremonies, and such practices are found among most primitive tribes, the pubescent members of the group are separated from their intimates, oftentimes forcibly, and subjected to periods of formal instruction which may last from several months to several years, depending upon traditional practice. Hart makes the significant observation that the personnel responsible for this period of instruction are different from the intimates of childhood because, among other reasons, the material of education, the manner of its preservation, and the urgency of its acquisition require a type of relationship and a type of knowledge that the group of intimates could not provide.

Hence, this responsibility is vested in "strangers" who even though they may be known to the initiates represent a different, sometimes hostile, segment of tribal organization. Where such internal divisions do not exist, and intimates carry out the initiation practices, the fiction of strangers is created by the use of masks.

Deeper understanding of the relevance of initiation ceremonies can be gained through a brief excursion into the theory of *rites de passage*.[12] Over a half century ago Van Gennep noted that those occasions on which an individual was in transition from one status or category to another were marked by ceremonies. These included the universal life crises of birth, puberty, marriage, and death, but also included other situations in which changes in behavior or group identification were involved. In many of these ceremonies there was a ritually enacted simulation of death and of a subsequent rebirth into the new condition. Van Gennep also noted a structural arrangement

[12] Arnold Van Gennep, *The Rites of Passage* (Chicago: University of Chicago Press, 1960).

of the sequences into three phases. The initial phase in which the connections with a current way of life were severed he called *separation*. The individuals, or, in the case of puberty ceremonies, the neophytes, then found themselves in an intermediate stage in which they were neither of one group nor another; they were *not-beings*.[13] This liminal condition was labelled *transition*. In the final stage of *incorporation* the individual returned to the group but into a different social niche and with altered behavior.

From a societal point of view the most significant *rite de passage* is initiation into tribal membership and adulthood at puberty. The ceremony marking this event may be quite brief, but it may also extend over a lengthy time period depending upon the nature of the instruction which must be given. Even among those groups which do not have formal observance of physiological puberty as the point in time for initiation, there are other occasions or educational devices which serve the same purposes and which incorporate the basic ritual and instructional aspects. The important point is that each society does have ways to *claim* the young.[14]

In those societies in which the origin and operation of the universe is viewed from the perspective of supernatural forces, instruction in and revelation of religious mysteries constitute a major portion of the knowledge which is transmitted during the period of initiation. In contrast, instruction is not in the mundane matters of how to make a living or to build a house, nor even in the private magical practices which accompany so many activities. This useful knowledge is gained elsewhere. In Australian tribes, for example, the neophytes are taught theology—the mythology which explains the origin and meaning of life, the sacred songs and prayers, and the ritual and dances of world-revival ceremonies. Much of this knowledge must be acquired so precisely that, in theory, there is no deviation from generation to generation in ceremonial performance.

Hart interprets postpubertal education as preparation for citizenship and argues, "Citizenship training in these societies . . . means

[13] Victor W. Turner, "Betwixt and Between: the Liminal period in Rites de Passage. Symposium on New Approaches to the Study of Religion," *Proceedings of the 1964 Annual Spring Meeting of the American Ethnological Society* (Seattle: University of Washington Press, 1964), pp. 4-20.

[14] Solon T. Kimball and James E. McClellan, Jr., *Education and the New America* (New York: Random House, 1962), chap. x.

exposing the boy under particularly stirring and impressive conditions to the continuity of the cultural tradition, to the awe and majesty of the society itself, emphasizing the subordination of the individual to the group at large and hence the mysteriousness, wonder, and sacredness of the whole individual-society relationship."[15]

If we turn once again to the particulars of Hopi culture, we can exemplify not only the relevance of the analysis but also extend our own perspective. The induced striving to achieve the "good heart" and to learn and follow the Hopi way of life is not an individual goal in our sense of the word. Our perspective could readily equate the individually centered orientation, as it has been described, with the ultimate goal of self-fulfillment which our own culture emphasizes. The similarity is a superficial one and to treat it otherwise would lead us astray.

For the Hopi, self-perfection serves a larger purpose. Their mythology posits a preestablished universal order, but in order that this cosmic orderliness be actualized it is necessary to have man's cooperation. In such a formulation we are again witness to the *interdependence* of basic Hopi thought and social behavior. Man is also a necessary aspect of the universe and without his contribution and only through the fulfillment of his part can that which might be exist. The responsibility constitutes a cosmic burden which can only be properly discharged by those whose moral rightness is manifested in the striving for the "good heart." Hence the linkage between the private life of the individual and the public life of the society. Hence also the distinction between the instruction and training received from one's intimates in childhood and the formal education which begins with a first initiation between the ages of six and ten, and a subsequent initiation ceremony eight to ten years later. The learning of the values, mythology, and ceremonies of the society is further extended in the years which follow.

It is true that the initiation ceremony marks the separation of the individual from his childhood and from other children, and his entry into the public and adult world, but it is also much more. When the Katchinas—the gods—are unmasked and the realization breaks through that these are mortal men among whom are some you know, there follows the destruction of the illusion, the loss of childhood

[15] *Ibid.,* p. 420.

innocence, the final separation from childhood, but also the realization of man's part in a great cosmic scheme.

Before we begin the next part of our analysis, it might be well to recapitulate briefly our original objectives and the relevance of the description and analysis to these. The search for an understanding of the conditions affecting the transmission of culture constitutes our primary goal. Toward this end we have, first of all, argued for the validity of the distinction between affective and cognitive learning. The stimulus-response paradigm appears as adequate to explain affective and skill learning although it is not realized through simple, additive repetition. It seems, however, that we must look to some other mechanism to explain cognitive learning. We were also interested in establishing the cultural fashioning of the how and what of learning and to show that the stimulus-response connection is itself a variable of the cultural environment.

We wanted to show next the distinction in the educational approach and personnel for prepubertal and postpubertal education and to relate this to subject matter and objective. In particular, we wanted to draw attention to the fact that the stuff of the deliberate and highly patterned instruction of the postpubertal period was knowledge, although we cannot exclude the influence of the affective context within which it was imparted, nor the affective disposition which the individual carried into the situation from childhood experience.

But the preschool learning includes much more than the organization of instincts and emotions—the ethos, as described by Bateson and Mead.[16] It also includes the acquisition of the tools with which the world can be apprehended symbolically, the facility of language and the patterns of differentiation of things, events, relationships, and processes. These are the intellectual tools which can be used quite apart from any affective predisposition. They constitute the basic *sine qua non* of intellectual efforts in learning the knowledge or subject matter of formal schooling. The instruction may focus upon mythology and sacred ceremonies as exemplified by initiation rites, or it may be organized in formal courses under the rubrics of mathematics, grammar, logic, and science.

[16] Gregory Bateson and Margaret Mead, *Balinese Character. A Photographic Analysis* (Reprinted 1962; New York: New York Academy of Science Special Publication, 1942).

There is, however, a basic similarity in the instructional content of either "bush" school or classroom. In both, not only is there transmitted knowledge and a way of thinking about such, the whole of which we may call world view, but also there is transmitted the criteria by which events may be analyzed and judged. The use of these criteria in the understanding process represents the epitome of cognitive learning. Among the Hopi, for example, everything ranging from simple good fortune to catastrophic drought can be placed in the interpretive reference of individual behavior or of cosmic process. Let it be said now that the problem is not one of testing the validity of such interpretations against our own explanations of the workings of the laws of nature. It is quite certain that each contestant examining a specific event from his own perspective would inevitably be guided by his own rules of evidence, logic, and process in rendering a decision. How else can we understand an Agassiz, a Darwin, a Hopi priest, or a Murngin elder? Nor is the problem of who is right or wrong ours to consider; it leads us astray. The problem is to make explicit the criteria and the mechanisms which explain cognition and ultimately to examine these for their relevance to formal education. It is to that problem that we now turn.

Culture and Cognition

There are several approaches to the study of the relation between culture and cognition that promise fruitful results, and eventually all of these should be used. The analysis of the internal structure of language, as developed by Whorf,[17] has yielded early rich rewards. His procedure shows that certain thought processes are derived from the structure of the language employed by the speakers. Language may also be examined as a tool in communication or studied semantically as a system of symbols. But its study may also be approached from the more purely cultural perspective in which it is treated as one aspect of culture.

The approach used by social anthropologists introduces a rather different perspective. Their intellectual tradition stems from Comte

---

[17] Benjamin Lee Whorf, "Language, Thought, and Reality," in John B. Carroll (ed.), *Selected Writings of Benjamin Lee Whorf* (Cambridge: Technology Press of Massachusetts Institute of Technology, 1942).

TRANSMISSION OF CULTURE

through Durkheim and Radcliffe-Brown, to those contemporary anthropologists who are seeking the processes of change through study of the structure of human groupings and their relation to other aspects of the environment. From this perspective all symbolism, of which language is a significant part, may be understood as a hypostatization of social reality. Warner utilizes this approach in his analysis of Murngin totemism.[18] Patterning of behavior as a function of culture has been utilized constantly. The specification of these approaches here recognizes their contribution and shows the breadth of the conceptual base from which this analysis proceeds. They will be implicit in much of what follows.

In this paper I have consistently insisted that the learning process must be viewed as an aspect of the cultural milieu. Since culture is transgenerational, we should find in culture those clues which could explain both what and how the child learns. But our effort must also be transcultural if we are to abstract that which has universal relevance. Since it is the screen of cultural perspective through which experience is received, ordered, and acted upon, our problem is to identify those commonalities which encompass all cultures irrespective of their substantive divergences.

There are three such commonalities which I believe to be universally present; namely, the categories of knowledge, the canons of discrimination, and process as a function of relationship between variables.

Each individual who has participated in the full range of cultural experiences appropriate to his sex and status possesses a set of categories which permits him to distinguish and classify individuals, things, qualities, events, and processes. The language which he speaks contains the verbal referents for all such distinctions and may itself be analyzed for grammatical structure. Among such other commonly agreed upon categories are those of order, class, number, shape, time, and space. These *agreed upons,* not just the label they carry but the basis upon which groupings of similar and dissimilar may be made, are part of the cultural heritage which is transmitted in a multitude of ways, and which makes possible meaningful communication among cultural similars. In our society those who operate from pri-

[18] W. L. Warner, *A Black Civilization* (New York: Harper and Row, 1937).

vate symbol systems are often institutionalized or, if they are artists, may be considered as avant-garde and tolerated in the hope that they may be expressing something significant.

The social base of such categories is readily apparent in the terminology of any kinship system and in the acquisition of identifying terms and appropriate behavior easily observable in parental teaching of the young. In the acquisition of such knowledge, the child also learns implicitly the more inclusive distinctions based upon sex, age, generation, descent, and sequence through birth order. For example, in the kinship terminology used by Navaho Indians, all those who use the reciprocal term of "sister" for each other are called "mother" by their children. The extension of the principle contained within this system of categorizing means that you apply the term "sister" to all those who are daughters of the persons you call "mother." The further fact that both classes of persons (mothers and sisters) are sexually taboo excludes them from the group from which one may choose a marriage partner. When categories and the process of categorizing is extended to all experience, we can see how extensive, comprehensive, or orderly is the cultural framework. We should also note its stability since it is embedded in the language, expressed in mythology, and governs the thought processes.

If the categories of knowledge are supraindividual, so also are the canons of discrimination.[19] Here we are concerned with two aspects, each one of which must be treated separately, although they are related. The learning of identities is only one step in acquiring a cognitive framework. The individual must also learn the criteria which make identification possible and which permit classification of the item of experience in the larger whole. Not only must each individual learn the basis upon which items are classified, but he must also learn the criteria which permit him to evaluate and hence to respond.

From our knowledge of how cultural interconnections exhibit an internal consistency we can infer that evaluative responses are expressions of a coherent system. Our analysis of Hopi affective patterns supports this view. Our goal, then, is not only to discover the canons which order the system, but also to make explicit the criteria

[19] Solon T. Kimball, "The External Source of Values" (unpublished manuscript, 1964).

upon which these are based. Being unstated assumptions of behavior, their exposure will not be easy. Knowledge of them cannot be gained by blunt question and answer approaches; they must be pried out through processes of inference utilizing linguistic, mythologic, and behavioral data. Only with the appearance of the conscious questing of the practitioners of science has it been possible for us to even begin to discover these wellsprings of human thought. We cannot assume, however, that they lie buried in the unconscious of the human psyche or that they spring from an assumed inner force. Rather, we shall gain knowledge of them from culture itself. If we accept the supraindividual sources of discrimination and of the canons which govern their use, then we must accept cultural variability in the criteria by which one identifies and evaluates. What is culturally universal is the process by which canons and criteria are transmitted.

This brings us to the consideration of process as the third member of our group of cultural commonalities. We have defined process as a function of change in the relationships among variables. Sometimes these changes may be seen as a consequence of modification in the magnitude or quality of variables, and sometimes they may be due to changes in the conditions within which a system operates. Further elaboration of this terse statement is necessary.

Relatively little attention has been given thus far to the analysis of the internal dynamics of culture as viewed from the internal vantage of a specific cultural perspective. The task would be far from easy, since it would require two sets of intellectual tools. It would require, first, an adequate general theory of social and cultural change; and, secondly, a theory of change, or process, viewed from within each culture. Few people would grant that a general theory now exists, although Marxian and Freudian theorists make such claims. Such a theory could be the base from which cultural data would be probed for the purpose of yielding another theory of change specific to the culture under study. It is quite probable that we shall win through to such a model only through the slow, laborious process of inductive empiricism. It *is* possible, however, to designate some of the data that must be examined and the direction in which we can proceed.

The simplest formulation of what we are seeking is contained in the question, "How do things happen?" Now the mythologies of the various cultures of the world provide an explanation to their members of how the universe came to be. In content these creation myths vary widely. Some specify set stages of development with the appearance of man in a culminating epoch. Others see the tension between natural forces as essential to creation. In some, a transcendental power effectuates a divine plan, or a mythological culture here prepares the way for man and lays down the rules of life. There are some cultures in which their myths express only a feebly developed sense of beginning. The direct comparison of the contextual material of differing cultures has been tried time and again and does not yield much, but there is another approach which holds great promise.

The difficult problem, of course, is to hit upon a method of analysis that will yield results of a kind we are seeking. If we could examine mythological events of a given people within their context of time, then we might begin to make meaningful the pattern of rhythm and sequence as they see it. If the cycle of birth and death, or the succession of the seasons or of other recurrences, are contained in these accounts, then we can compare them to seek for the framework of repetition. But we must also examine the explanations which accompany the descriptions. In these we must search for the relationships which explain emergence, becoming, being, and ending. Hopefully, this approach will yield the principles of process for which we seek.

The activity suggested above, however, is only one phase of our quest. We must subject the ongoing communal life to the same kind of examination, seeking out the time patterning as men join and separate in activities. And finally, we must see what the structure of language reveals. Hopefully, we might some day be able to establish the connections among all of these. The rich rewards garnered by the few who have begun the exploration give great promise.

Let us not forget that the same purposes are to be served in the applicability of this approach to modern science, philosophy, or theology. We must make explicit the pattern of the process by which we interpret events. We seek the processes of nature in the cyclotron, in experiments with substances and animals, and in the observation of plant and animal life in their ecological settings. But we must also make explicit the process by which we achieve results, for this is the essence of education. These are the tools of cognition. In the systems of categorization and discrimination and their associated criteria and in the conceptualization of process, we find cognitive commonalities which are transcultural.

Conclusion

If we view the primary function of education as the transmission of culture, then that which is unique to education are the conditions which govern its process. Process is a variable relationship of two systems, the social and cultural environment which prescribes the method and content of education and the individual in whom experience is organized and internalized.

From each segment of the culture comes knowledge of a different sort. Within the family the child is trained in bodily functions, kinship behavior, and household skills. In institutionalized schooling the child is taught by strangers. In both, the child learns body skills and affective and cognitive behavior, although the emphasis will vary from one to another. Presumably, experience is cumulative, but the differential of the limits for performance between training and cognitive development remains largely unexplored. It is possible that the affective disposition of most persons has been set in early childhood, particularly so if there are no changes in the conditions of life. Certainly one of the conditions which affect the transmission of culture is the nurturant environment of the infant. It is here that the individual is prepared to be culturally acquisitive. Since what happens here is apparently so crucial to what happens later, and because the content and method of education in early childhood is substantially different from that of formal schooling, knowledge of the process of the preparation of the infant for responding to cultural experience is a basic concern in education.

We must turn to the social and cultural environment itself to discover the other applicable conditions. We should distinguish, however, between those which we call operational and those which are conceptual. The former includes all those informal or institutional arrangements which a society provides for instruction. It should also include the organization of the presentation of subject matter and, as a separate category, the relationship between teacher and learner. In essence the operations in cultural transmission subsume the how to do it.

Although the conceptual conditions which affect the transmission of culture are of far greater significance, because in these are found the stuff of full humanity, they have been left largely implicit in educational theory. From these conditions comes the perspective which is reflected in world view. The rules which govern the organization and evaluation of knowledge and explain the processes of change are to be found here. In them are the oftentimes unstated assumptions which make experience meaningful. In them are the guideposts for learning itself.

All of the conditions which affect the transmission of culture constitute a proper, if not exclusive, concern of educators. It is my belief that in the study of the mechanisms of cognition, seen as functions of social and cultural reality, educators can gain that understanding which is essential to the process of education.

History and the Body of Knowledge Unique to the Profession of Education

Clara P. McMahon
The Johns Hopkins University

IT IS OF utmost importance to those who meet for the purpose of exchanging ideas about a particular subject or topic to make sure that they possess either a common denominator of agreement as to the meaning of the terms involved or to require that there be a clear and unequivocal explanation as to what each participant means by his use of certain key words in the topic under discussion. I therefore propose to indicate at once exactly what I mean when I use any of the following terms as they relate to the subject of this paper:

> *history*—the discipline which deals with "the past of mankind," the formal record of past events, particularly those pertaining to human affairs and events
> *body*—the main, central, or principal part
> *knowledge*—learning; cognition; the sum total of information
> *unique*—being without like or equal; unrivaled
> *profession*—a vocation which rests upon a "systematic body of knowledge of substantial intellectual content and which is entered upon by advanced degrees,"[1] such as theology, law, medicine, teaching
> *education*—systematic instruction, schooling, or training in preparation for the work of life; in other words, the "whole enterprise of schooling, from nursery school to university, or any other system of deliberate and organized schooling."[2]

---

[1] John B. Davis, editor of the *Princeton Alumni Bulletin,* writing in the *Harvard Alumni Bulletin* for March 17, 1962.

[2] See John Walton's brief discussion of this in "A Discipline of Education" in *The Discipline of Education,* ed. John Walton and James Kuethe (Madison: The

discipline—a body of knowledge and methods that can be taught, such as history or mathematics[3]

I shall attempt, then, in my presentation, to relate what the discipline of history has contributed to the discipline of education;[4] in other words, the relationship of history to that body of knowledge which comprises the study of the enterprise of schooling, first, as a body of subject matter, and second, as a method for advancing knowledge of the past, whereby the historian attempts to describe, analyze, and interpret that part of the human past which can be "meaningfully reconstructed" from its available records. This will involve of necessity a brief discussion of the nature of history, its place in the general education of man, and its research techniques, and a more detailed account of its importance in the history of education, from the standpoint of formal course work as well as the extension of our knowledge about the educational enterprise as it has emerged and developed from the remote past.

History has not always been considered a proper study for mankind . . . "a branch of learning to be studied for its own sake . . . a kind of knowledge which is useful to men in daily life."[5] On the

---

University of Wisconsin Press, 1963), pp. 5-6. A more recent expanded concept is offered by Bernard Bailyn in his *Education in the Forming of American Society* (Chapel Hill: The University of North Carolina Press, 1960), p. 14, when he defines education as the "entire process by which a culture transmits itself across the generations; when one is prepared to see . . . schools and universities fade into relative insignificance next to other social agencies; when one sees education in its elaborate, intricate involvements with the rest of society, and notes its shifting functions, meanings, and purposes." I shall treat this emphasis in more detail in another section of this paper.

[3] Marc Belth in his new book, *Education as a Discipline*, lists four criteria applicable to all disciplines: the level of abstraction of the concepts with which they are concerned; the modes of thinking by which they are characterized; the objectives they seek; and the types and manifestations by which they are limited and evaluated. Marc Belth, *Education as a Discipline* (Boston: Allyn and Bacon, 1965), pp. 6, ff.

[4] I want to emphasize at this point that this paper is not concerned with "proving" whether education is a unique discipline in itself or interdisciplinary in nature, but merely concerned with the *contribution* history has made to its study.

[5] Sir Charles Firth, quoted by A. L. Rowse, *The Use of History* (rev. ed. England: The English Universities Press, 1963), p. 17.

contrary—Napoleon is said to have remarked that "history is a fable agreed on," and Nietzsche warned that history was just a "belief in falsehood." Voltaire declared in *L'Ingenu* that it was no more than the record of crime and misfortune, a statement with which William Cullen Bryant agreed, somewhat flamboyantly, in his poem *Earth:*

> "The horrid tale of perjury and strife
> Murder and spoil, which we call history."

But thoughtful men of this generation and of generations past have not overlooked the fact that the present can mean nothing unless it is illuminated by the past. From Cicero to John of Salisbury and Hugo of St. Victor to Vives to Luther to Comenius to Rousseau to Priestly to Jefferson—to mention but a few[6]—has come the admonition to look to our past for help in understanding our present culture and institutions, in finding sustenance for a course of action, in making us good citizens (in the sense of becoming intelligent participators or wise leaders in the political arena of life). A really liberal education—the possession of which is the dream of all true educators for our youth—has a three-fold purpose, of which the study of history must be an integral part: to provide those elements of knowledge which we hold essential for our times; to cultivate the intellectual skills and habits of reasoning without which an individual cannot get along in our highly complex society; and to strengthen those traits of character and personality, both moral[7] and intellectual, which are basic to a "reasoned and responsible" life.[8] Teachers, perhaps more than other professional groups, in view of their commitment to the education of the young, must exhibit the characteristics of such a liberal education, and continue to be intellectually active, morally strong, and knowledgeable. A wide range

[6] See Henry Johnson, "History in the School Curriculum before 1890," *Teaching of History* (rev. ed. New York: The Macmillan Co., 1940) chap. ii, for one of the best available historical overviews of the place and importance of history.

[7] See Kenneth Lewalski, "The Study of History as a Moral Exercise," *Journal of Higher Education,* XVI (October, 1964), 237-245, for a good discussion of the evidence of moral weakness in Western culture, the need for historians to study the moral foundations of past and recent events, and the place of history in the restoration of moral strength.

[8] Earl McGrath, *Liberal Education in the Professions* (New York: Bureau of Publications, Teachers College, Columbia, 1959), *passim.*

of interests and knowledge sometimes makes the difference between a good teacher and a poor one when the more able students begin to ask questions outside the usual context of class subjects. The famous English historian, A. E. Rowse, once remarked that there was "nothing more boring for educated people in the society of the uneducated than the restriction of their conversation, the limitations of their mental world."[9] What frustration and disappointment must be experienced by a mentally alert student (and what deprivation by the not-so-alert) who finds himself serving a period of time under a teacher who has nothing in the way of intellectual stimulation to offer him. Students *deserve* interesting, literate, and cultured teachers, and those who are involved with the preparation of teachers must see to it that such teachers are produced. And surely there is no better way of producing such teachers than to make sure that the study of history is included in their program of study. Thomas Jefferson's comment on the didactic value of history as the core of education for everyone is still more or less valid today: "History, by apprizing them of the past, will enable them to judge the future; it will avail them of the experience of other times and other nations; it will qualify them as judges of the actions and designs of men."

A knowledge of history, then, is indispensable to a teacher, since it is an essential component of the mind of a cultivated man, the mark of a truly literate individual. The study of history is one sure way to help guard against the dichotomy of the two cultures C. P. Snow so forcefully warns us against, and the disappearance of that common bond of attachment which used to exist among all educated people, regardless of their professional interests, which is fast disappearing in a highly technological society that demands more and more specialization of its members.

One of the major characteristics history exhibits which has contributed to the discipline of education is its original and indispensable way of looking at and describing human nature.[10] History not only puts our temporary present in its place—and in the process colors our understanding of the past—it also recognizes that every

[9] Rowse, *op. cit.*, p. 163.

[10] For a description of the many-sided characteristics of history, including this one, see the *American Historical Association Newsletter*, II, No. 4 (April, 1964).

event, act, and individual is unique and can never be repeated, and reveals as well the unexpected complexities of human affairs. Since the so-called practical problems of society are constantly changing— in education, for example, the explosions of knowledge and population, and the demands of an automated society call for an entirely different approach not only to teaching but to the purposes of education, both of which have greatly changed in the past twenty years—the historian of today may have to look more closely at the aspects of the past which earlier historians could afford to neglect. The would-be historian, whether he is interested in social, political, cultural, or educational history, must be thoroughly at home in as many areas as possible which contribute to an understanding of our present problems (they are, of course, rooted in the past), areas such as anthropology, biology, sociology, psychology. All of these subjects throw light on human affairs, institutions, and events, and equip the historian with what, for want of a better term, I shall call "psychological insight." It is only a matter of common sense that the historian who has the greatest fund of knowledge, the most wisdom, and the widest range of experience will be more sensitive to the large number of possible analogies and contrasts that can be drawn. In order for him to reach an understanding of the past, the historian must of necessity look at his subject from the viewpoint of the present. He must bring all his knowledge, from whatever subject or variety of experience he can, to bear on the problem he is investigating. The historian of education, familiar with the school's efforts to help the disadvantaged child to adjust to an educational environment whose values and instructional patterns are seemingly at variance with his own needs, can perhaps help to make the process a smoother one by analyzing and drawing inferences about the school's efforts in the past to deal with a similar type of problem. At the close of the nineteenth century and the opening of the twentieth, for example, there was an attempt to educate the immigrant with his foreign ways, modes of behavior, and ways of thinking; and to incorporate him into American society with a minimum of disruption both to the immigrant and to the school and community. Is it not possible for the historian of education, in light of his present, more expanded knowledge and experience of urbanization, and psychological and cultural differences among peoples, to analyze, compare, and contrast the activities of our schools and other agencies then and now, and to draw some analogies from the past, dissimilar in some ways though the two situations may be, for present action? And will not this expanded knowledge of anthropology, sociology, and educational psychology not only help him in understanding the present, but act in reverse as well, so that the historian can draw some analogies to the events and episodes of the past? It is this latter "exploitation of the current events," as Gottschalk[11] calls it, which takes the place of the scientist's laboratory for the historian. Vann Woodward underlines this same point when he says that the "new look" in American history is not the result of new discoveries, but rather of the reading anew of the old evidence by historians with new sensitivities, identifications, preoccupations, and methods.[12] The historical process is a two-fold one, then, in which every fact of history has significance with respect first to its importance in the era of which it was a part, and second to its bearing upon the "genesis of contemporary culture." It is the latter part of the process, perhaps, which has greater value for the historian, particularly the educational historian.

In addition to this broad knowledge, the historian needs to be thoroughly trained in the five-fold technique of historical research: (1) the selection of a subject for investigation, sometimes phrased as a question to be answered or a tentative hypothesis to be proved or disproved; (2) the collection of data on the subject; (3) the subjection of the data to external criticism (examination of the data or sources for authenticity); (4) subjection of the data to internal criticism ("the extraction of the credible particulars from the sources"); and (5) the synthesis and imaginative recreation of the past from the data derived in the preceding steps. As carefully as the historian can, he follows the steps in historical analysis, but some element of subjectivity cannot help but insert itself. What is a determining factor in selecting a subject for investigation but the

[11] Louis Gottschalk, *Understanding History* (New York: Alfred A. Knopf, 1958), p. 276.
[12] Quoted by Belth, *op. cit.,* pp. 150-151. For an interesting description of the relation of education and other disciplines to mankind and its curiosity, see Robert Ulich (ed.), *Education and the Idea of Mankind* (New York: Harcourt, Brace, and World, 1964), pp. 270-271.

interest of the investigator? And is not the intellectual and educational background which the investigator possesses also a factor in determining his subject? What about the availability of data? Many an historian works in the field of nineteenth century American education not necessarily because he is genuinely interested in it, but because materials may be more accessible than those for the eighteenth century. Many investigators shy away from the medieval period because of the expenses that may be involved in traveling to reach the sources, or because they are not equipped with a knowledge of medieval Latin to read them.

Careful and thorough training in the techniques of historical research are not necessarily the exclusive domain of the historian, nor do the advantages of such a mental discipline accrue only to the professional. Every one of us must, at one time or another, draw inferences from the spoken or printed word; we are never free from the necessity of giving more or less weight to this or that document or authority. All of us need to know how to make a wise judgment, based on accurate information. The habit of right thinking is a must for everyone, and it is in this area that the value of history and historical analysis is uppermost. One of the most exciting and vivid statements on these intellectual values I have ever read was made by a scientist, Professor Hermann J. Muller, in discussing the role of science in inculcating this kind of mental activity in students, but it seems even more appropriate to the role of history:

It is of the utmost importance for our youth to experience, in part vicariously but also in part directly, this kind of objective quest, and to get to feel the thrill of the hunt for truth. They must undergo the emotions aroused by the disproof of some preconception, must learn to take objective criticism gracefully. They must form the habit of looking for wishful thinking and other flaws in their own positions as well as in those of others. They must have practice in searching for their own thoughts, in attempting to express them lucidly, and in interweaving their thoughts with those of others. They must learn to question all authority as such, including, of course, that of science, yet be ready to accept the conclusions that the evidence logically leads to.

There are several major values implicit in all this. Among them are the values of intellectual honesty, of communication unclogged by obfuscation and pretense, of readiness to admit one's mistakes, and of moral courage to maintain one's position in the face of condemnation as long as that position is founded on firm evidence. Another major value that emerges is the acceptance of the search for truth as an end in its own right. Along with this should also come a deep respect for the power of truth to lead men, by paths that had often been unsuspected previously, to means of benefitting the human lot. . . ."[13]

Muller concludes by saying that genuine thinkers (I am substituting "thinkers" for "scientists," and I am sure that Muller will agree that I am not violating the tenor of his thought) are "in their inner hearts, united in the cause of freedom of expression, unlimited criticism, unhampered challenging of authority, the right to pursue truth by whatever paths they may glimpse."

Every assumption, fact, theory, law, and principle in every field of knowledge, from art to zoology, has an historical antecedent, and that antecedent, no matter how recent or remote, is susceptible to the kind of investigation and interpretation which historians give their own subject. Indeed, every discipline or subject is richer and fuller when either some of its own practitioners or historians proper have attempted to place it in its setting. For example, one of the most explosive, far-reaching, belief-shattering theories of all times was the Darwinian theory of evolution; it has not only been one of the most provocative and fruitful stimuli to research in its own bailiwick, it has also affected investigation into every aspect of man and his environment; his religion, philosophy, political beliefs, literature, and education, to name but a few, have all been characterized at one time or another by the attempts of historians to gain new insights and knowledge of the growth and development of these aspects by using the so-called evolutionary approach. But education as a field of knowledge probably lends itself more readily to historical research than perhaps others because it is so vitally concerned with man's efforts to perpetuate and transmit his cultural heritage to succeeding generations. The educational process involves institutions, subjects, social practices, traditions, ideas, books, methods, teachers, pupils, curricula, attitude, vocations—its domain is almost limitless, and every segment or part of it is related in some way to every other part, and each one in turn has appeared at one time or another in the past, remote or recent, sometimes apparent to even the most casual observer, but at other times so intermingled and enmeshed with the strands of other developments that it is difficult

[13] Herman J. Muller, "The Role of Science Education in Value Formation," *Values in American Education;* ed. Theodore Brameld and Stanley Elam. (Bloomington, Indiana: Phi Delta Kappa, 1964). See especially pp. 96-97.

for even the most astute and dedicated investigator to disentangle them. When Juvenal two thousand years ago said, "Nihil humani mihi alienum est," he might have been describing education as a field of knowledge.

Education (or pedagogy as it was first titled) as a subject for study and investigation appeared in American colleges and universities toward the close of the nineteenth century—I might add that it has had a much longer (although sporadic) history as a subject in institutions of higher learning than most people, including educationists, realize[14]—and quickly fragmented into a number of courses, of which the history of education was a major one. Since research was an important function of the German universities (after which my own institution—The Johns Hopkins University—and subsequent American graduate schools were patterned), not only was the historical method at hand, but a corpus of historical knowledge was also available to be drawn on. Nineteenth century Germany[15] had produced a number of great historiographers—von Ranke, Waitz, Bluntschi, Mommsen, to name but a few—whose historical writings, critical scholarship, and teaching left an indelible impression on American professional historians, particularly Herbert Baxter Adams, who established the seminar method in history at The Johns Hopkins University and who from the first exhibited a strong interest in American educational history and in the training of public school teachers.[16] It is interesting to note that in the very decades in which

[14] See my article "Teacher Education in the Fifteenth Century," in the *Journal of Educational Research*, XLIV (October, 1950), pp. 134-137. See also William W. Brickman, "Revisionism and the Study of History of Education," *History of Education Quarterly*, IV (December, 1964), pp. 209-223, for examples of educational historiography in the 16th, 17th, and 18th centuries, with some isolated examples even earlier.

[15] I am limiting this very brief discussion to German influences, since it was in the German university that many American professional historians had trained, later importing their German teachers' techniques. This is not to say, of course, that there were not other European and English historians who exerted an influence —Stubbs, Maitland, and Maine in England, for example.

[16] He was editor of *Contributions to American Educational History*. Circulars of Information, United States Bureau of Education, Washington, D.C., Government Printing Office, 1887-1903. Adams wrote at least one of the monographs himself. He also conducted a series of lectures at the university for teachers for several years, as well as a seminar for those university students intending to teach.

education as a "scientific" study was struggling for a foothold in our institutions of higher learning, history was also struggling for recognition in this country as a research discipline, as a new learned discipline whose methodology for study was as exact and as rigorous as any other university study whose approach was not mathematical in nature. That this recognition in history was achieved by 1910 was due primarily to the work of such pioneers as Adams, John W. Burgess of Columbia University, and the students whom they trained.[17]

That history of education came to be firmly entrenched in the colleges and universities as a major subject in the training of teachers early in its academic history can be seen in the results of a questionnaire sent in 1900 to about fifty college and university professors of education who were asked to list the courses which they thought to be most essential in teacher preparation. History of education was listed more frequently than any other course (82 per cent).[18] By 1902, almost 200 institutions offered it; and in 1906, twenty-seven out of thirty-one colleges sampled in another investigation revealed that it was a part of their curriculum (more than any other course), and that the number of students—1,996—enrolled in the history of education course was larger than that in other offerings.[19]

The names of those who began to produce textbooks for the history of education courses in this early period (prior to World War I) and to add to the growing list of monographic literature included some of the "greats" of the early days in the profession. Paul Monroe, Ellwood Cubberley, Thomas Davison, A. O. Norton, Edwin G. Dexter, and those who trained under them embarked on a course of writing not only because there was so much to tell about the development of American education, but also because they had a sense of commitment, of tremendous responsibility toward this newest member of the academic world. Recent charges have been labelled against them that they were not professional historians but crusaders con-

---

[17] See John Herman Randall, Jr. and George Haines IV, "Controlling Assumptions in the Practice of American Historians," *Theory and Practice in Historical Study: A Report of the Committee on Historiography* (New York: Social Science Research Council, 1946). See especially pp. 23-43.

[18] G. W. A. Lucky, *The Professional Training of Secondary Teachers in the United States*. New York: 1903 (n.p.), pp. 160 ff.

[19] Henry Suzzallo, "The Professional Use of History of Education," *The History of Education as a Professional Subject* (New York: Teachers College, Columbia, 1903), pp. 34, 35.

cerned with "getting the story straight," who, in the course of the telling of the story, restricted it to that part of the educational process which is carried on in formal institutions of instruction and who in the doing reflected their assumption that the past was merely "the present writ small."[20] That they were not professional historians, however, does not necessarily mean that they could not write good history or carry out important historical research. Historians themselves would be the first to acknowledge that much good history has been written by those whose major concern was not in that field. As a matter of fact, some of these peripheral works are superior in many ways to those produced by plodding, less imaginative historicists. And as to the criticism that the professional interests of these pioneer historians of education accounted for their parochialism, other important forces were at work which to some extent, at least, might have accounted for the narrow point of view.[21] Remember that this was the "scientific" age of research, and that every academic discipline, including history as well as education, was trying fervently to "prove" that it could be scientific in its approach to research. Historians were attempting to fragment and compartmentalize (á la the German model) their materials by concentrating on institutions, each one of which was treated as if it were, in Handlin's words, "autonomous and . . . self-generating." This professionalization and institutionalization of the practice of history was taking place almost concurrently with that of the practice of educational history; Randall and Haines remark that this twofold factor had controlled the methods, aims, and concerns of the American historian for the last two generations (i.e., prior to 1946, when this statement was published).[22] Historians of education were not out of step, then, with what was going on at the time with their parent discipline. It is true, however, that as new interpretations and new advances in American history occurred, they were not always reflected in educational historiography. Accounts of American educational history remained more or less static, but there were other reasons involved.

The criticisms being made today by Bailyn and other historians

[20] Bailyn, *op. cit.*, pp. 5-13.
[21] Oscar Handlin, "Introductory Note," *Harvard Educational Review*, XXXI (Spring, 1961), 121-123.
[22] Randall and Haines, *loc. cit.*, p. 25.

against the professionalism and isolationism in the writings on history of education and, by implication, at least, in the subject matter content of its courses, however, were reflected in similar charges made by professional educators as far back as 1908. William H. Burnham of Clark University, writing in the Proceedings of the Society of College Teachers of Education of that year, contended, "It is time to . . . study educational movements in relation to the development of civilization, as a part of *Kulturgeschichte*."[23] He further argued that the study of education as an *isolated phenomenon* and the failure to examine its *wider cultural aspects*[24] had led to a narrow pedagogical view and the neglect of many other important educational factors. He listed a number of special "agents of education" which he felt had not been given their proper treatment: non-institutional forms of education such as clubs, unions, learned societies, and periodicals. A further criticism involved the kind of treatment that was given to such educational personalities as Comenius, Rousseau, Pestalozzi, Basedow, Froebel, Richter, Spencer, Husley, and Ruskin—not only had they either been neglected entirely or reduced to the "narrow limits of school pedagogy," with, in many instances, only a part of their writings being presented, but they had also been presented without regard to "their environment, the soil from which they came, and the influence of their work in the history of civilization." Quite an indictment! Burnham's recommendations included that the schools of a period be studied in relation to the social and industrial conditions and ideals; the educational movements in relation to contemporaneous literary, artistic, and political movements; educational doctrines in relation to prevailing philosophies, psychology, religions, and ethical ideals; and educational writers in relation to all of these. This is a blueprint which many of us in history of education even today would do well to follow.

Suzzallo, writing in the same volume, called attention to a situation which continued to exist for many years afterwards—in fact

---

[23] William H. Burnham, "The History of Education," *The History of Education as a Professional Subject* (New York: Teachers College, Columbia, 1908).

[24] Italics mine. This comment is very similar to the crux of Bailyn's argument for education to be conceived of as the entire process by which a culture transmits itself across the generation. *Op. cit.*, p. 14.

even today, unfortunately—the lack of scholarship in those who were teaching courses in the history of education: "Scholarship is very much needed in the history of education," he wrote, "for too many of the men who teach it, deeply interested in other aspects of education, are, in practice at any rate, somewhat indifferent to the scholarship required to teach the subject properly." But then he went on to warn ". . . scientific scholarship in history with its own peculiar points of view should not intrude itself beyond its proper function. It has the business of establishing facts as such, but the selection and treatment of these facts for cultural and practical purposes has its own standards and they should be observed. History in the department of history may be history, but history in the department of education is education."[25]

Suzzallo was quite aware that in the somewhat frantic attempts of education to establish a foothold in the academic arena both as a profession and as a discipline, there was a very real danger that it would become too narrowly professional. "The very first need, in the face of the present condition of our profession, may be more thoroughly to professionalize them (i.e., those preparing to become teachers) by giving them the wider view which has been demanded for the cultural student."[26] He, too, made some recommendations for a course in the history of education, some of which have a very modern ring:

1. It should present as a constant factor the relation of the school to society with its conditions and aspirations.

2. Materials should be selected upon the basis that they are relatively the most pertinent to an understanding of the present educational situation. The mere recency of an historic influence is by no means a guarantee of its worth in explaining the educational problems of today.

3. There must be an adequate and continuous tracing of the theoretical and practical influences which are related to the educational conditions and aspirations of American democracy in the twentieth century.[27]

History of education continued to be one of the major courses in

[25] Suzzallo, *loc. cit.*, p. 42.
[26] *Ibid.*, p. 47.
[27] *Ibid.*, pp. 55-67.

the curriculum for the preparation of teachers in ensuing years, although studies show that there was a great deal of criticism leveled at it by students and others.[28] The criticism was concerned primarily with the "practical value" of the courses, although some defenders of its subject matter argued that its shortcomings were due primarily to poor teaching and inadequate or poor materials, especially textbooks. A steady decline of the importance of history of education in teacher education programs began to set in, however, so that by the 1930's, although it still appeared as a subject, it no longer occupied a major role, nor was it recommended by national groups concerned with teacher preparation for inclusion in the program. Cremin points out that, while a number of texts in the field appeared during this time, some of them good, there was a decline in monographic literature. This was due in part to the scientific movement in education, which resulted in an increased output of scientific and statistical studies in educational psychology and administration.

Renewed interest in history of education both as a subject and as a field of research sprang up after World War II, and, while there has still been a lot of "grumbling," the interest seems to be healthy and widespread. In 1950 an investigation made by Arthur H. Moehlman under the sponsorship of the History of Education Section of the National Society of College Teachers of Education[29] revealed that 87 per cent of the institutions surveyed offered courses in the history of education and that the subject was a required one in one-fourth of them.[30]

In the past few years a fresh breath of air has stirred the sometimes desiccated leaves of the gnarled oak tree of education; general historians have finally become interested in the field of educational history, particularly American education, and have at long last begun to bring their tools of historical scholarship and their command of a wide historical background to supplement those who have been working so long in a field until now unappreciated by the general

[28] See Lawrence A. Cremin's excellent overview of this, "The Recent Development of the History of Education as a Field of Study in the United States," *History of Education Journal*, VII (Fall, 1955), 1-35.

[29] Formed in 1947; the Section, now called The History of Education Society, publishes the *History of Education Quarterly* (formerly *History of Education Journal*).

[30] Cited in Cremin, *loc. cit.*

historian. In December of 1954 and May of 1956, a committee of historians and two or three others met under the sponsorship of the Fund for the Advancement of Education to consider "The Role of Education in American History." The Committee asserted their belief that the relationship of society and education is a reciprocal one and that the impact of education on society has been less fully studied than the reverse and urged scholars "to examine education as a creative force in United States history."[31] The committee believes that intensive investigation and thoughtful interpretation of the role of education in certain great movements in American history might throw light on education as a creative force, and suggests that the following movements will prove fruitful:

1. The building of new communities on the frontier
2. The transformation of the immigrant into an American
3. The fulfillment of the promise of American life
4. The growth of distinctively American political institutions
5. The transformation of American society
6. The utilization of the immensely rich material resources of the nation
7. The adjustment of the foreign policy of the United States to its growing responsibilities as a world power
8. The growth of a distinctive American culture over a vast continental area[32]

As a means of encouraging such investigations, the Committee, through the Fund, will (and has already done so, in some instances) give assistance in such ways as awarding grants and fellowships, granting publication subsidies, supporting summer institutes or conferences for interested scholars, and establishing professional chairs in universities.

Along the lines of this new surge of interest in the history of education, the *Harvard Educational Review*[33] devoted a special issue to the topic of "Education and American History," with such contributors as Frank Freidel and Oscar Handlin, professors of history at

---

[31] Paul H. Buck *et al.*, *The Role of Education in American History* (New York: The Fund for the Advancement of Education, 1957), p. 6.
[32] *Ibid.*, pp. 10-15.
[33] *Harvard Educational Review*, XXXI (Spring, 1961).

Harvard; Frederick Rudolph, professor of history at Williams; Timothy L. Smith, professor and head of the Department of History at East Texas State College; Wilson Smith, now professor of history at Davis College, University of California; Richard J. Storr, associate professor of American history at the University of Chicago; and David B. Tyack, assistant professor of education and history at Reed College. All of these men, and of course others, are now putting their energies into and concentrating their efforts on some phase of American educational history. Up until now, however, there has been no indication of a similar interest in the history of non-American educational history.

Wilson Smith describes this new historian of education as being distinguished from his predecessor in two ways: by his use of broader historical references and by his wider, more humanistic, professional commitment, both of which he feels are having a liberating effect upon educational history.[34] He will branch out into whatever discipline may have something to offer him, using the methods and hypotheses of demographers, anthropologists, sociologists, philologists, and the like, whenever they may prove to be of value to him. As examples, the case study technique and the punch-card method of collecting materials have been used in *The Making of an American Community*;[35] the statistical approach is utilized in *New Trends in Education in the Eighteenth Century*.[36] The future appears limitless with regard both to methodology and to substance to the new historian of education.

As Paul Nash says, the educational historian must be involved, committed, and concerned; he must make judgments, evaluations, and interpretations, all of which involve responsibility and require competence.[37] Since, as he acknowledges, few of us can be competent in many areas—human limitations being what they are—he suggests

[34] Wilson Smith, "The New Historian of American Education," *Harvard Educational Review*, XXXI (Spring, 1961), 137-143.

[35] Merle Curti, et al., *The Making of an American Community: A Case Study of Democracy in a Frontier Country* (Stanford: Stanford University Press, 1959).

[36] Nicholas Hans, *New Trends in Education in the Eighteenth Century* (London: Routledge and Paul, 1951).

[37] Paul Nash, "History of Education," *Review of Educational Research*, XXXIV (February, 1964): *Philosophical and Social Framework of Education.*

that the most fruitful line of development in the field of educational history lies along the lines which historians of education have taken in the past three years: a single topic or problem, approached with wide and multiangled views. Good examples of such studies are Callahan's *Education and the Cult of Efficiency*,[38] Andreas Kazamias' "What Knowledge Is of Most Worth? An Historical Conception and a Modern Sequel,"[39] and Henry J. Perkinson's "Giambattista Vico and 'The Method of Studies in Our Times': A Criticism of Descartes' Influence on Modern Education."[40]

There are still many gaps, of course, in the field of history of education, of which both educators and historians have been aware for many years. In addition to the section on "History of Education" which appears in three-year intervals in *Review of Educational Research,* and which gives a rather thorough review of the historical research done in the preceding three years—both as to quality and comprehensiveness, as well as to areas still in need of investigation—there have appeared from time to time studies and books which attempt in part to do the same thing. Typical of such works are Brubacher's *History of the Problems of Education,*[41] containing a bibliographical commentary which surveys and assesses the work already done in the various topical and chronological periods under discussion, and in some instances, suggests further research. The larger section of Bailyn's *Education in the Forming of American Society* is a bibliographical essay (already referred to) which reveals the large gaps in our present knowledge of American educational history and suggests some needs and opportunities for study, particularly in the colonial period. Rudolph prefaces his section on bibliography in his volume *The American College and University* with these words: "It has seemed to me that the best service to historical scholarship would be to supplement a consideration of standard titles with some general observations on the development of the historiography of higher education in the United States and with some suggestions on

[38] Raymond Callahan, *Education and the Cult of Efficiency* (Chicago: The University of Chicago Press, 1962).
[39] *Harvard Educational Review,* XXX (Fall, 1960), 307-330.
[40] *History of Educational Quarterly,* II (March, 1962), 30-46.
[41] John Brubacher, *History of the Problems of Education* (New York: McGraw-Hill Book Co., 1947).

needs and opportunities in the field."[42] Cremin in his *Transformation of the School*[43] does the same thing for nineteenth century history of American education, emphasizing the progressive movement in education. Such studies as these are invaluable to the scholar in history of education and clearly demonstrate how exciting and challenging the efforts of such investigators can be in exploring the possibilities of further extension of knowledge about our educational enterprise.

We now seem to have come full circle again. Wilson Smith's admonition[44] that the educational historian must relate the institution to its social setting and to other cultural institutions around it, to expose the complexity of ideas and movements which educate different men in different times, to see the ways in which men and events at large control or are guided by educational themes and organizations, echo the thoughts of William Burnham and Henry Suzallo expressed some fifty-odd years ago. Let us hope that our half-century historical lag is a thing of the past, and that the succeeding years of this century will bring us a double millennium in educational history, when A.D. 2000 rolls around. And while we must agree with Robert Ulich[45] when he says that we "cannot say who helps the future more: the historian . . . the social scientist . . . or the biologist . . . ," we can agree that the discipline of history and education, working hand in hand, will help to throw more and more light on our educational past and to clarify more and more issues now facing us, and will help to prevent that eventuality which Thomas Carlyle so poignantly expressed: "That there should one man die ignorant who had a capacity for knowledge, I call a tragedy."

[42] Frederick Rudolph, *The American College and University* (New York: Alfred A. Knopf, 1962).
[43] Lawrence A. Cremin, *The Transformation of the School* (New York: Alfred A. Knopf, 1961).
[44] Wilson Smith, *loc. cit.*, p. 136.
[45] Ulich, *op. cit.*, p. 270.

The Study of Education for Professional Purposes

Donald P. Cottrell
The Ohio State University

THE QUIETLY philosophical discourse once carried on by scholars with reference to the education of teachers recently has become noisier and more intense. Many academic people, formerly unconcerned, have become persuaded that their primary interests are involved in educating teachers for the expanded educational program and are taking an active part in recommending the content of teacher education curricula. Since the educational system has become enormously expensive, by comparison with any fraction of the productive income of society formerly devoted to education, many laymen have come to express specific views regarding both the nature of school and college programs and the professional education of workers for those programs.

This heightened controversy has put college officers and professional certification authorities on guard and has frequently tended to crystallize their views with reference to the commitments they assume in teacher education. Some leaders of the organized profession of education have become understandably defensive at times against proposals which would seem to compromise their efforts for improved professional standing and performance. Other academic and public leaders have been concerned lest professional education in teaching should jeopardize the use of the educational enterprise in broad service to the diversified needs of a rapidly changing society. The aspiration of teachers for professional status, it has been argued, has been promoted to the detriment of the claims of other professions for the best human talent. This aspiration has tended to reduce the resources available for the development of other fields of scientific and humanistic interest for whatever purposes they might serve. Moreover, it has been alleged that the requirements for professional competence and status have often been too narrowly conceived, with the result that the broad education of the prospective teacher in intellectual and moral dimensions has been neglected.

Today there is wide diversity in educational and certification requirements for teachers. While the total amount of education required for teachers has been considerably increased in recent years, the component of that education which is directly calculated to serve the needs of professional practice has come to vary from a relatively modest fraction of preservice higher education, commonly one fourth to one fifth, in terms of academic credit hours, to virtually nothing, except a clinical internship, or even merely an apprenticeship on the job.

The practice of the learned professions of law and medicine in the United States has, in the past quarter century, come to be based upon a foundation of general collegiate education of two to four years, with the addition of three to eight years of strictly professional education. Such a heavy investment of time in preparation has been justified, not only by the increasingly high expectations of society for the performance of practitioners but also by the compensation which society has been willing to provide for their services. While teaching at the college and university level has generally been based upon comparable requirements, teaching in elementary and secondary schools is not built upon such exacting specifications. In fact, if the advice of the most extreme critics were to be followed, as virtually it is in a few locations, teaching in the schools could not properly be termed a professional occupation, by the criterion of direct professional education, for that component practically would be eliminated. Direct professional education is now incorporated in part in the collegiate years; and if it is provided with serious intent to conform to the standards of professional leaders, it is expensive, in terms of additional qualified staff to conduct it. For this reason, the casual view of the importance of direct professional education held by those extreme critics is appealing to some general college leaders. The time has therefore surely arrived for an appraisal of the importance of direct study of the field of education, with a view to professional practice in this field.

Education as a Field of Study

Since education is a phenomenon of human experience, it can be studied in concrete terms. It can be observed in both process and result. Theories can be propounded to explain it, and it can be controlled experimentally. Thus there can be little doubt that it is a field for scholarship.

The fact that education has been studied in a scholarly way by persons who are identified with other fields of academic concentration, such as psychology, sociology, history, philosophy, economics, and biology, should not obscure the identity of the field of education as a discrete reality. The cognate relationships of education and many other fields of scholarly inquiry are both real and important, but the fact that the studies of the psychologist with reference to education, for example, are often significant additions to the field of psychology does not remove their significance for the field of education. Nor does the need of the scholar in the field of education for appropriate orientation to the substance and method of cognate fields deny the reality of his own field of concentration.

Thus we may assume at the outset of this discussion that there is a place for the educationist in the company of scholarly workers, along the side of the psychologist, the historian, the philosopher, the biologist and others. If the phenomena of education seem invariably to invite and even to require an interdisciplinary scholarly approach for their full understanding and interpretation, this is no more true of education than of the phenomena of many other classes, such as politics, economics, social organization, or religion. The identification of these many classes of phenomena and their special scholarly study represent an often repeated historic pattern of academic development, namely, the division of previously unified work for the purpose of attaining greater clarity and depth of perception and understanding.

We may also assume that there is no issue as to whether the specialist who identifies himself as a professional worker in the conduct of educational activities and programs has a necessary body of knowledge to master. Nor is there an issue of any consequence as to whether his necessary knowledge is unique in all of its particulars and separate from knowledge necessary to other groups in society. There may be uniqueness to his total pattern of knowledge, while some or even all of the particulars are shared by other groups such as physicians or officials of government. The real and important issue is the nature of his requisite body of knowledge, whatever its relations may be to the knowledge necessary to the performance of the functions of other groups.

The concern of the present paper is neither to make an inventory nor to propound a form of systematic accounting for the elements which may be thought to be necessary for the professional worker in education. Such an endeavor would border on the encyclopedic and would leave many useful purposes unserved, even if it could be accomplished authoritatively, which is doubtful. Nor will any job survey or systematic analysis be undertaken here, since the completion of such an Herculean task would leave us with little more than a report of the hypothetical status of present performance of the educational profession. Instead, a much more modest objective is set for the present paper, namely, to describe some important types of problems inherent in the work of the educational profession, to illustrate the nature of their matrices in culture and society, and to point some cautions with respect to the methods of inquiry and the processes of professional development which would promise to yield relevant information for the solution of those problems.

Professional Practice in Education

The practitioner in education is more than a student of education. His primary function is to promote the process of education. He must be a specialist in doing something by way of such promotion. He must know how to do it, and his very professional pretentions also oblige him to know whether and why to do it. He must make himself responsible for the social and cultural consequences of what he does. He is necessarily a part of an enterprise involving directly a sizeable company of professional colleagues and indirectly the fortunes of everyone affected by the process he and his colleagues are promoting.

The professional person in education knows that his work is both dangerous and important. A misunderstood remark or gesture of his may alienate an individual and through a protracted chain reaction may shape a grotesque cultural product affecting a group of people of unknown size or power. He knows that the potential importance of his service is great, since some kinds of learning are virtually inevitable in community life and his influence may decide what kinds. He realizes the inherent challenge to his efforts, since the vital keys to individual and community life and development always have an experimental dimension. The possibility of desirable consequences is built into the process as truly as is failure or disaster.

The professional ideal and commitment require the practitioner not only to shoulder a heavy cultural responsibility for the program in which he serves but also to perform with the greatest possible technical effectiveness. No truly professional teacher can live with his conscience while using in his work methods or materials inherited from uncriticized tradition or adopted for the sole reason of their vogue. He studies his performance operations, not merely to make them acceptable, under the circumstances, but to perfect them as fully as possible. The practice of the profession imposes a rigorous discipline of responsible technical performance which inherently and continuously contrasts it with routinely skilled occupations.

Inquiry into Educational Practice

The prime question which logically presents itself to an inquirer into any given practical educational situation is: What is going on there? This seems to be a disarmingly simple question, but in reality it is both very complex and very difficult to answer. The station of a single child in school may be the window through which to observe a whole new world emerging from what may appear to be a kind of chrysalis of the past, if the observer has but the patience, sensitivity, and imagination to recognize what he sees. Perhaps a subliminal awareness of this fact and its baffling implications account for the superficial character of many status inquiries into education. There must be some obscure reason for the perennial preoccupation of surveyors with the readily answerable but often irrelevant questions, such as: How many people are visibly present in the location at any given time? How long do those people remain there before basically changing their configuration or their apparent main purpose? How much money is being spent on the maintenance of the given station and how does that amount of money compare with the amount spent elsewhere upon similar situations? What materials and equipment are in evidence? What signs and symbols are used to record people's judgments as to what is going on there? Whatever the need for answers to these latter questions, they are secondary to the main inquiry. Frequently, the most important knowledge about the status of a given educational operation, from the standpoint of the needs of the professional practitioner, is neglected; and for the lack of it, the practitioner cannot measure up to his professional ideals and standards. What the professional practitioner needs to know about a given educational situation, in order that he may decide what he should do to influence that situation, and thus to attempt to guide its further processes, concerns the insights being expressed, the values revealed, the statement of levels of understanding and purposes of the participants, and any and all diagnostically relevant evidence which will aid him to make his own experimental thrust toward possible educational advance. We need more imaginative inquiry into the terms by means of which the status description of the educational situation may be elevated in significance. Professional performance of educational practitioners hinges upon such inquiry.

While the meaningful description of a given educational incident, as the first requirement for judgments on the part of the practitioner, is difficult enough, he needs to know much more, in order to fulfill his professional function. In addition to knowing what in fact is happening, he must inquire into the limits of possibility as to what could happen, under the given set of circumstances. While the practitioner's own experimental thrust may be expected to yield some evidence as to the limits of the possible, he must be informed by some interpretation of the present incident as to how far to go, how much change in performance to try for, lest he use his opportunity wastefully, either by expecting too little or by overstepping his margin of tolerance and inducing failure. Thus, every educational incident must be seen as an outcropping of a continuous series of developments whose longitudinal sequence is informative. Any idea that education is a matter of a simple arrangement of situations wherein people are to be clothed according to objective measures and then observed, as the tailor measures clothes and then observes his model, is as far from reality as painting numbered squares is from true visual artistry. There is just more to it than readily meets the eye, as every professional practitioner knows.

The final blow to simplicity in the proper interpretation of an educational situation, as the professional worker must know it, lies in the necessity to decide what should happen in it. The professional person in education must know what is really happening, what could happen, what the odds may be on the success of a given thrust on his part, but he must also assess the consequences of a given development, both in terms of their utility for further educational advance and in terms of the values inherent in an advance in any given direction. This normative judgment is a matter partly for his mind and partly for his conscience. The fields of choice for normative judgments are usually finite, even if frequently somewhat obscure. Through intellectual analysis and projection, he can estimate the range and content of the choices, but in the end his action hinges upon what he wants for the people involved, not even what he can properly say he thinks he should want. This is obviously the most taxing part of the work of the professional person, for it pins down his own share in the possibly life-giving or life-preventing consequences of the educational situation. This is the point at which his whole character as a human being, his whole view of himself and the world he inhabits, comes into play. To add to the awe of it, usually his performance in this situation must be virtually instantaneous. There is often no time to make specifically instrumental studies, or even vaguely to think the matter over. Is there any more cogent reason for the contention that professional people engaged in education should be the ablest and most fully and deeply cultivated people we have in the community?

Thus it should be evident that inquiry into educational processes is inquiry into the deepest springs of human life, individual and social. It is inquiry into evidences of life-in-the-making. It is completely practical, in that it is conducted for no purpose of idle musing upon the nature of people, but only as a means of wise choices of possible actions by people whose professional responsibility it is to guide human development in all of the dimensions of performance, for understanding, for attaining self-hood, and for the realizations of significantly and wisely chosen values in the communities of men. Inquiry into individual educational situations, into schematic and sequential educational programs, and into all systematic educational machinery of the community must be undertaken in the matrix of cultural and social development. In no other way can such inquiry yield the information necessary for the proper performance of the professionally responsible educational practitioner.

Appropriateness of Methods of Inquiry

At this point it becomes evident that particular educational situations, being the direct objects of the inquiry, define the necessary methods and design of that inquiry. They impose their own discipline upon the inquirer. They admit of the use of methods of inquiry that have proved useful elsewhere, only provided those methods can be found to fit and to contribute to the successful completion of the inquiry immediately in hand. If the clinical or social psychologist, for example, seeks to inquire into an educational situation, he must first examine that situation to see what, if any, of the methods he knows may fit, rather than to assume that certain of the methods he knows may freely be selected for the present purpose, since he finds the educational situation to resemble other situations involving human beings in which his familiar methods have been forged and have had their utility tested. The fact that an educational situation may also be labeled as a particular case of a psychological situation does not justify the shifting of the orientation for the study of the educational situation to that previously found appropriate for the study of a psychological situation. This error of automatic classification of educational inquiry by the use of methodological categories used in other fields, with objects defined differently, has greatly retarded educational research in the past. The time has arrived, if educational research is to be made significantly more effective, when that particular kind of research must be treated as a field of inquiry in its own right—a discipline, if one pleases to dignify it by a presumption of rigor readily grasped by many other fields, with no more rational claim than is appropriately available to educational research. To bring to bear upon practical educational inquiry the research experience of other fields is indispensable to the full exploration of the implications of such inquiry, but interdisciplinary enrichment of the task does not justify surrendering control of the methods appropriate to the task.

The Education of the Professional Practitioner

To identify the character of the knowledge of education which is to be regarded as indispensable to the professional practice of education, it is necessary to discover its relations with other categories of knowledge. Educational programs embrace all types of knowledge and the professional practitioner of education must inevitably recognize the scope of knowledge and have some grasp of the schemes used to organize all knowledge, even though, like any other individual, he can never himself pretend to possess more than an infinitesimal portion of what is known to man.

Perhaps the foremost relationship of educational knowledge to all knowledge, which must be explored, is the degree to which educational knowledge necessarily consists in an understanding of the scope, character, and organization of all knowledge. That this relationship is commonly perceived to be significant is evidenced by the fact that for the professional educational practitioner the same general and specialized educational opportunity and achievement are usually presumed to be necessary as those required, across the board, for all other human beings at every given stage of their educational development. Whatever the additional special knowledge he is to be required to possess, in order to be worthy of special status as a professional practitioner of education, he is usually required to have the same elementary education, the same secondary education, largely, at least, the same collegiate education, and, in many dimensions, the same postgraduate education as other people with whom he is studying at those levels. Just how, why, and when differentiation of his education from that of other people is to be undertaken is a significant indication of the nature of the concept of his professional knowledge which is to be adopted. It has been suggested, for example, that in the elementary school consideration be given to motivating students to develop an interest in becoming teachers. If this is to be encouraged, as is frequently recommended, it indicates that such interest and motivation, in contradistinction to other possible interests and motivations, must constitute identifiable elements of professional knowledge, and, from the standpoint of basic human rights and needs, must be equivalent in value to alternative possibilities. The same is true of the recommendation that interest and motivation with respect to teaching careers should be cultivated in the secondary school by means of encouragement for secondary school pupils to observe teaching purposefully and even critically, and possibly to assist in various teaching situations with their own or earlier age groups in school. When college students are permitted and encouraged to specialize in education as a career outlet for pursuit after college, it must mean that such specialization is thought to have both significance as professional knowledge and equivalency with specialization in other fields as a focus for general collegiate education. This dual purpose of professional interest and motivation in the field of education must be assumed to imply that professional interest and motivation in education consist, at least in part, in the substance of the very formation of interest and motivation for any career outlet. The fact that professional and other controversy surrounds such anticipation of professional education, with some people contending that elementary, secondary, and collegiate education are compromised by it, does not dispute the main thesis that the projection of career choice and potential of the individual constitute a real element in the composite of professional knowledge, whenever they are undertaken and whatever other educational utility they may have.

Having observed at the outset that the very bent and direction of the individual's life-time continuum of education constitutes the orientation in which a professional motivation for teaching is generated and therefore constitutes the base line of professional education, we may now inquire as to the primary categories of constituent elements in such education. In doing so, we are immediately confronted with the difficult question as to whether such categories can be marked off clearly from all of the rest of the education of the individual. If the initial formation of motivation for teaching is hardly distinguishable in process from the formation of motivation for any other positive identification of career interest, is it also true that the understanding of the function of teaching and the ability thoughtfully to fulfill that function are indistinguishable substantially from competency in any other field? Some people argue that the career outlet of the work of a good learner takes no sure or confident form, or at least no form which is not readily alterable or interchangeable, until the advanced stages of that work. Since there are assumed, at least, to be no necessities in this respect, it is argued that the greatest possible flexibility for career applications of learning should be preserved as late as possible. Therefore, professional orientation toward any career is to be resisted and suppressed, in this view, until it is absolutely necessary to recognize it.

There is room for difference of opinion as to whether it may be wise to encourage the formation of career identification at an early stage in education, on the ground that it may preclude the choice of an alternative and equally promising identification. But on the face of it, the argument for postponing career identification for teaching or for any field whose substance is encompassed in the program of education currently being pursued seems singularly lacking in cogency. The very materials being handled and the very processes by which those materials are used in the student's education are the vital core of the substance of understanding which constitutes the foundation of professional education in those fields. As one learns how to learn by learning, one learns how to teach by being taught, even if the later and more mature requirements of either learning or teaching necessitate that those learnings be corrected or replaced by more nearly adequate concepts and experiences. Mathematical knowledge is now widely recognized as rapidly changing, but the very foundation of mathematical competence upon which today's mathematician must build, or which he must reconstruct basically, is that which he formed in his study of mathematics from the beginning of his own schooling. In like manner the teacher inevitably carries a heavy freight of his understanding of teaching from that which was formed through the influence of his own teachers. Such past understanding may be advantageous to his practical performance as a teacher, it may be virtually irrelevant, from the practical standpoint, or it may be a burden of concepts to be replaced or reconstructed as his own practical performance is developed. In any case, his professional education began as he first came under the influence of teachers, even if those teachers were parents, other adults, or possibly only children with whom he was associated in his own formative years. Thus it is evident that the professional education of the teacher has deep roots in the whole longitudinal development of the education of the individual. Any effort sharply to differentiate professional education from the rest of education is doomed to frustration. Such differentiation as is attempted is a matter of convenience at the relatively later stages of the education of the individual and concerns the fulfillment, supplementation, reconstruction, or displacement of concepts at the heart of his professional education which already have taken form in his very human nature and being. All of one's teachers are engaged in his professional education for teaching, whatever they may consciously be attempting to do, or whatever else they may in actuality be accomplishing.

Thus a good deal of the pseudo-sophisticated arithmetic with reference to the number of credit hours of professional courses and of "content" courses is irrelevant, if not mischievous. The question is not exactly how much professional education should be tolerated, since all of the individual's education has professional relevancy. The proper question is: Considering all that has gone before in the individual's education, what yet needs to be done, by way of fulfillment, supplementation, reconstruction or replacement of his education, in order that he may purposefully and with promise of success undertake to engage in professional practice as a teacher? This puts the professional component of the education of a teacher in a very different light from that in which often it is seen, and shifts the burden of professional education from the lone shoulders of the professional specialist to the whole company of professional practitioners who deal with the individual. The professional specialist in education is cast in the role of an expert contributor to a broad process, rather than a magician who is supposed to transform a scholarly individual into a teacher.

Methods of Teaching

Controversy, much of it quite idle and ineffectual, has long raged over the question of methods of teaching. This controversy has often ground serious efforts to improve teacher education to a halt, either because the efficacy of certain methods could not be established firmly or because those methods have seemed not to be transferable from one user to the next. Picayune details of procedure and obviously insignificant classroom arrangements have sometimes been identified with teaching methods. Inquiry into methods of teaching has at times proved so frustrating that some leaders have concluded fretfully that there is no way of estimating the comparative merits of teachers, except in gross and largely irrelevant terms.

From the level of such controversy, it would seem that the function of the teacher has been basically misconceived. A great deal of the discourse on teaching method seems to be in terms of a fatally inadequate analogy between teaching and manufacturing. The teacher is treated as the fabricator and the student as the product, with the subject of study being both the raw material and the tool to be used in the molding and finishing of the product. No such concept could be farther from the reality of teaching. Learning does not take place primarily by precept, but rather through the influence of example. The objective of teaching is not direct action to hang upon an indifferent frame certain raw material to fashion it in terms of a predetermined pattern. The objective of teaching is to start and facilitate the progression of a process in a person who has all of the complexity of motive, sensitivity, acuity, and will which characterize humanity. Authoritative precept, as often as not, is completely abortive in engendering the animation of the student which properly is to be sought. Where it seems to succeed, doubtless the precept is simply tolerated as a facet of the example which the student expects and wishes the teacher to set. The problem of the teacher is to do the things he wishes the student to be able to do, to embody the attributes he wishes the student to come to possess, and to constitute a live example of the results he hopes to have the students achieve. Nothing is so contagious as example and, in learning and teaching, nothing so dead and impotent as the authority figure or symbol who commands such miracles to take place as are embodied in the birth of new insights and aspirations in learners. While the teacher must have his own concepts of the appropriate results from his efforts at given stages, together with his reasons for believing those results to be appropriate at such stages, he must be guided in his every step, not by a blueprint yet incompletely transferred into reality, but by his observations of emerging developments in the performance of the ultimately self-directing individual student. If he has an exact blueprint, he will find that never, except by accident, does the end result exactly follow its lines. This should disturb no one, since it verifies the proper objective of teaching, namely, to get individuals constructively into motion toward creatively conceived goals, whether or not those goals have been fully anticipated by the teacher. Methods of teaching are thus ways of setting an example for students. There is nothing abstract about them, since they are ways of doing or being something which is hopefully the common objective of the teacher and those taught. If that hope proves to be impossible of realization or temporarily evanescent, under the circumstances, little if any teaching is being accomplished. The teacher's business is to keep on trying thoughtfully to make example do its miraculous work. Sometimes this fails to happen and intelligible reasons for the failure must be sought as guides to renewed and continued effort on the part of the teacher. An appropriate analogy for teaching, if one must be found, would lie in the practice of medicine. Drugs and surgery have their importance to the practitioner, but it is "Mother Nature" who really cures the patient. And preventive medicine is the highest hope for the safeguard of health.

Transaction in Teaching

One of the frustrations of the researcher who seeks to facilitate the improvement of the performance of teachers is to obtain empirical data. Observations of what teachers do are always qualified by what students seem to think the teacher is doing and, by the same token, what the students think is only readily apparent in the overt response the students give to what the teacher does. This frustration stems from the old philosophical problem of appearance and reality. It has plagued research on teaching method to the point that many researchers cease to concern themselves with what the teacher says he intends to accomplish, and are content to assume that the teacher teaches, whether or not it can be shown that learning results. The improvement effort is thus swamped in a sea of empiricism.

Teaching is a transaction between teacher and student. Both retain control of their actions and their intentions and purposes, and both modify themselves and their behavior as a result of mutual expressions in the situation. The expression they make to each other is empirical information, but the meaning of such information is only discovered as both parties revise, refine, and develop their expression to reveal in ever greater clarity their intentions and purposes. Thus the continuous process by which such meaning is projected is the prime evidence of teaching, rather than any tightly time-bound performance by either teacher or student. Teaching is accomplished through the continuum of the transaction, if at all, as the ground for further action of both parties is reorganized. It cannot be known to be accomplished through the performance of any set of prescribed exercises by the teacher, any more than learning can be demonstrated as the result of a similar set of student exercises.

Functions of the Teacher

From the standpoint of such a revised concept of the nature of teaching, we may now turn to the question of the specific functions in educational, social, and cultural life to be performed by teachers. The series which follows represents one way of describing the work of teaching and illustrates the integral relationship between teaching method and the substance of learning which is vital to the performance of the teacher and to the education he needs for such performance.

1. The teacher is a demonstrator of learning. He not only sets the stage and performs the role of a person at a given level of understanding faced with a given set of circumstances but, perhaps even more significantly, he demonstrates learning by revealing himself as a learner at his own level of understanding and faced by the circumstances of his own life. The actor-coach performance of the teacher rapidly loses its appeal when it is disconnected from the reality of a person able to reveal honestly his own levels of understanding and his own needs and efforts for further understanding.

2. The teacher is an analyst of knowledge. He builds, tests, and constantly reorganizes the patterns of relationships in his areas of knowledge, searching for improved perceptions of particulars that may be revealed by the ground against which the figure is set. He must be a skilled technician, with a thorough grasp of the materials he is undertaking to analyze, and he must also constantly display an alertness as to the interpretive import of each analytical pattern. Thus he reveals the purposes of every analytical operation and, insofar as possible, he identifies the consequences which ensue upon the pursuit of those purposes. Analysis thereby is learned as a tool of interpretation, rather than merely as a game to while away otherwise idle time, or as a skill proficiency to be displayed for the wonderment of observers.

3. The teacher is a diagnostician of understanding. Much of the accomplishment of the teacher hinges upon his ability to help the student to discover the level of understanding which he possesses at any given moment. While this is an examining function, in part, the examination does not carry its own fulfillment in diagnosis. The objective of the diagnostic function lies in the utility to which the examination is put and the resolve which flows from the data of the examination. It is the student's perception of his own next steps which the diagnosis reveals and which the teacher seeks to establish. Much confusion surrounds this point and if one tenth of the energy spent by many teachers on busy work with examinations could be captured for

true diagnostic interpretation, the efficiency of learning would be greatly enhanced.

4. The teacher is a guide to human development. Rudimentary developmental processes in human beings are hard to suppress, under conditions of associative living. Without critical assessment and thoughtful cultivation, weird distortions of physical, intellectual, aesthetic, and moral development frequently occur, as is evident in any study of individual and group behavior under conditions of deprivation. It is for the refinements of development that education is conducted. The teacher may make the difference between blunting or abortion of developmental potential and discriminating release and fruitful fulfillment of such potential. The teacher knows what comes naturally under the infinite variety of conditions which obstruct the refinement of developmental tendencies and he endeavors to select the preferable natural conditions and counteract the unfavorable natural conditions for the purpose of such refinement. His guiding touch in the sequence of development is one of the great secrets of his effectiveness.

5. The teacher is a model of human nature. Whatever erudition he may reveal, whatever adroitness and skill he may display, whatever articulateness may characterize his utterances, whatever acuity of penetration his intelligence may exhibit, whatever fame he may have earned, and whatever attractiveness his personality characteristics may yield, all of these have their meaning and force through their enclosure within the unity which is a human being. Whether he intends it or not, the teacher is always some kind of a model for his students. He will be emulated by them, whether they know it or not. He may be fought by them, but he will teach them how to fight. He may be the object of their affections, but those affections are tailored to his image. This is the sobering fact of the relationship of the teacher and those taught in all cultures. Thus a conscious awareness of his image and a responsible effort to constitute a proper model are a part of the human capital of the professional teacher. He fulfills a good part of his total function through his influence as a model of human nature.

6. The teacher is an artist in expression. Correct usage in the languages or media of human expression is hard to define. Insofar as acceptable standards are available, obviously the teacher, above all others, should follow them. But more than correctness is necessary.

Artistry implies sensitive perception and responsiveness. It implies appreciation and discrimination between the significant and the trivial. It implies alertness and awareness, rather than satiation and ennui with the flow of experience. But most of all, it implies assertion. Neither coyness, nor evasiveness, nor any form of deliberate misrepresentation are tolerable to the artist. His mission is to foster integrity, purposefulness, and forthrightness of statement in human beings. The true teacher is the outgoing person who can be depended upon to give whatever he possesses, and by his lights the best of what he possesses, to further the growth of learners. Thus inarticulateness in a teacher is a contradiction in terms. By the same token, the fullest expression of himself, at his highest possible level of potential significance, is the key to the performance of the professional teacher.

7. The teacher is a builder of community among men. Common cause, the most essential ingredient in all societies, requires constant cultivation. Without that cultivation, society tends to disintegrate into atomistic particles, or what may appear to be a society may never have functional reality. While common cause necessitates an intellectual foundation of understanding of common interests and fortunes among individuals and groups, it is primarily a matter of conviction, commitment, and will. All societies are in greater or lesser degree unstable, depending upon the continuous regeneration and renewal of both the awareness of common interests and fortunes and the will to minister to their fulfillment by common effort. Common cause thus represents moral judgments regarding values to be conserved and moral determinations regarding actions related to the purpose. Community is the instrument for the realization of such judgments and actions. All learning has either evident or obscure consequences for community, because it changes people. Every teacher, whether he knows it or not, exercises an influence upon the formation of community. The professional teacher knows it, makes himself responsible for the influence he has, and prepares himself to exercise this influence as constructively as possible. The urgency of this function in teaching at the present time need hardly be argued, since rapid, fundamental, and threatening change in the foundations of community among men is probably the most staggering fact of our present generation.

8. The teacher is an architect of the culture. Nothing is learned in

isolation, for knowledge is defined by relationships. If science is currently being over-emphasized in education, as is widely being argued, this only means that burgeoning scientific discovery is being poorly learned, without adequate exploration of the humanistic field in which this discovery is set and to which its utility ultimately refers. If today we are learning a concept of the universe as a toy for the amusement of men, as has been suggested, this superficiality represents both insufficient pursuit of the integral relationships of scientifically derived knowledge and neglect of the prime teaching function of helping people to learn the basis upon which a good human life is to be erected. Every teacher works at the point of control of the substance and design of the culture. Many teachers do not know their own strength in this respect. Both processes and programs of education should be designed in terms of a responsible assertion as to the character of the culture which will result from their fruition. Every generation pays something for its own failures of responsibility in planning its education to build a proper cultural design and unhappily it hands on a great share of the cost to oncoming generations. The teacher who has not considered this dimension of his responsibility can hardly be said to have received a sufficient professional education.

Programs of Education

The argument to this point has laid great stress upon the process of education and the practice of fostering that process in the individual where ultimately it takes place. Organized societies, however, only accomplish their educational purposes in programs conducted through groups of individuals. The effectiveness of educational programs is estimated in many different ways. A program must be built to fit the cultural characteristics of the particular society. A program must both foster individual achievement and capitalize upon the associative opportunities and advantages of the groups which it organizes for educative purposes. A program must be expected and permitted to exercise its creative potential for the modifications of the society. A program must possess the stability and continuity to permit its processes and results to mesh with the other seminal social and cultural institutional processes (the economy, the political system, the communication agencies, the religious institutions, the organized intellectual forces, and the like), and it must also possess the flexibility necessary to its own development and maturation. A program must embrace a sufficient proportion of the population to serve the developing needs of the society for education. Thus a large segment of the field of education consists in the design, operation, and evaluation of educational programs which may be expected to meet such criteria of effectiveness.

Some of the newly developing societies of the world today are in a position to design their educational programs almost from the beginning to meet the necessary criteria, even though the full implementation of their programs will be postponed for some time. Educational programs in the older societies, however, seldom respond to such comprehensive efforts for originality. They are composed of the residue of long and deep traditions, and sweeping innovations come with great difficulty. Prudence and caution often seem unduly influential in such situations. Occasional comprehensive critical reviews are made in such societies and usually visible changes, sometimes quite fundamental ones, and occasionally, ultimately far-reaching ones, result from such reviews. Recent Royal Commission reports on education in Great Britain seem to have had some such results. In the United States of America the vast geographical territory, the varied social conditions encompassed therein, and the studied aspiration for cultural pluralism impose severe limitations upon freedom to make broadly applicable educational program plans. Fear of educational standardization is widespread in the United States at a time when enormous trends of cultural standardization have been set in motion by recent advances in communication and transportation, as well as by the increased mobility of the population incident to the advance of technology. Moreover, this very technology has put audio-visual tools at the disposal of educational programs, which are now being furnished with accompanying content by authoritative national scholarly bodies. The materials and means for national educational programs seem suddenly to be appearing in profusion, even though the formation and application of such programs is still hotly debated by individual critics, by various agencies of local and state government, and by a complex of professional associations. Thus the technical educational questions of programmed learning are presently somewhat overshadowed by the questions of public policy for educational programs. Proper knowledgeability with reference to all of these questions, together with their alternative possible answers, today obviously constitute an area of the field of education with vital significance for the responsible professional practitioner.

THE TEACHER EDUCATION CURRICULUM

In the light of the individual reference of all education and the necessity to program education for group operations, what may be said of the frame of the teacher education curriculum? In the first place, all that has been said of learning and teaching, of the learner and the teacher, necessarily also applies in principle to the teacher of teachers. No more can teacher education programs be reduced to acceptable uniform patterns than is true of good education anywhere else. The first consideration is repeated diagnosis, upon the basis of which the curriculum pattern is shaped and the courses of instruction designed. The student's achievement obviously is estimated, and the curriculum evaluated, upon the basis of the projection indicated by diagnosis.

Should a particular minimum set of courses be required? Good institutions build up experience which indicates the value of particular courses and sequences for considerable numbers, perhaps all, of their students. Such courses will be required as will assure the ability of each individual to fulfill such functions as have been described in the preceding paragraph, upon the basis of diagnostic evidence indicated by a particular student body.

One thing becomes increasingly clear in recent experience with teacher education. Namely, full and significant understanding of education does not result simply from the study of other subjects, any more than a person becomes properly knowledgeable in geography by studying mathematics. Thus the thought that broad general education, coupled with specialization in some teaching field, may simply be applied on the job, with a little conference or seminar talk on the side, in the hope of producing an intelligent teacher, is obviously ridiculous. Systematic study is required in education as in other fields.

Thus there will be differing patterns of higher education for teachers, incorporating the types of integral sequences of studies which represent the creative product of the experience of different institutions. One of the dangers of the present situation with respect to education is that, in the interest of narrow concepts of efficiency, we shall be persuaded or forced to surrender experimental initiative. Let the curriculum be built and continuously revised to reflect the genius of every faculty working in its collaborative relationships with practitioners and responsible public leaders. Let minimum standards clearly represent their cooperative judgment as to the best educational interests of the community. Let the authoritative wisdom of professional and scholarly leaders be respected after it is fairly checked for practical applicability and for its representation of the public interest. Let the compulsive will of every group be softened in good faith to accommodate honest examination of the results of purposeful experience in preparing teachers.

Urgent Current Problem Areas

No field of learning is completely static. Unused accumulations of intellectual treasure tend to wither and to lose their value. New dimensions of inquiry add to the working capital of a field. Some fields change more rapidly and fundamentally, at any given stage of history, than do others. The best clue to the current meaning and definition of a field lies in the problems its professors are studying and, more particularly, in the problems they see for further investigation.

The field of education is now in a stage of burgeoning development, both for the reason of its pursuit by scholars from cognate fields and because its prime interests have been found to lie deeper in the subsoil of culture than often had been supposed previously. The functions of the teacher and the effects of educational programs are being reconceived in the light of new evidence of their fundamental significance. While it has long been suspected and sometimes assumed to be so, the educational process has been identified, through the work of clinical and theoretical psychologists and psychiatrists, to be an important facet of the process of psychic development. The levels of the educational potential of individuals have been found, not merely supposed, to be shaped, influenced, and even in some particulars determined, for increase or decrease early and throughout life by the kind and amount of educational nourishment or deprivation which is afforded. Changes of social culture are being found to exercise an increasingly forceful and accelerating impact upon both educational aptitude and educational achievement. Large school and college enrollments are verifying the efficacy, or proving the ineffectuality, of many new techniques and approaches to teaching and learning. Whole new cultural dimensions among political, racial, ethnic, minority, and majority groups in a shrinking world are emerging to require educational recognition and mastery. An increasing necessity is appearing to treat educational programs as instruments of economic development and of public policies of various kinds. These and many other new horizons are bringing the educationist out of his previously narrower technical role and placing him in the company of major contributors to the highest reaches of scholarship, with responsibility for primary leadership in cultural development.

Leaders of thought in education are now concerned with the reach of their field into a vast array of significant areas for inquiry. Their problems for investigation range all the way from the effect upon educability of physiological nutrition and pharmaceutical tolerances in medication to the influence of an educational program upon a viable theory of the state. Among them there must be and are persons who, in addition to their primary orientation of training in the field of education, bring special scholarship in the methods and materials of history, philosophy, medicine, behavioral sciences, economics, anthropology, politics, administration and management, sociology, communications, and many other fields. Lively controversy is current over methods of research design and interpretation in each type of problem area. The long standing preoccupation with exact quantification of all research data in education is giving way to basic reexamination of the canons of truth which are relevant to the field.

A brief discussion of the professional field of education can afford only a few simple illustrations of the types of problems which now seem to be on the growing edge of the field. The following are such illustrations:

1. Mountainous accretions of knowledge have been built recently in many fields, particularly in those fields in which refinements of the scientific method and technological data processing have most readily been brought into play. For the specialist in those fields, the accretion has its own logic and proceeds at an accelerating rate. Increasing difficulty is apparent for the student who would cut into the process, so to speak, and join forces with those who are guiding the acquisition of new knowledge. Some telescoping of the accumulation through selection of essential supportive concepts is indispensable. Concentration upon teaching the structure of the field becomes the

only means of renewing its supply of knowledgeable personnel. To make matters more difficult, the process of learning the structure of a field is often different from the process of building that structure logically. Thus the teacher is faced, not only with the necessity of mastering the logical structure, but also with devising a sequential process of mastering that structure which can be used by the neophyte student, whether he be a beginner or one at a later stage of study. Teaching has become a necessary consideration for the scholar. The work of devising teaching structures and methods must now be pressed forward rapidly.

2. Since scholarship in teaching and scholarship in the substantive structure of the disciplines are now necessarily related integrally, the question arises as to the terms upon which both strands of interest may be pursued with no fatal loss to either in the process. In the past, competition between the two types of interest has nearly destroyed the chance of survival and development of the teaching interest, especially in the cases of prospective college and university teachers. Teaching responsibilities have been performed without serious efforts toward preparation for them and the quality of teaching has suffered, especially in terms of motivation, originality, and continuous cultivation for improvement. A new collaboration of academic and professional specialists must now be devised.

3. The necessities of selection of students at various levels of the total educational enterprise have generated a depressant force which is impending the full utilization of human talent. A system of examinations excludes students with increasing reliability and validity, but it does very little to redirect those who are rejected at different stages to more promising avenues for achievement. Increasingly widespread standardized formalism in instructional procedures depresses student originality. Thus the entire school and college system is coming dangerously to be pervaded by a certain fear of failure, with the consequent invitation for students to invent means of circumvention of the methods of control. How can the power of success be put in the place of fear of failure as the prime motivation? Hunting for errors and penalizing shortcomings should give way to means of capitalizing upon strengths of whatever kind. This is an urgent problem with major dimensions and implications for educational processes and programs.

4. The rapid expansion of education has prevented uniform adherence to the best we know in education for the profession. Compromises in the proper qualifications for professional practitioners have been made for more than a generation. As a consequence, the general public has much too limited a view of proper standards for the educational profession. How can such standards be presented to the public and significant advance made in their application, in the face of the widespread nihilism on this subject in the general community? Division among scholars and professional leaders has abetted the spread of negative attitudes and must be alleviated if the educational profession is ever to be in a position to take pride in its authority to do its work, but public support must also be generated on better terms. To bring these things about is a major practical problem of the field.

5. Interpenetration of cultures around the world is now a fact, and no longer merely a cause to be espoused or frustrated, according to one's views. Sometimes this is clearly a two-way flow of influence. Sometimes it is not, as in many technical assistance programs manned by people who have no intention to export the ways of one country into another, but who find imitation of their own ways, nevertheless. Sometimes cultural amalgamation is felicitous and sometimes it generates unbelievably great frictions. Prudence, however, if not high purpose, dictates that intercultural understanding be a major objective of educational systems. This phenomenon must be studied to discover its meaning, its implications, and its consequences, and it must be understood widely in the population. How can professional educational personnel be made sufficiently knowledgeable and how can programs be reformed to update them in this respect? This is one of the new responsibilities of the field of education.

Concluding Statement

The position of this paper is that the substance of knowledge in the field of education is defined by the occurrence of the phenomena of education, past and present, the changes which those phenomena typically now are undergoing, and the explorations of knowledgeable educational leaders with respect to the solution of recognized educational problems. Knowledge of education is that knowledge which is used by persons responsible for the conduct of the educational

STUDY OF EDUCATION

process, regardless of where that knowledge supposedly came from or whatever other uses it may have.

Thus an effort has been made to portray the field of education as presently a tremendously dynamic field responding to the challenges of new social and cultural conditions, events, and trends. It has been suggested that education is one of the truly comprehensive disciplines, in that it properly should embrace portions of the work of scholars in many other fields which might be applied to the illumination of educational questions and issues. Furthermore, it has been observed that the interdisciplinary collaboration of educationists increasingly is recognized as a vital contribution to its cognate fields.

A level of scholarly achievement and opportunity is appearing in the field of education which promises a fortunate future development, particularly if some past forms of provincial contentiousness among scholarly and professional leaders can be completely eradicated and the general community adequately informed of the vital interest of all citizens in high professional standards for educational practitioners.

Cultural Factors in Remediation
Allison Davis
The University of Chicago

DURING THE last few years, the education of the *culturally deprived* has become a major concern of both public and private schools. Like the nationwide emphasis in schools during previous decades upon *individual differences* or *progressive education,* or understanding *child development,* or more recently upon *delinquency* or *dropouts,* the current efforts to improve the education of the *culturally deprived* will encounter stubborn difficulties, both with respect to theory, which in this field is derived from too little research, most of it using incorrectly defined samples, and also with respect to the classroom application of cultural principles and cultural learning theory.

The culturally deprived—a misnomer: The first difficulty with most current research and remedial work with the *culturally deprived* is that most of the research staff and school personnel attempting to work in this area do not understand the nature of culture, nor its interactions with personality, and its influence upon nearly all learning. Furthermore, they do not know from their own experience and firsthand observations the social and cultural behavior of low cultural groups in America. The fact that nearly all these staffs consist of people having middle-class cultural behavior and value systems means that they usually do not perceive most slum children's behavior and values as, in fact, cultural. Thus we have fallen into the trap of using the concept *culturally deprived,* which most researchers and teachers in this field now vaguely recognize as a false concept, without *recognizing* the error in cultural analysis.

All human groups and members of groups have a very complex

CULTURAL FACTORS IN REMEDIATION

and strongly sanctioned culture—language, child-rearing practices, sexual controls, kinship relationships, parent-child roles, and group goals concerning husband-wife, parent-child, and Superhuman-human relationships. The *low-income groups,* or *lower classes,* or *economically deprived,* or *slum groups,* or *the poor,* have, in fact, cultural patterns of behavior, values, and learned emotions, which organize all the major areas of behavior mentioned in the preceding sentence. They are not culturally deprived in the *generic* sense; they are deprived, specifically, of many of the cultural skills and goals of *middle-class* American groups. The term *culturally deprived,* in the usual generic sense, is a natural and inevitable expression of middle-class cultural perception. The slum, or lower class, or low-income, or poor groups are not deprived of a culture; in fact, they have learned as a group, and as individuals, a complex and powerfully motivating culture, which all the efforts of the school have relatively little success in changing, except over generations.

These low-status groups are deprived, then, to speak exactly, of certain skills and values possessed by most middle-class groups. The point for the staffs of schools and of the other institutions concerned with remediation is that certain of those skills and values common to middle-class people would be socially and economically adaptive for many low-status people, because such skills and values would enable them to compete in our economy.

Children of the poor, or the lower classes, or the slum groups already have learned a complex change-resistant system of culture, a *survival system,* before they enter the kindergarten or first grade. To be explicit, low-status groups are disadvantaged in our economy, in our schools, and in our social system because they have to learn a new cultural pattern of behavior, including: (1) habits of speech and writing, use of books, and other skills; and (2) new modes of sublimating or socializing the sexual, acquisitive, and aggressive drives which middle-class children and adolescents learn in their families.

Cultural problems in the classroom: My wife, who is a courageous person, began the most difficult work of a substitute schoolteacher after our sons had gone away to college. She taught in both the primary and elementary grades in many public schools. All of the schools, except one, were in a Negro slum. Her previous training in social anthropology at Radcliffe, at the University of London, and as a field anthropologist in the study of Negro-white communities in Mississippi was far more valuable to her than her six courses in education, for it enabled her to deal with many apparently insoluble learning problems in slum schools, and to make observations which are valuable to all teachers.

In a first grade of slum children, she found little comprehension of the abstract problems in arithmetic. Knowing that the children deal much more effectively with three-dimensional—concrete—problems, she asked them to stand in groups of four, or five, or six. For each group, she then said, "Now two (or three, or four, or more) of you go over to play with this other group. How many are left in this first group? How many are now in this second group?"

These disadvantaged first-grade children played out the arithmetic problems excitedly and learned the correct remainders and sums rapidly. But their walking and running from one group to another and their laughter and talking made *noise,* and brought the very punitive and insecure principal to the room. The classroom had to be returned to the deathlike *quiet* which is required in some penal instuitions, and in most slum schools.

In a second grade, my wife found several children, including one nine-year-old boy, who could not count beyond two or three. Since the following day was to be St. Valentine's day, she had brought some candy hearts to school. She told the children they could have as many candy hearts as they could count. *The nine-year-old boy thereupon counted fourteen candy hearts.* The significant improvement in problem solving by pupils of *low* cultural status when they are offered concrete rewards such as soft drinks, candy, or movie tickets has been demonstrated by Haggard,[1] using data gathered on 516 pupils by Eells and Davis.

In a seventh-grade class of Negro students, aged twelve to fifteen years, from poor families, my wife found the reading assigned by their regular teacher was a story of a Swedish girl who was in tears because her hair was straight and could not be made to take a wave or curl. Most of the retarded thirteen-to-fifteen-year-olds in this seventh grade class were boys, who of course had no interest in a girl's problems of hairdressing. Furthermore, all of the class, boys and

[1] Ernest A. Haggard, "Social Status and Intelligence: An Experimental Study," *Genetic Psychology Monographs,* 1954, 49, 141-186.

girls, were Negroes, who had been taught by this society to want straight hair, like that of the white movie and television stars, and to depreciate their own curly or crinkly hair. Attempting to teach reading with the culturally meaningless story of the Swedish girl who cried for curly hair was impossible. She substituted cowboy stories, civil rights stories from newspapers, love stories for the girls, and accounts of sports heroes for the boys. The class came awake, and read.

All teachers of such culturally *low-status* children, and all social workers, poverty program workers, and youth club workers need to use the principles which my wife applied. To do so, they must have firsthand experience with these children and youth, their families and peer groups, and they must have the insight and courage, as she did, to try new and more realistic approaches. To do so, they must learn the culture at close range, and apply their knowledge to their professional activities. In schools, this approach means the selection and discovery of new materials and new methods, and the discovery of ways to encourage and approve these students who have experienced little except disapproval, stigma, and failure in the age-old stereotyped curriculum of the school.

Cultural distortion in perception: **Efforts to deal with such pupils' cultural behavior as if it were *stupid, immoral,* or *lazy,* or attempts to stigmatize it in other value terms, are certain to fail. The naive do-gooders, the humanitarians untrained in comparative psychology and sociology, and those lacking firsthand knowledge of these children and their families will fail, as the moralistic old-style settlement house or social-work approach failed. A new way of life, of skills and values, cannot be given to or forced upon either children or adolescents. It has to be learned. To help anyone learn, one must analyze that person's present pattern of behavior and values, and always withhold judgment. One must also withhold advice and guidance until one learns to understand this behavior as influenced by low-income culture, and by the stigmatizing demands of the middle-class teacher, middle-class tests, middle-class curriculum, and middle-class guidance.

It is naive to expect the school bureaucracy, or the social work bureaucracy, or the poverty program bureaucracy to know how to change the culture of the low-status groups, even when these *educated* staffs have the best intentions in the world. In the history of *social uplift* the hell of failure and alienation is paved with good intentions. School staffs, and those of other social agencies, must get down to the bedrock of face-to-face participation with families, churches, and peer groups of children and adolescents. We must learn the present behavior of the pupil, in terms of habits, skills, and values, and start exactly where he is. We must abandon deliberately and finally the prim, sheltered, traditional world of the classroom for nice middle-class children, and start dealing with the strange, harsh, and sometimes frightening realities of the real slum world, and the behavior of the child. Life often *is* hard, cruel, and dirty for these pupils. They cannot be reached by those who want to keep their hands *germ-free* and their minds neatly arranged into the conventional *lesson plans*.

The ominous and disheartening truth about the large-scale *projects* being initiated by federal agencies, private foundations, and school systems is simply this: Virtually none of the people who plan these *projects* has lived among slum groups, nor studied them objectively and intensively. They are *outsiders,* alien to the culture of those masses which they are honestly hoping to change. They have to depend, therefore, upon hearsay and anecdotes, and upon quantitative estimates of retardation, familial disorganization, delinquency, and other indices too gross to afford any insight into the causes, dynamics, and meaning of the lower-status culture and child. Even more destructive to such projects is the fact that probably something like 90 per cent of the professional staffs of such projects also have no intensive firsthand knowledge of slum homes and people. They are social workers, or other college graduates, or volunteers, most of whom, like 85 per cent of urban teachers, have lived only in middle-class homes, and learned to understand only educated culture and values.

How, then, are they to understand the work problems of an unskilled or semi-skilled man or woman? How are they to understand the problems of getting enough food for one's children, or winter coats, or shoes, or the minimum heat to keep them from suffering?

How is the middle-class person to understand the sexual life of people most of whom are not ashamed of sex, and who find in sexual love the manhood and womanhood which poverty and oppression constantly operate to deny them in all other areas of behavior?

Most important of all, what understanding do those who make policy, or those who implement it, possess concerning the children, themselves, those for whom the program is designed? How can we understand this child's life in his family, his social development, his life in the streets, and his behavior in the school when the schools and most of his teachers cannot understand his behavior? Yet his teacher is with him thirty hours a week.

These certainly are fair questions, since no social agency can work effectively with any group unless its policy makers and staff have an objective knowledge of that group's behavior. There are no miracles in changing a group's culture. We must learn, by face-to-face visiting, participation, and observation in these neighborhoods, how families and children live, are motivated, regard the school and the teachers, and how they *survive,* when we ourselves would not be able to escape the bludgeoning attacks from life and society which they have to bear.

Teacher-child relationship: In her intensive studies in the homes of white families of the lowest economic level in Chicago, Miss Elizabeth Bott, formerly my research assistant, pointed out that these children were more spontaneous, more lively, more vigorous in the expression of their emotions, than the typical middle-class child. She documented this behavior with respect to their language, including their intonation, use of verbs, and emphasis upon verbs by placement in the sentence; their gestures; the expressiveness of their bodies in play, dancing, conversation, and other types of social activities. The same kind of zest and expressiveness seems even more general among Negro children from working families, and among Mexican-American children in southern California. In the schools, however, the child from low economic groups is likely to inhibit his expressiveness and zest after he finishes the kindergarten, unless he has a very insightful and skilled teacher.

Moreover, spontaneity and expressiveness must not be confused with self-confidence and self-esteem. The child of low-status culture usually loses early in school his confidence in his ability and in his future. Since his parents usually do not encourage him to compete in school, he usually lacks the drive for achievement which is the prime incentive taught by middle-class parents to their children.

Moreover, the school itself, including the reading-readiness tests, which will not predict reading achievement a year or two later; the educational-aptitude tests; the primers; the readers; and the curriculum as a whole soon damage severely the confidence and the basic self-esteem of the child from low socio-economic groups. Finally, his low place in society, and that of his parents, friends, and neighbors, tends to weaken his self-esteem. This self-depreciation is typical of all low-status groups, and is the result of their having been severely stigmatized in most relationships with dominant groups. It results in self-depreciation and in hidden self-contempt beneath the facade of hostility and resentment.

These children need teachers who will encourage them to try, to hope, to believe in their futures, and to believe in themselves and their abilities. They are hungry for hope, for encouragement, for some reason to have confidence in themselves against the dead weight of the social and economic pressures which drive them down to self-deprecation and sullen resentment.

The only knowledge and understanding we have gained on the slum has come from those social anthropologists, sociologists, social psychologists, and a few social workers or settlement house workers who have actually lived in and studied slum communities. Ninety *per cent* of teachers, young or old, are *sociological strangers* to these communities. They have access to the children thirty hours a week in school, but do not learn to study them, nor to understand their behavior, nor to change curriculum materials, nor teaching methods, nor their own attitudes, so as to help them learn more effectively.

Teachers flee from these groups. Thus in Chicago in 1964, the median number of years of experience by regularly appointed teachers in *inner-city slum* areas is only four years. The average number of years' experience of teachers in *high-status areas* is nineteen.[2] A gigantic 84 per cent of all substitute teachers in Chicago are in the inner-city schools; only one *per cent* are in high-status schools. In short, teachers flee the slum school, where they feel they are hopelessly alien—sociological strangers. Many educators are struggling with the sociological problem of keeping white pupils in schools with Negro pupils, but who is trying to stem the flood of regularly assigned teachers, rushing away from schools for the low-status cultural groups, which constitute one third of our school population?

First, we must help prospective teachers, and in-service teachers

[2] Robert J. Havighurst, *The Public Schools of Chicago* (Chicago: The Board of Education of the City of Chicago, 1964), p. 170.

learn how to work with these children, and to find situations and materials which possess intrinsic motivation. The lack of attention, the failure to listen, the crippled drive to learn and to compete in school, on the part of these children, result, in part, from their cultural handicap. They discover at the very beginning of their school life that they do not know many objects, words, pictures, and concepts which many of the other (middle-class) children know.

An equally powerful deterrent to achievement, however, is their fear and distrust of the school and the teacher, which constitute an alien environment, and their failure to identify with the stranger (the teacher) and her behavior. The so-called *lack* of attention, *lack* of desire to learn, and *lack* of competitive drive in school are expressions of urgent realities of *fear* and feelings of inadequacy, and the consequent *resentment* toward the teacher and the school tasks.

The chief emphasis in the kindergarten and the primary grades, therefore, should be placed upon the establishment of a strong relationship of trust and mutual acceptance between the teacher and pupil. The first step in education is to train the pupil to trust the teacher. If he trusts the teacher, he will later learn to *respect* the teacher and *will want to win her approval.* The feeling of liking and trusting the teacher develops into respect and the desire to win her approval. It is just this step which is missing in the early school life of most Negro and white children from low socio-economic groups, and which must be developed at the preschool and primary level. The teacher must find enjoyable informal activities, such as story reading and games; she must give the child freedom to tell his *own stories* about his *own* life or fantasies, in whatever words he knows. Free talk, together with songs, dances, and little plays, can establish a bridge between the culture of the teacher and that of the low-status child.

Across this bridge the teacher can lead the child into new learning and new behavior, into a new world of letters, numbers, and writing which now becomes invested with the importance and the feeling which the child attaches to the teacher, and to *whatever she values.* From the good relationships with the teacher comes interest in the school, in the materials, in reading, writing, and working in school. It is this spark struck by the relationships with the teacher which illuminates and enlivens the world of the mind even in the first grade.

Therefore we need to bring the Negro and white child from low economic groups into a relationship with such a teacher as early as possible, and we need to structure this relationship so that it will be rewarding to both pupil and teacher.

Cultural behavior defined: In the development of a teacher, probably the most important and most useful concept to be learned is the sociological and anthropological concept of culture. The writer's experience with teachers both twenty-five years ago and today, as well as experience with the staffs of many other types of social agencies, has been that the vast majority of them do not understand the nature of culture, and cannot use cultural analysis and cultural learning theory in their work with individual children or with groups of pupils. In colleges and universities, and in school systems, few teachers have learned either the basic meaning of sociological culture, or the effects of subcultures upon the learning of that particular culture which the school staff attempts to teach.

Within each group of people, culture includes all that behavior which the individual *learns* from that group. He learns from many groups, ranging in size from his immediate family to the factory or institution in which he works. For the child, the basic social groups which *socialize* him (channel his cultural learning into specific types of language, values, inferences, and sublimational patterns) are the family, the peer group of his own sex, and the school. When the child has been socialized in a family and peer group whose culture is different from that of the middle-class American culture, such a child is confronted by a strange cultural pattern when he enters school, a new culture which conflicts with that already learned by him. If the child becomes ambitious to learn this new culture, he also will have to move gradually into new peer groups which approve this culture.

While culture includes all behavior learned from (or exhibited in conformity with) a social group, culture exists *only* within individuals, of course. Culture is, therefore, in the last analysis, a psychological system since it consists of the responses of individuals. It is composed of the perceptions, thoughts, concepts of *reasonable* inferences, concepts of right and wrong, language, and other skills, and roles appropriate for the individual within such a group. In the sense that cultural behavior consists of acts of perception, thought, emotional patterning, and social response, culture clearly is psychological.

As contrasted with other psychological systems of behavior, however, culture includes only that cognitive and emotional behavior of the individual which has been learned from social groups. It excludes genetically determined behavior, and other idiosyncratic behavior which has been learned not in order to conform to the demands or standards of a group, but in the effort to come to terms with the *individual* system of perceptions, emotions, and drives. For instance, although influenced by culture, what we vaguely call *personality* and *intelligence* consist chiefly of individual psychological behaviors, and *differ within cultural groups.* Cultural behaviors *within* the same group vary much less than genetic or emotional dynamics, because the group authority figures—mother, father, peer-group leaders, teachers—provide daily models for identification, and also exert sanctions to motivate conformity.

Learning a new culture: Many thousands of children and adolescents, born into low-status families, learn enough, chiefly through the school—the educated culture—to obtain white-collar positions later. The proportion of all children born in slum families who learn this new culture is less than 10 per cent, but the numbers are impressive, and the proportion certainly can be doubled by better curricula and more skillful teachers. Under our present system of upward social movement, the successful student from the severely disadvantaged groups usually is the boy or girl who has identified with the teacher or other middle-class persons, has a verbal I.Q. above 98, and has good work habits in school. He also must have developed sufficient control of his hostility to enable him to be cooperative with the teacher and people of higher status.

Such a climber out of the ranks of the disadvantaged has identified with a new culture, a new set of values, as represented in the teacher or other middle-class persons. He has sought earnestly to take this new culture into himself because he admires it and considers it superior to that which he first learned. This process of incorporating the values and behavior of the admired *educated* group is the basic learning process in the ambitious, upward-climbing student from the lower depths of American communities. Identification with the culture of a socially higher group, the conviction that their culture is more intelligent, more rewarded, more desirable, also helps to reduce the resentment and hostility felt by the slum child toward that group.

Culture and academic learning: For both white and Negro low-status groups, the school should be a powerful factor in changing their cultural behavior. But the schools and our whole educational system are operating far below their potential effectiveness in training these children.

We know, for instance, that a third of the white children of unskilled and semiskilled families in a middle western city already are retarded in grade placement by the time they are nine and ten years old.[3] By the time white children from these lowest occupational groups are in their tenth year, they are about one year behind the children from the top occupational families in reading, and ten points lower in I.Q. ratings. In the sixth grade, Negro children of the lowest economic group are about a year behind the white lowest economic group in reading, and seven points lower in I.Q.[4]

But both groups have improved markedly in the last generation. The average I.Q. of white children of unskilled and semiskilled parents in Chicago is 102.3, actually above the national average for all children.[5] The average I.Q. of Negro children born in Philadelphia is 97.[6] Klineberg and Lee have shown, moreover, that the I.Q.'s of Negro children born in the South improve steadily with length of residence in New York or Philadelphia.[7,8] This trend is statistically significant and continuous. Such improvement, in an overall measure of educational aptitude, indicates the great power of acculturation, both in the school and in the community. We need, however, to accelerate the pace of acculturation of these groups in our schools.

Here, I should like to consider first the norms of academic behavior for different socio-economic groups, and secondly to focus upon the *great variation within each of these groups.*

[3] Kenneth Eells, Allison Davis, Robert J. Havighurst, Virgil E. Herrick, and Ralph W. Tyler, under the chairmanship of Allison Davis, *Intelligence and Cultural Differences* (Chicago: University of Chicago Press, 1951), p. 112.

[4] Robert D. Hess, "An Experimental Culture-Fair Test of Mental Ability" (unpublished Ph.D. dissertation, Committee on Human Development, the University of Chicago, 1950), p. 97.

[5] R. D. Hess, *op. cit.,* p. 91.

[6] Everett S. Lee, "Negro Intelligence and Selective Migration," *American Sociological Review,* XVI (1951), p. 231.

[7] Otto Klineberg, *Negro Intelligence and Selective Migration* (New York: Columbia University Press, 1935), p. 59.

[8] Lee, *op. cit.,* pp. 213-232.

CULTURAL FACTORS IN REMEDIATION

First, if we are to attempt to change part of the culture, and especially the language culture and educational motivation of the low socio-economic groups, we need to know what their present culture is. It should be stated at once that we do not know much about the culture of the lowest socio-economic groups as a whole. Furthermore, what we do know has often been stated incorrectly, so that social scientists fall into useless controversies, only to discover that they are talking about different parts of the *working class* or about different *segments* of the total range of behavior within the lowest economic group.

All attempts to define cultural behavior must face constantly the problem of finding the ways in which a group may be said *to behave in some systematic way, as a group,* and at the same time explain the tremendous variation of individual members from the norm of the group. When the traits or behavior being studied are continuous, that is, when the behavior varies over or may be classified into many degrees on a scale, the only way to describe the consensus of the group is by getting an average or some other measure of central tendency. Such a central tendency in the behavior of girls, as compared with boys, is expressed by an average height, or I.Q., or reading score. There still remains, however, the far more intricate and revealing work of explaining not only the difference in average behavior between the two cultural groups, but also the individual variation between one girl and another, or one boy and another.

Like all sciences, child psychology must seek to identify and explain the factors which differentiate between the *behavior* of *groups* such as: (a) six-year-olds and ten-year-olds, (b) Americans and English, or (c) slum children and upper-middle-class children. At the same time, we must observe and explain the *individual variation* within these cultural groups.

We can identify groups by their average behavior, or by a single trait which they have in common, such as age or sex. But nearly all differences between the groups will be matters of degree. No matter how a group of children is defined, there will be tremendous variation within the groups, and this intra-group variation will be as large in nearly all cases as the inter-group variation. Average weight, height, reading age, or vocabulary scores will differ as between ten-year-old boys and ten-year-old girls, but there will be as great a difference, usually, between *one* ten-year-old boy and *another* ten-year-old boy as between the *average* for boys and that for girls.

Individual differences: A similar task confronts physical and biological scientists, of course. In human genetic behavior, the variation is certainly as great as in cultural behavior. As Jerry Hirsch has pointed out, the probability that brothers will be exactly the same genetically is $(\frac{1}{2}^{23})^2$ or less than one chance in a trillion.[9] This is the chance that one sibling will have exactly the same hereditary structure as the other. This virtually infinite variation among human beings, genetically, results from the fact that man has 23 pairs of chromosomes, and thus each gamete may have any of 2^{23} alternative genomes. Thus any gamete contributed by either parent is chosen from 8,388,608 alternatives.

Human groups with their almost infinite genetic variability are socialized in families whose cultural behavior varies through a wide range of child-rearing methods, dogmas, and values. Finally, in addition to the tremendous variability of *both* the *genetic* factors and *cultural* types of behavior, a third force, namely the interaction between the genetic and social behavior, gives rise to an even larger number of emotional and personality variables. Thus, it is not surprising that the social scientist rarely finds any two variables which correlate significantly. Later we shall consider two such variables which do correlate in children's lives. They are socio-economic status and various types of academic behavior. The fact that these two sets of behaviors always correlate significantly at the elementary school level is a result of the structure of our society itself, and of basic significance to all those interested in improving and extending education.

The scientific effort to identify and compare so-called *cultural behaviors* depends chiefly, however, not upon intercorrelation-analysis but upon measures of the *central tendency in behaviors,* or consensus. Comparisons of different cultures, as well as definitions of cultural behaviors depend chiefly upon measures of central tendency, the identification of norms of behavior. Such measurement of central tendency of the behaviors is especially needed in the study of the basic, universal American types of cultural behavior.

Cultural influences upon test skills: Cultural differences within the

---

[9] Jerry Hirsch, "Individual Differences in Behavior and their Genetic Basis," in E. L. Bliss (ed.), *Roots of Behavior* (New York: Harper and Brothers, 1962), pp. 5-6.

school are shown in an intensive study of cultural differences in performance on intellectual tests, initiated by the writer and a group of social scientists at the University of Chicago. Kenneth Eells found that *slum* white children of *old-American* stock performed significantly less well, at both ages nine to ten and thirteen to fourteen, than did the white children from upper and middle classes. The difference between the mean I.Q.'s of the two social status groups ranged from eight to twenty-one points on the I.Q. scale, depending upon which of the nine group tests was considered.[10] The difference in the behavior of the two groups is more clearly revealed, however, when Eells divides the entire range of I.Q.'s found for these pupils into quarters, so that every individual's I.Q. can be described as being in the top quarter, the second quarter, the third quarter, or the bottom quarter. Now the effect of the cultural status factor is more clearly seen—*57 per cent of the white upper-class and upper-middle-class pupils had I.Q.'s in the top quarter.* The full effect of the cultural and developmental difference is made even clearer when Eells considers the bottom quarter of the range. *Between 40 per cent and 50 per cent of the slum children had I.Q.'s in the bottom quarter of the range, depending upon the particular test used, whereas only 5 per cent of the upper-class and upper-middle-class children scored in the bottom quarter.* Such a preponderance of upper-middle-class children in the top quarter, and an equally large preponderance of slum children in the bottom quarter, is as clear a statement of the *cultural* difference in performance on educational aptitude tests as we can get. Moreover, even those who are inclined to ascribe group differences on intelligence test scores to genetics would find no support from geneticists in assigning differences of this size to genetic group differences.

We have just used a highly reliable (though not equally valid) scale, such as intelligence tests, to illustrate the meaning of *cultural norms* and of differences between social groups. But the equally important fact of individual variation within each group, with respect to scores on these tests, is perhaps more revealing than the central tendencies of this behavior for each group. The range of I.Q.'s for upper-class and upper-middle-class children on one test was from an I.Q. of 70 to an I.Q. of more than 150. For slum children, the range was from an I.Q. of 60 to an I.Q. of 139. How can such tremendous

[10] Eells, *et. al., op. cit.,* pp. 156-157; 158.

variation *within cultural* or social-status *groups* be explained? *The fact is that 24 per cent of the white slum children, who have I.Q.'s above 109, are superior to 37 per cent of the white upper-class and upper-middle-class children who have I.Q.'s below 109.*[11] Such variation within each social level, as well as the superiority of many slum children to many children from professional families, will have to be studied in different ways.

So far as the average variation within these two cultural status groups is concerned, all our studies agree that the performance of the lower or slum group is more variable than that of the upper and upper-middle-class children. This difference, of course, is also one of degree. But since it is a *persistent* group difference, it is to be regarded as related chiefly to the environmental factors, including culture and training in school. We found that for the bottom socio-economic group, ages thirteen to fourteen, the standard deviation was significantly higher than for the top socio-economic group of pupils, with respect to both grade placement and I.Q. This finding means that at ages thirteen to fourteen there was a statistically significant tendency for the high-status children to be more highly concentrated around their mean I.Q., than was the case for the lowest socio-economic group,[12] and for the *low* economic group to be *more variable*, as a group, in its behavior on these tests.

Thus we are confronted by two major types of variation in this behavior, namely an intra-group variability which is large for each group, and also an inter-group difference in degree of variability which is significantly greater for the low economic group. The first type of variation is to be regarded as primarily the result of the operation of many factors which influence the behavior of individuals in different degree. That is, the combined effect of such factors as genetic, social, and personality forces is to constantly *differentiate* behavior in solving the test problems. The result in this sample is a *range of I.Q.'s* for the *high socio-economic group* of 70 to over 150. Similarly, the interrelationships of all these highly varied systems of behavior result in an even *greater variability within the low socio-economic group,* as indicated by a greater range of scores than that in the high economic group.

[11] Eells, *et. al., op. cit.,* p. 154.
[12] *Ibid.,* p. 155.

This high degree of variability within groups cannot be explained alone by cultural variation between families, or between neighborhoods, or between the degree of test motivation and test practice experienced by different individuals. In the opinion of the present author, which I stated in my first paper on intelligence, the system which exerts the greatest effect upon problem solving of this kind is that of genetic, or hereditary, *intelligence* factors. I am still of the opinion that genetic factors account for more than half of the individual variance, with cultural and other developmental forces, such as emotional factors, inter-family cultural variation, and degree of test motivation and practice accounting for most of the remaining variance. I should hasten to add that, although I think the weight of evidence points to the genetic factor as the most powerful one in differentiating this behavior, *I do not find any satisfactory evidence that the genetic factors for intelligence are unequally distributed by socio-economic groups.* In any system of random mating involving tens of millions of animals, over hundreds of years, and in which there are no barnyard fences to prevent intermating, there is every reason to believe that the genes for intelligence are distributed randomly throughout every such vast population.

Our research and that of many other psychologists has established, however, that there is a powerful cultural influence upon problem-solving behavior, such as that in educational aptitude tests. This cultural learning and the resultant behavior are of course the essential knowledge, skills, and motivation upon which the genetic factors work in all pupils in all socio-economic groups. The evidence that the cultural factors are different in degree as between different socio-economic groups is expressed not only in the different proportions of such groups which score in the top and bottom quarters of the I.Q. range, but also by the correlation of about .4 between I.Q. and socio-economic status.

In our research, two groups of children from unskilled or semi-skilled families were tested. One was an *old-American* group, the other a second generation *Italian-American* group. On no test was there any significant difference in mean I.Q. between the *old-American-low*, and *ethnic-low* economic groups. This fact, in itself, is a testimony to the power of the schools and other institutions in acculturation. In addition, the standard deviation of scores was higher among the *Ital-*

ian-American pupils than among the *old-American*. Both these facts may be attributed, in part, to the learning and motivation for upward social mobility, which Warner, Srole, and others have found evidenced in the rise of ethnic groups to a higher socio-economic position with each generation in America—a rise from a preponderantly slum group to a preponderantly upper-working-class group, in the first generation or two, and then toward a markedly increasing proportion attaining lower-middle-class position.

It should be added that *there is no decline in the average performance of the low economic group as they grow older*. In an item analysis of four group intelligence tests administered to nine-to-ten-year-olds, and of five tests given to thirteen-to-fourteen-year-olds, Eells found, "When allowance is made for the variation in the proportion of verbal and non-verbal items in the tests given to pupils of different ages, no significant changes in the size of status differences appear with advancing age."[13] It is the much higher proportion of verbal items on the tests for older students which increases the socio-economic differential on tests at the higher ages. But there is no relative decline in average performance by low-economic groups on either verbal or non-verbal items, with increasing age.

Acculturation and academic skills of Negroes: The best evidence we have concerning the marked effects of acculturation upon the academic behavior of Negro students has been provided by studies of educational aptitude and achievement tests. The Selective Service System administered an educational qualifying test to candidates for the draft during World War II. Results of the analysis, by color groups, supported the findings on intelligence tests given by the Army in World War I. The rates of failure were much higher for whites in every southern state for which figures were available than for Negroes in Chicago, New York, or Massachusetts. Whereas only 2.5 per cent of the Negroes tested by Selective Service in Illinois failed this minimum educational requirement test, the following proportions of whites failed it: in Alabama, 8.5 per cent; in Virginia, 8.4 per cent; in Texas, 10.4 per cent; in Arkansas, 9.8 per cent; in Georgia, 8.2 per cent; in Kentucky, 6.1 per cent; in North Carolina, 10.7 per cent, and so on for the sixteen states in which the percentage of

---

[13] K. Eells, *et. al., op. cit.,* p. 66.

CULTURAL FACTORS IN REMEDIATION

whites failing the test was higher than the percentage of Negroes failing it in Illinois, New York, or Massachusetts.[14]

The best studies of the effect of migration to northern cities in raising the performance of Negro children on intelligence tests are those, cited above, by Professor Otto Klineberg on Negro migrant children in New York City, and by Professor Everett S. Lee on Negro migrant children in Philadelphia. Klineberg, using different samples at each age level, found that on the *Stanford-Binet* and the *National Intelligence Test* the scores of migrants increased with increasing length of residence in New York, and tended, after several years, to approximate those of the New York-born. Of particular interest to those attempting to improve the language skills of Negro low economic groups is Klineberg's finding that only tests with a definite linguistic component showed such clear gains with length of stay in New York. With performance tests, "this result is not so clear."[15] In a similar study in New Orleans of twelve-year-old Negro boys who had been born in rural areas, Klineberg found that there was a marked increase in their scores on the *National Intelligence Test,* from the first year of urban residence to the seventh. For instance, those rural boys who had lived in New Orleans only two years had an average score of 43.2, whereas those who had been in New Orleans seven or more years had an average score of 68.7. Whether there was selective migration or not, these studies make it clear that *urbanization* and the new cultural learning that accompany life and schooling in the city have the same order of effect upon the academic behavior of rural-born Negro children as does migration from the South to the North.

Lee's study of Negro migrant children in Philadelphia dealt with the same group of children tested at grades 1A, 2B, 4B, 6B, and 9A, with the *Philadelphia Tests of Verbal and Mental Ability,* the *Chicago Tests of Primary Mental Abilities,* and the *Minnesota Paper Form Board Test.* On the Philadelphia tests, equal scores on tests standardized for different grades represent equal distances, in terms of standard deviations, from the mean scores of the groups upon

---

[14] Selective Service System, *Special Monograph,* No. 10, Vol. I, Test, "Special Groups" (Washington, D.C.: Government Printing Office, 1953), p. 147.

[15] Otto Klineberg, *Race Differences,* (New York: Harper and Brothers, 1935), pp. 185-187; 197.

which the tests were standardized. The same scores at different ages of the same pupil define the same I.Q. status, therefore.

Lee's study provides us with a test of the hypothesis that *acculturation in northern cities results in an increase in I.Q., which is correlated with the length of time the migrant child has been in the northern city.* He found "a statistically significant and continuous upward trend in the intelligence test ratings of southern-born Negro children as their length of residence in Philadelphia increases. This increase manifests itself not only on a general intelligence test, but also on each of the sub-tests of the *Chicago Tests of Primary Mental Abilities,* with the single exception of memory. The increase in general score cannot, therefore, be attributed to an increase in any one specific ability. Nor can the increase be laid to increasing familiarity with the tests or the testing situation, or to a general trend to be found among all students, since there is no such increase in the scores of the Philadelphia-born students. It can further be shown that the migrant children who entered the first grade in Philadelphia are on the first three tests definitely inferior to the Philadelphia-born but by the time they have reached the sixth grade there is no significant difference between their test ratings and those of the Philadelphia-born group, who, like them, had not attended kindergarten."[16]

Lee's study has other highly suggestive implications for the education of children from low socio-economic groups. He found that whereas by the sixth grade there was no significant difference in I.Q. ratings between the migrant group and the Philadelphia-born group which had *not* attended kindergarten, there was a significant superiority in Philadelphia-born pupils who *had* attended kindergarten, over migrants, at all grades through 9A. This finding indicates the likelihood that preschool training leads to a permanent increase in test ratings for a deprived cultural group. Even more striking is the fact that there is a difference of ten I.Q. points between the mean I.Q. of New York-born Negro children, aged ten, tested in 1934 with the *Stanford-Binet* by Klineberg (mean I.Q. 87.3) and the Philadelphia-born Negro children in either the fourth or sixth grade, tested by Lee about fifteen years after Klineberg's sample was tested (mean I.Q. 97.2 and 97.5).

[16] Lee, *op. cit.,* pp. 232-233.

CULTURAL FACTORS IN REMEDIATION

Although it is generally agreed by students of the South-North migration that the more able and ambitious Negroes came in the first waves, *the fact seems to be that the mean I.Q. of Negro children in northern cities has been rising steadily in the past twenty years.* There is evidence that the average I.Q. of Negro children in the first four grades in Chicago is over 95, for Professor Robert Hess found in 1949 that the mean I.Q. of a sample of Negro children, all from *unskilled* and *semiskilled* families, was 91.7 at age seven and a half and 94.8 at age nine and a half on the Kuhlmann-Anderson Tests.[17] Since this group is the lowest occupational group, accounting for about 60 per cent of the Negro population in Chicago, it is likely that the average I.Q. of the total population of Negro children is about 97 at age nine. The I.Q.'s obtained by Klineberg and others, fifteen to twenty years *before,* on representative samples of Negro children in Chicago and New York had a mean of 84 to 87.3, that is, from seven to ten points *beneath* those obtained on the *lowest* economic level of Negro children fifteen years later in Philadelphia and Chicago. *In less than one generation, the total process of acculturation, including the learning of linguistic and academic habits, has raised the average I.Q. of Negro children by about ten I.Q. points.*

Conclusion: This marked improvement, over just twenty years, in basic academic problem solving, involving verbal, arithmetical, and other cognitive skills, constitutes most convincing evidence that our largest culturally disadvantaged group, Negro Americans, is rapidly learning the symbol systems and cognitive behavior valued by the school.

The evidence in Klineberg's and Lee's classic researches is that, given the better teaching, equipment, and longer school year available in cities like New York, Chicago, and Philadelphia, the Negro pupils who come from the South consistently improve in educational aptitude and skills, especially in *language,* which is the central skill in academic achievement. The average I.Q. for the nation as a whole is 100, and that for Negroes in the cities referred to is 97. In another decade there will be no difference.

Wider participation by Negro Americans in the American culture and economy, with the opening of more skilled jobs, more access to libraries, museums, art galleries, and other such educational institu-

[17] R. D. Hess, *op. cit.,* p. 91.

tions (which in the South were not open to Negroes) has been a major force in cultural relearning by Negro children and adolescents. Finally, the stimulus of the more complex industrial urban society and the resultant development of more complex responses and needs, of new cultural aspirations and desires, has been a powerful force in changing their culture.

The effect of such economic and cultural opportunities for their parents and the new hope of fuller opportunities for themselves has been to lead to the rebirth of the American dream. The school should direct and implement this drive for a higher standard of living, and fuller cultural opportunity into a drive for better education and industrious efforts to learn the culture of the teacher.

MODERATOR AND PARTICIPANTS PLOT THE COURSE OF THE COLLOQUY

II
THE COLLOQUY

The Colloquy

Moderator: In the presentation of position papers such as we have before us there are always many relevant ideas which cannot be developed fully within the limitations set. There are instances, undoubtedly, where you might have elaborated specific points. We are going to give each panel member an opportunity to examine his second thoughts, or to indicate any modifications in his position since the original paper was prepared. All panel members have indicated their willingness to have questions raised by other members of the panel at various points during each presentation, so please feel free at any time to direct questions to the person commenting.

Dr. Ferree, may we ask you to comment further on some of the important ideas in your paper or on some of the second thoughts you may have had on points that you have made.

Dr. Ferree: I would treat "knowledge" in the context of this topic as a body of statements. It is accurate to say that we can formulate a great many statements; we do this regularly about how to perform. We say that if we do this, then this will occur. If there is some sort of knowledge which is not capable of being formulated in statements, or can be acquired only by performing, I don't regard such knowledge as a part of the body of knowledge unique to the profession of education. But I do want to include a vast corpus of sentences that talk about *how*. In fact, I thought I made it fairly clear in my paper that there is an important vital relationship between *knowledge that* and *knowledge how*.

I began by raising the question "What does the expression 'body of knowledge' signify?" I arrived at the position that a "body of knowledge" is an ordered set of statements that have been confirmed as true, or at least as highly probable, which treat of the same sorts of questions (in contrast to a mere miscellany of sentences). I suggested the definition of the term "statement" as a sentence which admits of truth or falsity. But there's still the question whether directive sentences of ethics, normative ones that contain the words *should* or *ought,* are statements. "You ought to love your neighbor" or "You ought not to love your neighbor"—are these statements, that is, do they admit of truth or falsity? From Hans Reichenbach's point of view these sentences are directives; they exhibit what some philosophic semanticists call the emotive use of language. They are more of the nature of directives like "Shut the door." "You ought to love your neighbor" means "Love your neighbor." Commands and requests, though very important in practical human affairs, simply do not admit of truth or falsity. If I said, "Let us all go to the theater this afternoon," and someone said, "That's true," you would shake your head, because, though it might be a very delightful suggestion, and I think it is, it is simply not the sort of sentence that admits of truth or falsity. Reichenbach thinks that ethical sentences are much closer to directives and suggests that they are not the kind of sentences which clearly admit of truth or falsity.

There is a basic issue here even if you accept my stipulated definition of "body of knowledge." There is the issue of what sentences constitute statements and beyond that there is the issue of confirmation, that is, a whole set of issues involved in statistical inference. I have a colleague who relies heavily on mystical intuition. Some of the sentences he asserts as true I would hold suspect. There are a number of positions even within a given philosophic camp about the degree of confirmation of a given statement, and these issues have to be taken into account in assessing the adequacy of my stipulated definition.

I defend my stipulation because I think it does bring into sharp relief basic epistemological considerations which, from my point of view, any adequate conception of a body of knowledge invariably must face. We cannot dodge these questions. These are fundamental, linguistic, philosophic questions which we must come to terms with, I think, if we are to have any rigorous conception of a body of knowledge unique to the profession of education. We have all kinds of sentences in educational literature containing the words *should* or *ought,* don't we? Now are these knowledge claims? We have to face this question sooner or later with the philosophers who, incidentally, have not answered the question to the satisfaction of everyone but who are helping to clarify the problems involved in answering the question.

I would contend that even though the view of this essay allows thinkers to disagree about whether certain sentences embody knowledge, it nonetheless enables them to find substantial areas of consensus. Thinkers as divergent in their views about what constitutes knowledge as Roman Catholic Thomists, on the one hand, and tough-minded logical empiricists, on the other, can agree about a considerable number of statements in history, mathematics, and various sciences if they accept my stipulated signification of "body of knowledge." Although they may not concur about all sentences, they can agree on a great many, and they can identify the bases of their agreements and disagreements if they use the notion of "body of knowledge" which I have proposed.

My first question, then, was "What constitutes a body of knowledge?" I stipulated a definition to the effect that a body of knowledge is an ordered set of statements that have been confirmed as true, or at least as highly probable, and which treat of the same sorts of questions. Then I went to the question of whether there is a defensible notion of a body of knowledge *unique* to the profession of education. At first I said, "No," rather bluntly and hastily. Then I backtracked and said, "Oh, yes, there is." If the question "Is there a body of knowledge unique to the profession of education?" is a question whether there is some body of knowledge called educational knowledge which is completely different from all other identifiable bodies of knowledge, all the statements of which are subsumable solely under the rubric of education and under no other rubrics, then I question whether there is any body of knowledge unique to the profession of education, and I am questioning it, I think, from a logical point of view. I can't imagine a body of knowledge about education that is unique and autonomous in the sense that it contains no statements whatever that could be considered as appropriate to psychology or sociology or anthropology or political science or any of the various other bodies of knowledge.

Dr. McMahon: Wouldn't you say, however, that engineering and medicine have a larger fund of knowledge than education?

Dr. Ferree: Yes, I agree with you.

Dr. McMahon: Then, if you would expurgate medicine's collection of statements, a medical man might say, "Let us treat arthritis with cortisone." Would you consider this the same type of statement as "Let us train our young people to be good citizens" or "We should produce good citizens in our schools"? In other words, I am referring to the section of your paper in which you mentioned hortatory injunctions, and I am asking whether you would classify "Let us treat arthritis with cortisone" as a hortatory injunction.

Dr. Ferree: There is no hortatory injunction at all in that statement. It is a probability statement. I would phrase the sentence a little differently. I would say, if it is knowledge, the statement would go like this: If one injects cortisone into a person who has a certain sort of malady, it is highly probable that he will respond in these ways.

Dr. McMahon: Then could we say, "If we teach certain skills to our students—"

Dr. Ferree: If we submit students to certain sorts of experiences, it is highly probable that these sorts of results will occur. When I taught English, I submitted students to certain sorts of experiences which I hoped would make it probable that some of them would write better paragraphs than they did before they came to me. One can deal with questions of method in terms of hypothetical statements; for example, if we do this with students in this setting, then it is probable that these sorts of results will occur. I don't think one needs to try to derive hortatory normative propositions at all. If psychology is broadly defined as concerned with human behavior, all the propositions of educational discourse will by definition then be of concern to the psychologist.

Dr. Albee: I think what you say is true, but can you find any profession which has knowledge unique unto itself?

Dr. Ferree: No, and I am not contending that. I would say that medicine draws from bacteriology, pharmacology, and various other biological sciences; engineering draws from physics; education draws from psychology, sociology, anthropology, and other fields. I am not contending that certain other professions have a unique body of knowledge but education does not. I would contend that just as medicine draws from various disciplines, so does education.

Dr. Cottrell: You do not reject the reality of a knowledge of education simply because some of its knowledge is also claimed as relevant to other fields?

Dr. Ferree: Not at all. In fact, a substantial part of my paper is a defense of the concept of a "body of knowledge unique to the profession of education." I am simply saying that if you have some very rigorous conception of a body of knowledge unique to the profession of education, it would have a set of sentences that are all clean and self-contained; and these would then not be the province of any other people. Of course, there isn't any such animal. But if you have a more liberal conception of a body of knowledge unique to the profession of education which draws from a variety of sources in a certain way—if the statements which are drawn from the various sources are uniquely selected and formulated so that their pertinence to educational context is made explicit, then and only then, from my point of view, do you have a body of knowledge unique to the profession of education.

Dr. Cottrell: Not necessarily. You may have a body of knowledge significant to the profession of education, but is it unique? A statement can be significant to two fields at once.

Dr. Ferree: From my point of view, such a body of knowledge is drawn from a variety of sources, but the statements are uniquely formulated and ordered so as to make clear their relevance to the work of educational practitioners. In that sense the body of knowledge is unique. Such statements are not just pulled from hither and yon but selected and organized in such a way that their relevance to the practical concerns of teachers and administrators is made clear.

Dr. Kimball: I think this is a crucial point. This is really the crux of the answer to the question that was formulated. *There is no unique knowledge.*

Dr. Cottrell: We all agree on that, I think.

Dr. Kimball: I think we do, but I think it is necessary to underline this so that it is clear that this is the answer to the question.

Dr. Ferree: We've been discussing *unique* knowledge. Granted it applies knowledge from some other disciplines to practical concerns, but there is nothing wrong with knowledge about applications to practical educational contexts. Bringing together knowledge from parent disciplines and showing the application to educational context is nonetheless knowledge. If a teacher does this, then what will probably occur is a knowledge claim. It is concerned with answering an educational question and in that sense it is unique to education. It has a kind of uniqueness that is identifiable from my point of view.

Dr. Kimball: Do you make any distinction between theory and knowledge?

Dr. Ferree: Sometimes. I use the term "theory" in a number of ways, depending on the context. In rigorous scientific discussions I use the term "theory" to signify a set of fairly well confirmed hypothetical statements, or a set of laws or law-like statements that have a high degree of confirmation. In that context I use the term "theory" almost as a synonym for "body of knowledge." There are other uses, though, that include sentences of an ethical or a normative sort. I want to make it clear that I use the word "theory" in a number of ways depending on the context. I haven't used the term "theory" here at all.

Dr. Kimball: There certainly is a body of knowledge associated with the practice of farming. In the study of plant processes, for example, there developed a theory related to the practice of farming. Would you include both the theory about the practice of farming and the practice of farming as constituting the body of knowledge?

Dr. Ferree: When you say there's a theory of farming, you aren't talking just about soils or decomposition of matter; you're talking about farming, making statements about farming. Is that right?

Dr. Kimball: That's right. I would include such statements as "If you apply certain kinds of organic or inorganic materials to the soil, certain things will happen." This is a statement, but beyond the statement there are theoretical propositions about which the farmer need not know in order to be a successful farmer. Let me pursue this question a little further. In 1916, Abraham Flexner addressed the national conference on social welfare and shocked the social workers of the day by saying that social work was not a profession because it did not have a theory; that it was borrowing knowledge from a variety of fields and then applying this knowledge in its daily work, but until it had its own theory in the field of social work, it could not be a profession. This statement caused social work to spend the next thirty years trying to find itself a theory so that it could be a profession. I think this question touches on this same point. It may be that the field of education applies knowledge uniquely to the situation, but medi-

THE COLLOQUY

cine has a germ theory of disease which is a fairly well-confirmed theory.

Dr. Ferree: Is that just medicine's theory or is that bacteriology?

Dr. Kimball: That's an interesting point. It is bacteriology.

Dr. Ferree: Is this what you mean when you raise the question about theory?

Dr. Kimball: Yes. You are talking about education having a body of knowledge, but then you raise the question "Does there necessarily have to be a theory?"

Dr. Ferree: You made the claim that the farmer doesn't have to have a command of such theoretical knowledge in order to be a successful farmer. I'm not sure of that. In any case, I'd claim that the farmer who does have the command of the theoretical knowledge is going to be a more successful farmer than the one who does not.

Dr. McMahon: Not necessarily. The man who has the theory would not necessarily go out and dig a ditch and put certain kinds of organic substances in it.

Dr. Ferree: We're talking about the theorist farmer.

Dr. McMahon: Oh, we are! Are there such things? This question, I think, is very pertinent to education, because a teacher need not necessarily be a professional person in the sense of having a theory or applying theoretical knowledge.

Dr. Ferree: We're making a clarification between theory and practice which I wonder—

Dr. Kimball: All professions, inevitably—there is a sociological law here—spend endless time teaching theory to neophytes before they allow them to practice. It may not be a theory unique to that field, but all professions that want to be dignified by that term first subject their neophytes to a considerable amount of verbal learning of theoretical content before they allow them to practice.

Dr. Ferree: I wonder if you are using "theory" here in the sense of a body of highly confirmed knowledge claims that are pertinent to the practice of the profession.

Dr. Kimball: Statements that are interrelated—that can be used to deduce other principles—

Dr. Ferree: —can be used to guide practice?

Dr. Kimball: Yes, and can also be used to stimulate research in areas not yet clear.

Dr. Cottrell: I thought a theory was a tool for determining truth or investigating the possible truthfulness of an assertion.

Dr. Ferree: That's one way to define "theory."

Dr. Kimball: Yes, but behind this lie certain kinds of operations by which one creates theory. These involve criteria, processes of logic, and so forth.

Dr. Cottrell: That's right.

Dr. Ferree: It seems to me that your question was essentially whether teachers really need a command of the theory in order to be highly successful in the classroom.

Dr. Kimball: I'm not quite asking that question. In any kind of enterprise these days, there are people who operate at different levels. There are the abstract mathematicians; there are the physicists; and so on down the line. It isn't necessary that all levels know abstract mathematics or that the abstract mathematician know mechanics.

Dr. Ferree: Oh, I'm beginning to follow you.

Dr. Kimball: If you have an operating discipline, it would seem to me that one of the characteristics of such a discipline would be persons working at different levels contributing to the whole; one of these levels would be that of a theoretical concern. So my question is "When you're using the term 'body of knowledge' in education, how extensive is the theoretical knowledge?"

Dr. Ferree: I would want to claim that some nexus has to be made between theoretical knowledge and practical educational concerns. But this doesn't mean that the theorist, in this sense of theory, shouldn't at times back way off from the practical realm and theorize. But eventually, if his theory is to be part of the body of knowledge unique to the profession of education, there must be some sort of nexus, some class of sentences which links up his theory with doings in education. I guess I'm simply saying that, if there is no such nexus at some point, then, I'm not willing to consider theoretical knowledge as a part of the body of knowledge unique to the profession of education. But I'm not denying the right of the theorist to engage in his work at some distance from the practical concerns of educators. The point at which his theory becomes a part of the body of knowledge unique to the profession or education is the point at which some nexus is established between his work and educational doings. I intuit that in psychology, anthropology, and sociology there is a great deal of knowledge at the theoretical level and other levels which could be pertinent to the work of educational practitioners, but there is no nexus. Now I'm all for the theoretical deliberations of psychologists, sociologists, and anthropologists, but their work doesn't become a part of the body of knowledge unique to the profession of education until it is so formulated and ordered. This doesn't mean that every other sentence has to discuss education, but that at certain points its pertinence to education has to be made somewhat explicit.

Dr. Cottrell: This reminds me of Dr. Kimball's point that a theory is a systematic phenomenon. A hypothesis need not be; it may be very particularized.

Dr. Ferree: Yes, a theory is an interconnected set of hypotheses.

Dr. Cottrell: And, when you develop a system of hypotheses that have both integrity as a system and demonstrable relevance to the concerns of the practitioner, you begin to get a theory of education. If I understand you, that's what you are saying.

Dr. Ferree: Yes. In fact, my third question is "Do we *now* have a body of knowledge unique to the profession of education?" This is an empirical question. We have to go look and see, and I didn't conduct a scientific investigation. I based my observations on my own experience. I suggest that right now, in terms of my definition, our body of knowledge is relatively modest in scope and character.

Dr. McMahon: But it's relatively modest, perhaps, because not enough of us know about the fund of knowledge or relevant statements to bring them into the realm of education.

Dr. Ferree: Yes, I hastened to point that out in this section. I specified why, in my judgment, the body of knowledge unique to the profession of education is limited, if it is limited.

Dr. Cottrell: In your paper you say bluntly that our professional knowledge is meagre. Now you say your experience, from what you know and how you interpret this experience—would you not consider as knowledge the interpretation you just made of your own experience? Is this a statement of fact? Is this a knowledge statement or is this something that you still want to reject as knowledge?

Dr. Ferree: If I were doing a scientific treatise on the matter, I wouldn't want to call this a confirmed statement at this point. I'd want to investigate much more. I'd want to get a research team to go out and examine the statements that we have before I would make this claim. If I have been too blunt in saying our knowledge in education is meagre, forgive me. This intuitive statement or hunch is a potential hypothesis to be confirmed. And, by the way, that is the place of hunches in scientific investigation; hunches provide us with hypotheses to be tested. Once a hypothesis is tested, you can affirm or deny it is knowledge.

Dr. Cottrell: I don't see why you should apologize. I think your intuitive statement is your knowledge as of the present state of your intellectual analysis. That raises the question as to whether the knowledge of the profession of education has to be unanimously accepted as confirmed truth or whether knowledge can be substantiated to various degrees.

Dr. Ferree: Scientists prize very highly the canon of intersubjective testability. Any knowledge claim that really is worth its salt must be of the sort that any human being, given the knowledge and the technical devices, can confirm or disconfirm himself. "Fresh water boils at 212° F. under standard atmospheric conditions" is the classic example. Presumably any person, even my ten-year-old son, if he had the right devices for establishing standard conditions in testing, could confirm or disconfirm this knowledge claim. I think my claim that the body of knowledge unique to the profession of education is currently meagre is, in principle, capable of such intersubjective tests, though such tests would be very, very difficult to perform.

Dr. Cottrell: Suppose I should come along and say that in my experience and from my level of understanding, the body of knowledge in education is very extensive.

Dr. Ferree: We would have two contrary hypotheses which could be put to the empirical test. It would take considerable work to do it; but I have defined "body of knowledge" in such a way that presumably we could identify statements that are highly confirmed and that are shown to be pertinent to education. We could go look and see. I think that if a group of rigorous researchers investigated the question, they could come up with an answer, in principle. In practice, I don't know. Some questions are answerable in principle, but in practice, because of the technical problems involved, they are virtually unanswerable. In principle, we could count the grains of sand in the ocean and on the beach, but practically speaking we cannot. A great number of persons who have conducted research to formulate knowledge of the kind that is includable in the body of knowledge unique to the profession of education have lacked the necessary sophistication in parent bodies of knowledge pertinent to the inquiry. This is a way of saying that many who have called themselves educational psychologists, educational sociologists, or educational philosophers really haven't known very much about psychology or sociology or philosophy. They have at times, I think, had keen insight into the problems of education and some of its practical demands; but, lacking insight into parent disciplines pertinent to the definition and clarification of some of their problematic situations, they haven't been able to get very far with their research.

Dr. Kimball: Did you also ask yourself the question why this was so?

Dr. Ferree: Yes, but I find it very difficult to give a simple answer. I think it is a complicated question. Why is it more respectable, at least from some vantage points, to be a psychologist than an educational psychologist, or to be a philosopher in academic philosophy rather than in educational philosophy? I think this question is pertinent to the one you are raising. This is an interesting sociological phenomenon, and I think that you may be equipped to answer it a little better, Dr. Kimball.

Dr. Kimball: Actually, the sense of my question was not sociological. It was "What is there in the nature of the preparation of people who do research in education that leaves them with these deficiencies to which you seem to refer?"

Dr. Cottrell: Well, one thing is that they don't have twenty-five to fifty years to spend in preparing.

Dr. Ferree: It is my conviction that the person who is going to be adequate as a philosopher of education has to have doctoral-level sophistication in both philosophy and education, and who of us is willing to devote his energies to attaining these levels of sophistication? It takes so much time.

Dr. Cottrell: By analogy, it is interesting to observe that the scientists are beginning to be aware of exactly this same reality and contend that a man, in order to be a physicist, must have a lifetime of work in mathematics, in biological sciences, and in cosmology, and all sorts of things.

Dr. Kimball: That's four lives right there.

Dr. Ferree: I don't point the finger merely at researchers in the field of education. I suggest that far too often scholars in the behavioral sciences and certain other provinces of knowledge have neglected, if not eschewed, questions about education even when such questions have been quite appropriate to their spheres of inquiry. I cite history as an example. Until the last decade or so, professional historians have given very little attention to the history of education.

Dr. McMahon: Not even the last decade, except rarely.

Dr. Ferree: And these historians sometimes are the very ones who maintain that the institutions of society are functionally interrelated.

Dr. Kimball: Could the same statement not be made concerning the neglect of the history of physics, medicine, nursing, or engineering? This is not a unique situation so far as education is concerned.

Dr. McMahon: And now the problem begins to resolve itself by such subjects becoming disciplines in themselves. You find a history of science department, for example. The man who directs that program cuts himself off, to some extent, from science and, to some extent, from history.

Dr. Ferree: Your observation is an interesting one. On the other hand, one might maintain that, although your observation is accurate, the relative influence of educational institutions in human life is far greater than some of these other fields to which you have alluded. Hence, the neglect of the history of education is far more reprehensible than the neglect of the history of basket weaving.

Dr. McMahon: Except that the historians are now saying that the trouble with educational historians is that they have looked only at the institutional aspect.

Dr. Ferree: This is how they impugn the educational historian.

Dr. McMahon: I think there are various levels of people engaged in this whole field of education. For example, a school principal who is faced with a problem child cannot stop to think, "What body of knowledge can I draw upon to justify my behavior with this child?"

Dr. Ferree: Don't you think he is so steeped in theoretical orientation and in a background of the body of knowledge in education that he responds in second-nature fashion in a manner that is consonant with theory?

Dr. McMahon: Very often it is the action which generates the theory.

Dr. Ferree: Oh, I believe this. I also believe that one canon of a good theory is the way it gives guidance to practice.

Dr. Cottrell: That's the nexus you were talking about.

Dr. Ferree: Yes. And another point that I make is that scholars in various parent disciplines may be sympathetic to education in a general way, but insensitive to the many complex questions and problems faced by its practitioners. Hence, they have trouble in relating their knowledge to education in any useful way. For example, I'd like to see a mathematical logician sit in a history classroom for a week, examining the logic of explanation in history and bringing his knowledge to bear on the concrete reality of teaching history to eleventh graders. In a way, this is what B. Othanel Smith is attempting to do in some of his research. He has gone into classrooms and observed the language with which teachers teach; he has classified the uses of language in various ways, for example, historical explanation, scientific explanation, and explanation in literature. Here would be prime subject matter for a general methods course, since teachers generally engage in the business of definition, explanation, and clarification in identifying and dealing with ambiguity and vagueness. Why not develop a course which brings to prospective teachers the best available knowledge on the logic of explanation, the logic of definition, the types of definitions appropriate for one context or another, the identification of ambiguities, and so forth? How much more useful this might be to a practitioner than some of the vague generalities that are often included!

Dr. Cottrell: Our colleagues in the humanities may say, "You are omitting a whole dimension of thought and of concern when you reject the symbolism of literature as truth. You are so ready as positivists, scientifically preoccupied people, to say that you know only that which can be explicitly defined and substantiated by some rigorous method of confirmation; yet the life of Faust somehow or other escapes you. If we give these boys and girls an opportunity to experience with Faust the great mystery of life, in his terms, the truth that finally comes through is a truth you never could have presented to them in empirically confirmed statements, much less hope that they would understand." As a logician and a former English teacher, what would your answer be, Dr. Ferree?

Dr. Ferree: Is it a truth that you can distill and formulate in a sentence?

Dr. Cottrell: If you do that, you are going to miss it entirely. Students have to live this thing.

Dr. Ferree: That's the whole point of the literary mode of discourse as opposed to the scientific mode.

Dr. Cottrell: My question is "What do you do to honor symbolism as a vehicle for the expression of knowledge?"

Dr. Ferree: I think many interpreters of the analytic movement in philosophy falsely assume that because analytic philosophers have a tough-minded conception of science and knowledge, they have no sensitivities and no concern for things aesthetic, and this is erroneous. What many analytic philosophers do deny is that literary discourse is a vehicle for the communication of truth. It is interesting to see a piece of poetry analyzed by a linguist. I. A. Richards is a good example of a literary analyst and critic who made this emotive referential distinction. Science dwells largely upon the referential use of language; and literature, upon the emotive. Emotion is a large part of human life and is important, but it is very dangerous to confuse the emotive use of language with its referential use. It doesn't bother some of us linguistic analysts that literature is not regarded as a vehicle for making knowledge claims. Nonetheless, it is very important in human affairs; it should have a very large place in education. You have caught me at a weak point, because even though I am saying these things, I admit that somewhere down within me I have a sneaking suspicion that there is a defensible way of talking about literary works of art as vehicles for the communication of truth. But this is heresy!

Moderator: Dr. Ferree, in your general methods course, would you include the bases for decision-making?

Dr. Ferree: I might. I don't know much about the research in decision-making, but if we know anything that is pertinent to our practical tasks of decision-making, then I say let's bring the knowledge to bear.

Dr. McMahon: How would you treat art and music in the schools?

Dr. Ferree: I'm all in favor of them whether or not their statements can be shown to be justified. I'm simply saying that it may be questionable as to whether the justification of a normative sentence and the logic of the justification is the same thing as the verification of a scientific statement. They may be two different activities. I think art and music and literature ought to be included in the experience of children and young people in school.

Dr. Kimball: Doesn't an understanding of the aesthetics of human behavior operate by rules quite different from those which are so-called "scientific"? Applying the methods of logic which operate in scientific inquiry to problems of aesthetic appreciation seems to me to be taking methods which work in one area and trying to apply them to another area.

Dr. Ferree: Well, I'm sure you'd agree that a psychologist can study the phenomenon of aesthetic satisfaction. But one should not confuse the psychologist's method of looking at aesthetic experience or the anthropologist's with what goes on in human beings.

Dr. Cottrell: There are those who will say that aesthetic experience escapes the psychologist because of his scientific predilection. I have an art school and a music school in my college, and these people in the arts are constantly saying this.

Dr. Ferree: There is a perspective that one does get from another medium. Literature is in the mode of direct experience. Reading good literature is like looking into and feeling into a slice of life; and that is different from the abstract general propositions of science, though each has its points. But the logic of discriminating at this point, Dr.

Cottrell, is difficult for me. It's an area of inquiry for me, and one of these days I am going to write something on that.

At one point in my paper I question the parent disciplines from which education is presumably derivative. I ask just how much psychology, sociology, and anthropology have to deliver at this point. I am on ground that I don't know very well; but I cite Ernest Nagel, philosopher, scientist, and logician, who claims that the social sciences of today possess no wide-ranging systems of explanations judged as adequate by the majority of professionally competent students. The social sciences are characterized by serious disagreement on methodological as well as substantive questions. It would seem to me that, when a comparison is made with the basic laws and theories that are available in the physical sciences, the social sciences have a long way to go. We just don't have, in the social sciences, basic theories comparable in their level of explanatory power to some of the theories in the physical sciences. And if this is the case, then it follows that, insofar as education draws upon such theories, education is correspondingly limited. It hardly seems reasonable to expect more of education than of the parent disciplines from which it derives. The amount and type of knowledge available for application by educators may be limited by whatever limitations exist within the young sciences of psychology, sociology, anthropology, and the like.

Granted that the resources from which we draw may have their limitations, has the present body of knowledge unique to the profession of education made use of all the resources available to it? Or, and here is another empirical question, is there existent knowledge which is relevant to educational concerns but which has not been appropriated and formulated so as to make its pertinence to education explicit? I think there is evidence that there is knowledge out there that could be made relevant to educational concerns which, in fact, has not been appropriated. B. O. Smith has concluded that the knowledge in logic, psychology, philosophy, and science have implications for the teaching of concepts that are far more extensive than the suggestions found in textbooks on educational psychology and teaching methods. Perhaps he would agree with me that there is knowledge about the logic of explanation which has not been drawn together, formulated, and ordered in such a way that its pertinence to education is clear. In other words, we are not using what is available.

Dr. Albee, in his paper, points out that certain sorts of knowledge which are pertinent to practical work in education have not been drawn together and presented in a way that get them to the practitioners.

Dr. Kimball: Do you have any practical suggestions for how to accomplish this?

Dr. Ferree: I think that a practical consideration is "What plan of organization is appropriate to the body of knowledge unique to the profession of education?" That is, if we could gather all these statements from the supporting disciplines, how should they be ordered? How should they be put together?

Dr. McMahon: The prime question is not how are we going to put them together, but how are we going to get these statements and then put them together?

Dr. Ferree: Suppose we get a taxonomy of teacher behaviors which affords us a classification scheme under which we can subsume relevant knowledge and which will guide our search for new knowledge. Such a taxonomy may very well be useful as a convenient way of classifying knowledge pertinent to one kind of teaching behavior or another, but, beyond that, the very existence of the taxonomy may give us a new perception of questions to raise—questions that we may have in mind vaguely when we are investigating various kinds of related discourse but ones which we haven't formulated specifically. In that sense, it might help a little in the task of identifying relevant knowledge.

I raise the question of whether the body of knowledge unique to the profession of education, or portions of it, should be logically organized in the same manner for preservice instruction as for graduate-level researchers in education. B. O. Smith suggests that the knowledge about education ought to be organized around what he calls protocol material, or descriptions of teacher activities. At the graduate level, however, it is much more appropriate for knowledge about education to be ordered around parent disciplines and their logics, so that you have educational psychology, educational sociology, and the philosophy of education organized on the basis of the logic of the parent discipline.

Dr. Cottrell: That's the difference between H. S. Broudy and B. O.

Smith, the two men working on the same project. Broudy uses this latter approach.

Dr. Ferree: Yes, I think we have much to learn; considerable work to do. I suggest that we need to experiment with some of these alternative modes of organization in the preparation of teachers and see what happens.

Dr. Ferree: Let me conclude in a positive way. I'm going to read my final paragraph.

> The future of the body of knowledge unique to the profession of education is contingent upon the extent to which the challenges posed in this essay are met. Happily there have been some heartening signs of late—not the least of which is the present colloquy—that these challenges are not being ignored. A number of thinkers within the field of education recognize their need for and are seeking to secure depth in the behavioral sciences and other bodies of knowledge pertinent to their educational work. Moreover, many scholars outside of the field of education are showing an increased interest in education and a willingness to engage in conjoint teaching and research enterprises with thinkers in education. Currently, too, there are some serious projects under way to bring new knowledge to bear upon educational questions and to experiment with new ways of organizing knowledge about education. All of these things signalize the possibility of a new era in education. We may well be hopeful that the next several decades will see the emergence of a much more precise, complete, and useful body of knowledge unique to the profession of education.

Moderator: Dr. Albee, may I ask you to highlight certain aspects of your paper or make any additional comments that you would like to present.

Dr. Albee: Perhaps my discussion of "What is a profession?" complements Dr. Ferree's examination of "What is knowledge?" In my paper, I have considered those areas of knowledge which are shared by psychology and education, particularly those areas of psychology that are directly relevant to the business of educating teachers.

In my paper, before touching on these concepts, which are quite familiar to all of you, I dealt first with the general question "What is a profession?"

In my own view, the development of psychology has been seriously distorted by its movement in the direction of psychopathology. If psychology is the study of human behavior, and I think this is the definition that most psychologists accept, then it certainly ought to be

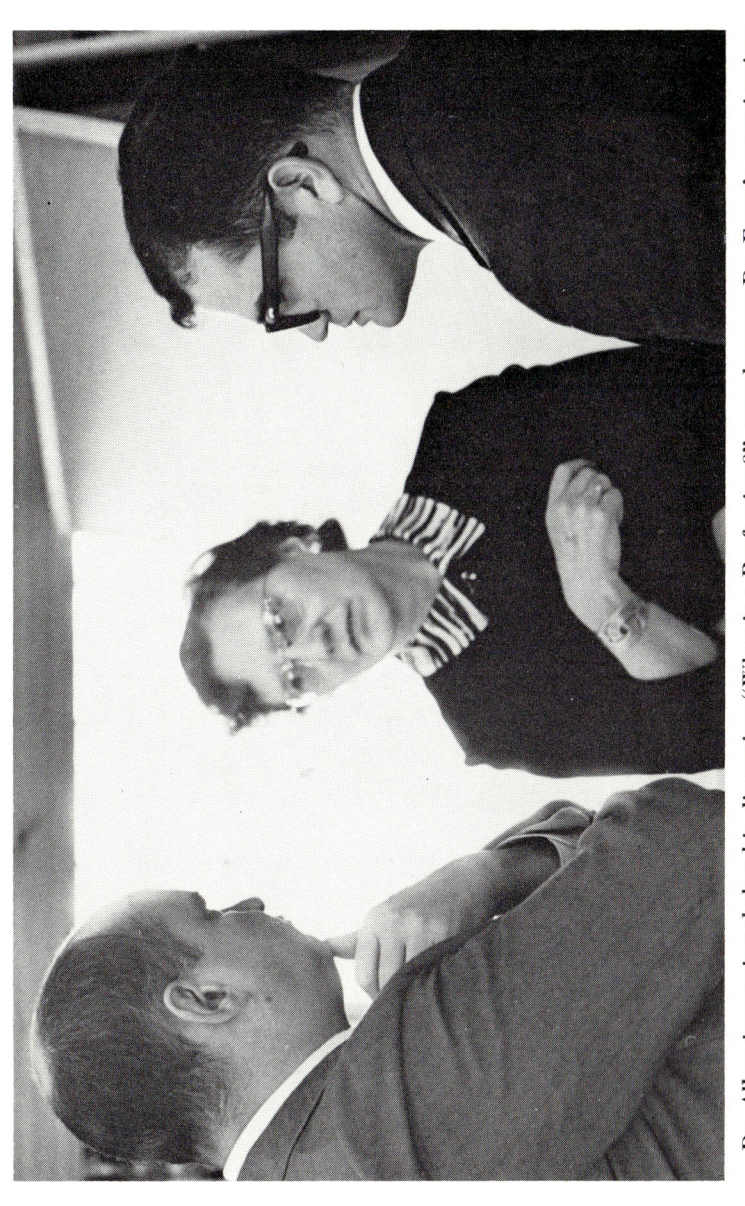

Dr. Albee is convinced that his discussion "What is a Profession?" complements Dr. Feree's examination of "What is Knowledge?" The Moderator listens carefully.

the study of all human behavior and, primarily, of normal human behavior. But at least 50 per cent of graduate students in psychology are now engaged in preparing for a professional role which involves the treatment of persons who suffer from some form of adult psychopathology. It is my conviction that this is the wrong direction for psychology to take, and there are beginning signs that a number of people now feel this way. Perhaps, if enough people feel this way, psychology will be able to return to its more proper concern with normal human behavior and, particularly, with the normal development of children. I think it is a blind alley for us to train thousands of individual psychotherapists to do psychotherapy for high fees with upper-middle-class neurotics in high-income suburbs. This is just not, in my view, a proper activity for psychologists. They have the right to do this, legally, and I would defend their constitutional right to do psychotherapy, but this is not primarily what psychologists should be doing and this is not how our energies should be channeled.

Moderator: Dr. Albee, may I inject a question at this point? Some of the people who are pursuing psychopathology say that there is much that we can learn about the normal from the abnormal. Are you discounting this?

Dr. Albee: No, indeed. I think this is true. But I don't think we need to learn the same thing over and over again. Very honestly, I think a great many of our insights into personality development have come from the experiences of psychotherapists, and I think psychotherapy should continue to be practiced by psychologists as an investigative method, as a research technique. Sigmund Freud himself said he would rather spend 300 hours with a single person than one hour with each of 300 people. He felt he learned more about human nature, and I think this is true. But I don't think that all psychologists need to engage in psychotherapy. The fact of the matter is that most psychotherapists in the field of psychology are not feeding information back into the field. They are sitting in their lonely private offices in suburbia seeing one client after another and making a very good income in the process, but they are not feeding information back into the mainstream of psychology. If we are really going to enrich our knowledge of human development, we ought to do psychotherapy with some people other than the groups who can afford to pay for it. Nicholas Hobbs of Peabody College pointed out, in prepared testimony before Congress last year, that if he had responsibility for spending the funds available in the area of mental health, he would earmark at least 50 per cent of all research, training, and education funds for work with children, or for preparing people in the mental health professions to work with children. All of the energy and all of the effort that we spend in attempting to do something about middle-aged neurotics really does not solve any of the major social problems confronting us. If we were to spend an equal amount of our resources in working with children—trying to understand the things that go wrong in child development, studying the development of emotional disorders in children, and preparing people to teach emotionally disturbed children—we would be farther ahead in solving society's problems than if we trained more people to be adult psychotherapists.

Now let me turn briefly to a consideration of the characteristics of professions in general. Only in the last half century have we really begun to examine the characteristics of professions; and only in the last fifteen or twenty years have we begun a serious sociological approach to the study of professions. Professions evolve if they satisfy clear-cut and definite social needs and if they have a specific number of identifiable characteristics.

Certainly the first criterion of a profession is knowledge, and perhaps theoretical knowledge. Abraham Flexner, in his consideration of the medical profession, and subsequently of other groups, stressed the importance of the intellectual nature of professional activities, their dependence on science and learning, and the necessity for their having theoretical content. If we look at what is happening in a number of professions that have grown up outside the "halls of the academe," we see how right Flexner was in predicting the essential nature of professions. He pointed out that whenever a group aspires to be a profession, it moves its training into the college or university.

Nursing, as you probably know, is now engaged in a valiant struggle to close, or to de-emphasize, the hospital schools of nursing. The leaders in the profession of nursing can become very eloquent and very emotional about how they feel about the hospital-diploma schools. They would like to see all nurses' training carried out in colleges and universities. In fact, all around the country there is a move to put nursing education into the community college, or into regular colleges, sending students to hospitals for field work but controlling the actual course content and training in the academic institution. Less than three years ago, the last proprietary school of occupational therapy was closed. Now all schools of occupational therapy are safely housed in universities. I think that, without being deliberately conscious of the reason for this move, they are following certain sociological laws, first stated clearly by Flexner.

Flexner also observed that professional training programs tend to get longer and longer. Even at a time when there are desperate shortages in the various professions, we see the length of training inevitably extended for longer and longer periods of time. It's certainly true in psychology, where it used to be that a master's degree was sufficient but where the Ph. D. has now become a requirement.

Another characteristic of professions is the relative privacy or uniqueness of the knowledge and skills of a professional group. The public really has to rely on the competence of the profession. One goes to a dentist or a physician and places complete faith, really, in his hands. Here, I think, the profession of education is different from most other professions because every parent has at some time been a pupil, and everyone has had direct contact with the educational system. While we like to think that much of our knowledge in education is private and unique, we have all kinds of people putting pressure on us. There aren't many people giving advice to the physician on how to treat illness, nor are many of us inclined to tell our dentists what they should be doing when they treat our children's cavitites; but certainly we are all looking over the shoulders of educators and teachers, telling them what they should or should not be doing. In this respect the profession of education is at a disadvantage when compared with the other professions.

Moderator: May I raise another question? To what extent do we bring this pressure on ourselves? I'm thinking in terms of some of the recent "systems" of teaching reading. I wonder if some of these have not arisen because some people ask for patterns. In other words, they want the security, perhaps, of steps one, two, and three; yet the people who are really proficient in education may not think such specificity is possible. However, when someone who knows less about the problems that are involved comes along and sets up a pattern, all too frequently there are some who are willing to buy it.

Dr. Albee: Dr. Cottrell, how do you feel about this?

Dr. Cottrell: I think we feel insecure in coping with these difficult problems, and teaching reading is one of these. Many teachers are very self-effacing, and inclined to be unduly self-critical, more so, I think, than people in many other professions. This uncertainty opens the way for commercial publishing houses to set up series of books and sell them widely; and people buy them because they don't know —the new books may not be any worse than what they already have and they may be a little better. I think this idea of preparing packaged materials is spreading. I view this development with a considerable amount of anxiety, as I do some of the new materials in the sciences and various other branches. I think it is high time that we let the authorities—scholars who know the field—put before their peers and put before us as practitioners the best that they know, based on research. But let us also see that we bring to the evaluation of each proposal the best that we know, and not accept it just because the authorities recommend it.

Dr. Albee: I would like to emphasize one other characteristic of professions. Because, as professional people, we have power over the public welfare, we always have to seek public sanction to do what we do. This takes the form of certification or licensing of professional workers and accreditation of training centers. This requires us to set up ethical codes so that we can discipline those members of our group who have exceeded the bounds of their authority or their public protective responsibility. We develop our own private cultural language, a professional jargon, which enables us, at least in part, to keep our meaning from being perfectly clear to the nonprofessional.

Now let me turn to my statement of the fundamental concepts that education and psychology share, which might properly be considered part of the body of knowledge in which all educators and all teachers should be thoroughly grounded. One is the pervasive value system that we might label "scientific." It has been in only the last 300 years that we have regarded nature as orderly. Someone pointed out that if we compare the time that man has been on earth to a twenty-four hour day, then the age of science is only about the last 1/100 of a second in that twenty-four hour day. The fantastic development that has taken place in science has really occurred in the last eyeblink of time. We sometimes get a little impatient with the slowness with which concepts percolate through from one field to another, but actually we've made fantastic progress in the last 300 years. This point of view, that we live in a world or in a universe that is orderly and is lawful rather than capricious, is a fairly recent notion. We have the logic, we have the philosophical armamentarium which is required for us to make tremendous strides in the acquisition of knowledge that fulfills the criterion of the logician and the philosopher. This is one of the most basic, and often overlooked, concepts in the field of education and, indeed, in all fields which regard the world as being lawful.

Dr. Kimball: I agree with what you have said thus far, except for the fact that theology also provided an orderly view of the universe and of its origins and its processes. I get the sense here that you are making your contrast between order and a former period of capriciousness. I would argue that former periods were not capricious at all.

Dr. Albee: I think we have to refer this disagreement to Dr. Ferree, who, I think, has made a distinction between testable statements and untestable concepts. While we may accept or reject theological descriptions of the order of the universe, many of these defy scientific proof, whereas most of the concepts and most of the statements that can be made in a scientific context are testable.

Dr. Kimball: I have no quarrel with this whatever, but my only point was that most peoples of the universe, since a long, long time ago, have lived under a system of thought in which they saw the world as quite orderly. The sun rose and set. The only point at hand is the extent to which you put your emphasis, that is, between an orderly view and a capricious one previously.

Dr. Albee: On the last page of my paper, and very briefly, I tried to bring in the difference that the state of development of the culture makes in terms of the kinds of concepts that education uses. I refer particularly to the organization of society in a conceptual model by David Reisman, where the tradition-directed culture demands a certain kind of educational model simply because there is so little leisure time and so little demand for education. Superstition, ritual, or a primitive form of religion gives explanation of phenomena in the tradition-directed culture but it can't stand the critical scientific test to which we subject our concepts and theories today. I'm not sure I'm responding satisfactorily to your question.

Dr. Kimball: It wasn't necessary to give an elaborate response. It was just an impression I got that you were contrasting the age of science with a previous capriciousness.

Dr. Albee: Let me say, further, that it is possible with our present conceptual tools to make fairly accurate predictions about the future. This is one of the urgent human needs, to predict the future using a scientific model. I use the example of statistics here and of the mathematical orderliness of most natural phenomena. It is possible to take samples from the present and to extrapolate to the future. I suspect that this was less possible under strictly theological models. I don't know whether you agree with that or not.

Dr. Kimball: It wasn't empirically possible, but you didn't need empiricists. All you needed was divine revelation.

Dr. Albee: Except that this didn't satisfy the human need to predict the future. Everything was either the will of God or the intervention of the fates. Do you have anything to add to this, Dr. Ferree?

Dr. Ferree: Dr. Kimball has emphasized that people for a long time have sought for structure and order through theology, magic, or some scheme of things prior to the era of modern science; and, in that sense, for a long, long time prior to the last several centuries people had looked upon the universe in some sense as orderly and tried to find order in the universe. I think your response is quite defensible. Although some theological systems of the past were very well structured and ordered, and logically self-consistent, they failed to meet the canon which many of us now demand in looking for a system of propositions to be called scientific, namely, the canon of bringing about capacity for prediction. If we prize prediction, I would like to select pragmatically the system that enables us to make accurate predictions which can be verified by experience. In talking about knowledge that teachers share in common with other professionals, one commonality is that the universe is one which admits of prediction.

Dr. Albee: Let me just say that, in discussing the orderliness and the predictability of the universe, I still was uncomfortable and so I said that there is a limit to what we can expect from scientific prediction. It is a fact that a great deal of man's existence is not answerable in any scientific operation. So there is a kind of concept of "ultimate inscrutability," which I use for want of a better term, which education and psychology and the other disciplines all share. We are in a universe that we did not make, that long preceded our existence, and that probably will continue long after we have disappeared. So we have to share this sort of uncomfortable inscrutability, and I think this touches on some of the things we were discussing earlier—the importance of art and literature and all of the other attempts to arrive at some kind of feeling for the meaning of existence that cannot be satisfied by scientific endeavors.

Dr. Ferree: I'd like to go on record as being a supporter of this doctrine, too. I think you are referring to what the contemporary existentialists sometimes call the absurd character of human existence—

Dr. Albee:—which is never analyzable or documentable by scientific operations.

Dr. Ferree: There are some dimensions of human existence which can't be explained by reference to anything prior—in that sense, maybe the fact of existence itself.

Dr. Kimball: I don't quite understand, because certainly the work in genetics and biology—

Dr. Ferree: To what do you refer to explain the raw brute facts of existence itself?

Dr. Albee: That's a good question. What concepts can we formulate to explain sheer existence?

Dr. Ferree: But I also agree with Ludwig Wittgenstein, who said, "Whereof one cannot speak, thereof one ought to be silent."

Dr. Albee: Or one ought not try to put this into a scientific model.

Dr. Ferree: I think there is much discussion of what you call ultimate inscrutability.

Dr. Kimball: I know, but these are cultural definitions, and it so happens that in the period between Søren Kierkegaard and the present time this has been one of the kinds of casts of mind which characterize our age, and it isn't necessarily the cast of mind that characterizes the age that follows or the one that preceded it.

Dr. Albee: I think we find evidence of philosophical speculation about the puzzle of human existence long before Kierkegaard. This might be called a generic human problem. On the basis of the operational studies we've been doing, man is the only animal truly conscious of his existence, of his extension in time.

Dr. Ferree: Isn't there always, out there, something that we still don't know? There's always an inscrutable area to be questioned; there are dimensions of our experience, the reality that we do culturally define and perceive, which forever escape us.

Dr. Albee: I think the point I was trying to make here is that we cannot settle for a scientific model and say this is it so far as education is concerned. We cannot simply train our students in statistics and scientific methods and say we have now armed them with all of the conceptual tools they need to be educators. We must also recognize that there are ways of knowing or ways of approaching an awareness of life's mystery other than the scientific model.

Dr. McMahon: In reality, though, you are denying this by your discussion, I think. Do you agree?

Dr. Albee: I think these are two different dimensions, two different levels of conceptualization. I am satisfied to work with a scientific model. I think this is what we must teach our students because this is what we have that is the most powerful; but this is not all. We must also at least make our students and ourselves aware that there are other approaches to the mystery of existence; and this includes preperation in art, in literature, and in music. I think this is why we have programs in these areas in our schools and this is why we prepare teachers in these areas because these are other ways of reaching out, never achieving, but reaching out for the mystery of existence.

Dr. Ferree: Maybe one could link up these observations with our earlier discussion of what one can learn through the medium of a literary work of art. I am quite willing to admit that there is something that one gets through reading a good novel or seeing a play that he may never, never get through the discussions of the scientists—two modes for treating the same—

Dr. Kimball: Are you in effect agreeing with C. P. Snow in terms of the two cultures, scientific and humanistic? Whatever his theories are, is it a recognition that there really are two cultures?

Dr. Albee: I think there definitely are. Whenever we discuss basic concepts, we need to recognize that there are these two different levels of organization or of ordering our knowledge of the universe. One approach conceives of the universe as a great big clock that has been wound up and is running and if we study it long enough we can understand the mechanism. This approach also regards a human being as some kind of mysterious mechanism with all its parts harmonizing and assumes that if we just study it long enough, we will find some explanation for human behavior. This mechanical model has not been abandoned but it has been supplemented with the recognition that there are other approaches to the understanding of human existence and human behavior.

Dr. Ferree: I was thinking of the lines from Herbert Feigl, who, I suppose, is one of the noteworthy exemplars of logical empiricism in American society in recent decades. He tries to argue that there is no fundamental incompatibility between the scientific and the nonscientific modes that we're talking about, but he suggests that—and these are his examples—when listening to a beautiful violin selection, one need not think about horsehair scraping against catgut, or when experiencing the ecstasies of love, one need not dwell upon the mysteries of endocrinology. It all depends on the setting.

Dr. Albee: I believe I recognize a good exit line. Let's turn to another area of my paper. I considered, next, some of the areas that have been of concern to psychology and that of necessity must be of concern to the profession of education. One is the area of individual differences. It's hard, I think, to realize that the first attempts to measure individual differences in cognitive functioning were made as recently as 1904.

You are all familar with the enormous elaboration of techniques for the measurement of individual differences. There has been considerable discussion in the last few years about the value of testing, but I don't think we need to get into the details of this controversy. Although tests certainly have been misused and misapplied, testing still remains one of the most powerful techniques available to psychology and education in their attempt to predict what the future holds for a given child or a given group of children.

Another area that I touch on is that of maturation, the knowledge of the mysterious unfolding of growth processes in the human being so that no matter what, within very broad limits, certain characteristic patterns of physical development and behavior unfold and develop, seemingly irrespective of external factors. Related to this, as I point out, is the concept of readiness, the theory that, as the human organism matures in a biological sense, there are certain critical periods when it is most efficacious to introduce certain kinds of learning experiences. It is important to distinguish between what is empirically determined and what is authoritative opinion about the proper time to introduce subject matter. Research that is going on at the present time suggests lowering the age at which we believe it is appropriate to introduce instruction in new concepts and skills.

Dr. Kimball: What has been done in the area of determining the process of readiness? Is readiness treated as a state which every individual reaches inevitably, although there is variability in the chronological time at which it might be reached? Or is it conceived as a function of diverse influences coming together to move an individual toward readiness?

Dr. Albee: It is indeed diverse influences that make up the readiness; we don't ever rear children in isolation without all kinds of external factors impinging on them. However, I've seen some dramatic examples of organisms being ready to respond in a differential way in the absence of any overt signs of such readiness. To give you one example, Bernard Z. Friedlander of our Mental Development Center has designed a very ingenious device which can be attached to a crib or suspended above the child in the crib. There are two plastic balls in which colored lights are strung. If the child hits one of the balls in a particular way, the lights flash and music sounds; if he hits the other one in a different pattern (and these can be ordered), then a different sequence of lights results. In other words, a different response has to be learned. He took this device to a ward for mentally retarded children where there was a ten-pound boy who, at five years of age, had never made any discernably intelligent response to his environment. Yet, in three hours, this very severely handicapped child was showing a differential response in order to get the reinforcement in this particular situation. Now this very severely retarded child was ready to learn something, but we had not found a way to test his readiness. I think that we need to develop more ingenious ways of testing readiness, not just of severely retarded children but of all children. In some schools geometry is now introduced at the end of the first grade. Yet, for some reason, we used to think that geometry was a subject that had to be taught in high school.

Dr. Cottrell: Isn't that last sentence the key? Isn't there some reason to interpret the concept of readiness in terms of the purpose and expectations of those who are in a position to teach and influence the child? Is it not possible to teach a foreign language to normal children of three and to teach it so fast and so well that they are communicating at the level of high school seniors when they are perhaps six years old? The question is what do we want? I've often heard parents badgering teacher-education folk for not insisting upon a reading competence at the end of the first grade that is demonstrable and clear-cut. I've said, "We could do that. Now here's the price you pay for it: if we do that, we can't do this and this and this."

Dr. Albee: I think that if what you've just said is true, then I'd have to go along; but is this true? That is, is the teaching of languages at an early age going to take away from teaching something else, or is the child much more receptive to learning in the early years, and are we not really taking advantage of this hunger for acquisition?

Dr. Cottrell: As a general principle, I don't think that can be disputed. Children are very much more able to learn than we've ever dreamed and much more avid to do so. I think the question, however, of the limitations of human attention still has to be raised. You can't do everything at once; if you do one thing, you don't do the other. I think a good deal of this readiness to do things depends on what children sense as adults' expectations and what they can, somehow or other, do to satisfy these expectations.

Dr. Kimball: Dr. Cottrell, why have we been so slow in discovering this ability of young children to learn?

Dr. Cottrell: I think the key reason is that we have preoccupied ourselves with the things to be taught, but we have not studied sufficiently the learning and the teaching processes and the maturation of children.

Dr. Albee: And we've really closed our eyes to specific examples of readiness for early learning. I recently spent a sabbatical year in Rome, and my oldest child, who was then aged four, went to a public Italian kindergarten. By the time we left Italy he was speaking fluent, beautiful Italian. In a year he soaked this up without effort. This didn't take away from his being interested in other things, but he was "ready" and he learned the language. I went for three nights a week to the Dante Alighieri Society and I studied my verbs; but when someone would come to the door, I would call my son Alec and ask, "What is this man saying?" and he would interpret for me. I think the point is that the four-year-old—or who knows what the limits are here—is ready to master areas of knowledge that we just have not exposed him to.

Dr. McMahon: I think this is just a cultural lag. For centuries we have thought children should go to school at six or seven years of age.

Dr. Albee: Because the philosophers told us that the age of reason was seven, we took this as a declarative sentence that was true. We have been told for years that one must have a mental age of six and a half to learn to read and now we have found that this isn't true.

I think we can build a technology around the fact that organisms, particularly young children, are hungry for experience and for order. Knowing what motivates them seriously, we can then enrich the materials that we expose them to. This gets us into the whole subject of operant technology which I will resist the temptation to consider here.

Dr. McMahon: Do you predict that, with this greater knowledge of the readiness of children to learn at so much earlier an age, there will be schools beginning at a much earlier age level and, therefore, children will complete high school at the age of twelve to fifteen instead of the present age of seventeen or eighteen?

Dr. Albee: No. I think we have to keep teenagers off the labor market in our present society, and so we will expand the educational process in both directions. We already see moves to send every child not just through high school but through two years of a community college. I'm not sure of our motivation here; I think it's economic. I would predict a movement to push back to earlier years the beginning of formal schooling. The current revival of interest in Maria Montessori's methods is probably a good indication that we are on the verge of this movement. In the earlier discussion, Dr. Kimball was saying that it now takes three or four lifetimes for a person to be educated. Perhaps, if we started a little earlier and made education a little more intensive, the child could master more of the subject matter that he needs to know. I'm sure that today's children will know more mathematics at an earlier age than we did in our day. They can then build on that foundation. Another point that is relevant here is the fact that if you have not made a contribution in certain fields by age twenty-five, you are probably not going to make one. This is especially true in mathematics; most of the great mathematical discoveries have been made by persons under age twenty-five. If we can provide the tools for mathematical discovery at an earlier age and at a more intensive level, we may get further multiplication of contributions in this field.

Another area of considerable concern to both education and psychology is the whole subject of motivation. Theoretically we know that motivation has a hierarchical structure. As educators, we must be aware of the work of Abraham Maslow and others which indicates that when there is frustration, or unresolved motivation at a very basic level, higher-order motives don't operate. The child, indeed the whole human organism at whatever age, requires the satisfaction of physiological needs and the needs for safety, that is, for an orderly and predictable world. Above this in the hierarchy of needs come love and affection. In working with children from deprived socio-cultural groups, we cannot utilize the striving-for-achievement factor which is such an important part of the motivational structure of the middle-class child. If the child comes to school hungry or if he does not enjoy a feeling of safety in his environment, then the frustrations at these very fundamental levels of motivation cause him to be unable to use higher-order motives. We as educators must recognize these basic needs, and we must take some social action to help insure that the fundamental motivational needs of children from culturally deprived areas are satisfied. A child cannot be expected to try his best to learn if he comes to school terrified of the world because he doesn't experience a sense of safety in, or love and affection from, his family.

The final area that I treat in some detail is the whole field of learning theory, which is currently a central area of attention in psychology, at least experimental psychology. Certainly there is a tremendous mutual interest in learning theory on the part of both psychology and education. Things are happening almost yearly in the field of learning theory which are going to have tremendous repercussions in the whole educational effort. At this point, I don't want to take time to get into a discussion of operant technology and the automated learning devices, but I think we are just on the threshold of tremendous developments in the area of automated instruction. These mechanical devices are not going to replace the teacher by any means, but they are going to provide the means for helping students acquire a tremendous amount of factual information, a tremendous amount of verbal concept learning that they would not otherwise get. One of the very simple principles of operant technology is that the learning process benefits enormously from immediate feedback information on success. Instead of having to write his spelling words, hand them in, and get them back the next day, the child is told immediately after he has spelled a word whether it is right or wrong. This principle of immediate feedback of knowledge is one of the fundamental bases of the automated instructional devices.

I also discussed the principle of reinforcement, that punishment is relatively ineffective but reinforcement is a tremendously powerful agent. I think this summarizes the essential points in my paper.

Moderator: The panel has imposed a second obligation upon Dr. Kimball, who is going to speak next. Since Dr. Davis could not attend the colloquy, we have asked Dr. Kimball to include comments relative to sociology as well as to anthropology.

Dr. Kimball: In making my final decision on the focus that I would give my paper, I had to reject several other possibilities.

One possibility would have been to select those aspects of anthropology that would be relevant to the knowledge in education and to the practice of education. For example, considerable research has been done in the area of culture and personality, particularly with respect to child-training practices. Some attention has been paid to the rites of passage—those celebrations or observances which mark the transition of a person from one stage of his life career to another. This particular aspect of anthropology is being received with considerable enthusiasm by many people in guidance because certain theories involved in the rites of passage literature are particularly relevant to students as they move from one stage of their education to another.

Another possibility was that I could have focused my attention on the methodology of anthropology. The processes by which an anthropologist gathers his data and analyzes them could have implications for the study of the teaching-learning process.

Still another possibility would have been for me to have paid considerable attention to a fascinating field, that of socialization of the child, and, on a comparative basis, the socialization of the great apes, because certain very interesting contributions have appeared in this field.

The topic which I finally selected is one that I consider to be of paramount significance to the field of education, that is, the transmission of culture. I have attempted to weave in some of the areas I have just mentioned and show their relevance to education. I have discussed them in terms of my focus of the topic "Transmission of Culture." Now within this general pattern of thought, I would make a distinction among the terms: (1) *knowledge,* (2) *theory explaining knowledge,* (3) *the practices which are related to knowledge,* and (4) *the ethical considerations which govern the gathering and analysis of the knowledge itself.*

When we consider the specific problem of the transmission of culture, there is the question of whether one can make distinctions among the types of learning that an individual experiences. It has seemed useful to me to distinguish the different types of learning: (1) technical learning, the acquisition of mechanical skills; (2) affective learning, the development of emotional responses; and (3) cognitive learning, which is related to the intellectual processes. I make no particular claim for this classification other than that it was useful to me in organizing my material.

In my judgment, no profession can be fully developed or can continue to grow unless adequate attention is paid to the theories basic to the knowledge and practices of that particular profession. Although this kind of higher level abstraction often leads us up blind alleys, we frequently get insights into behavior which either help us to understand what we are working with or provide a rationale for modifications in what we are doing.

In very large measure, I am concerned with consideration of some theoretical aspects which seem to be important for that knowledge which is acquired and utilized in education and which finds its way into practice and against which book knowledge and practice can then be examined. I am also interested in the nature of the relationship between the educational enterprise and the social characteristics of the environment in which that enterprise operates. There is an assumption here which has been expressed by others—nothing new about it —that there needs to be a relevant relationship between the nature of an educational system and the society in which it operates. It isn't that education necessarily should be used to reconstruct a society or that education should follow changes within society, but that people who work in the field of education should be sociologically sophisticated about the nature of the social world in which they are operating, not only in order to understand what they are doing but also to understand what kind of modifications should be made in the more concrete aspects of educational endeavor.

In my judgment, American society is undergoing extreme, rapid, and revolutionary changes in the nature of our social groups and the culture that is associated with our society. For example, American society has changed in less than a century from a pattern of small towns and rural countryside to a pattern of a few great metropolitan centers with their enormously complex organizational systems. These changes are evident in the institutions of family and government, and hopefully in education itself. Sometimes one is a little pessimistic, however, about the rate at which these kinds of organizational changes are being incorporated into education.

At this point in American history, educational organization, the content of the educational materials, and the processes by which education is carried on must all be reexamined and consciously changed. They are going to be changed anyway. The forces which are operating are too great to permit any aspect of society to remain apart from the rest. The point is that the educators have a responsibility to bring their best knowledge to bear, and to utilize the knowledge of others, as to what kinds of changes we can make.

Behind all educational endeavor, of course, there is an implicit or explicit educational philosophy. I would not attempt to describe to you what that philosophy is in the United States at the moment because, first of all, I don't know what it is. But, by contrast, I do want to show you what I mean by an implicit and explicit assumption about the nature of learning and the function of an educational system. For example, the basic goal of education in Peru is to accomplish what is contained in the Spanish word *formacion,* which means "to form," so that the purpose of the educational experience within the classroom is to shape the child. The questions for which the child needs to have answers are determined for him by external authorities—both religious and civil. The answers to these questions are also determined for him. Hence, the basic educational experience which the young person receives in Peru involves memorization of materials provided by the school, the teachers, or the textbooks. The student's degree of success is measured in terms of his ability to reply to the questions *verbatim* in a series of examinations which actually determine his future career. I have labeled such a system "catechismal education" because of its similarity to the nature of the teaching within religious denominations of questions and answers from the catechism. This type of education is one which maintains the status quo. It fits a society which is in a static condition. The type of education which would fit a society in change is something different from the one which I have been describing to you.

An anthropologist would use the comparative approach in order to come to grips with this particular question, "What is the proper function of education and what is the nature of a philosophical orientation toward it?" By examining a series of educational systems, modern or primitive, and by attempting to derive the kinds of uniformities which characterize these systems, we begin to get at the kind of universals which need to be known by educators, irrespective of the type of education which they advocate.

The only way in which one can begin to understand the qualities of a cultural item (whether it is a picture, a ritual, or a practice) is to see its relationship to other items within the culture. For example, to understand a child-training practice, one needs to see this practice in terms of other practices which are prevalent within the cultural situation which is being examined.

Now the conditions within which the learning process occurs are those which include: (1) the individual himself and his characteristics; (2) the nature of the social groups in the society in which he grows to maturity; (3) the nature of the cultural system, which means the series of beliefs and practices and values which are also a part of his cultural environment; and (4) the instruments, both operational and conceptual, by which learning is accomplished.

In my position paper, I have focused attention on the relationship between the individual and his environment which I perceive as one of intricate interdependency. It is necessary to examine the environment as carefully as we examine the individual who is a consequence of this environment. One of the points of view which has become accepted within anthropology in the last two decades is that man as a biological organism does not have the innate capacity to become a mature adult specimen outside the setting of a socio-cultural environment. If it had not been for the development of language and the ability to use manual tools, the creature which we now know as man could not possibly have appeared. There is an interesting relationship between the appearance of modern man and his physical characteristics and the growth of what might be called protoculture or early culture. The human infant born into a contemporary society is incapable of becoming fully human, either in a cultural sense or in a physiological sense, except within the characteristics of a cultural setting.

The informal as well as the formal aspects of the training and education of the individual help to make him a participating member of his society. Different cultures in the world can be distinguished and compared on the basis of what I call the perspective for the world view. There are certain aspects of each world view which can be submitted to a comparative examination. Crucial aspects of the world view have to do with concepts of time, of space, of order, and of what I call cognitive patterns of thought. Among most peoples of the world there exists a pattern of thought which represents a division of experience into dualities, for example, into good or evil, into black or white. But this is not true of all cultures of the world. There are certain cultures in which time is seen as cyclical—there is no change; there is only recurrence. Ancient Chinese culture saw the world as a constantly recurring succession of seasons with which they associated all the other dualities which were present within their cognitive system. These dualities were those of the earth and the sky, of male and female, of right and wrong, and the like.

The environment into which the child is born contains within it certain perspectives which are transmitted to him and provide him with this perspective or world view by which he then organizes and judges all experiences. One illustration which I gave of a world view was that of the great scientific naturalist, Louis Agassiz, whose point of view was that God was the first great scientist, that He created and ordered the universe, but that it was man's divine goal to unravel the mysteries of the universe and make explicit the plan which God had created. Agassiz could remain committed to a supernatural explanation of the origin of the earth and yet, at the same time, find no conflict whatever with the nature of the scientific findings which he was accumulating from his examination of the geologic and fossil past. Thus, an individual can make his experience conform to the nature of the world view which he holds.

During our earlier discussion of the orderliness of the universe and

THE COLLOQUY

the usefulness of scientific method, I was reminded of an experience reported by Vilhjalmur Stefansson, the Arctic explorer. He carried with him a telescope, and he told the Eskimos that if they would look through his telescope, they would be able to see things on the moon that they couldn't possibly see with the human eye. But the Eskimos weren't interested. They replied that "white man" was very far behind the Eskimos in these matters. They said that when they wanted to find out what was on the moon, they dissociated the soul from the body and went and visited the moon and then came back and reported.

Further examples seem unnecessary to establish the point that a part of each culture is a system of identifying and interpreting the things and events which constitute experience. In fact, without a culturally induced perspective, experience is meaningless. And, furthermore, we may posit that each such system operates within a framework of logic and consistency. Work in anthropology has shown that there is an orderliness which exists between the separate parts of a given people's culture, although it may not appear so to the outsider at first.

Dr. Cottrell: Are you imposing a new kind of determinism upon the individual, a kind of cultural determinism? I don't think you want to do this. The present world demonstrates the sometimes nefarious purpose of man to reconstruct the culture and the social system and, indeed, to reconstruct the universe. If the individual is in fact so deeply influenced by the pattern of the culture, how can he do this godlike work of making a new world in his mind? Concerning this interdependence of individual and culture, I see from one side that the culture influences the individual, that the individual is dependent upon the culture. But I don't yet see clearly in your theory how culture is dependent upon man.

Dr. Kimball: Among anthropologists, Leslie White would be characterized as the extreme cultural determinist. He says that man is caught within culture, that he cannot modify culture, that culture operates according to its own laws, its own dispositions, that it is something apart from man and that, therefore, in a very real sense there is cultural determinism. This is one view in anthropology, but it is not the view which I am expressing here. A number of variables affect the behavior of any human group. One of them is population. If you have a group of only 1,000 people and if for some reason that group doubles in size in two or three generations, there then is a change in the nature of the relationships among people. New kinds of stabilized groupings appear to take care of new problems which appear because of the mere magnitude of the numbers of persons with which one is dealing. The new problems of metropolitan life and the new kind of agencies we are creating to deal with these problems might be considered as examples of the changes which an increase in population may bring.

Secondly, although of lesser importance today, modifications in the physical environment can occur without any intent on the part of man. For example, ocean currents move according to other principles of natural phenomena. These, too, have their effects upon the nature of human behavior. Social conditions external to a group also have their influences. For example, when Adolf Hitler began to operate within Europe, his activities had reverberations throughout the entire world. One of the difficulties which White gets himself into is that he fails to see culture in relationship to any of these other things and attempts to explain it from within itself. Therefore, without man's intervention, you still must explain human behavior or human physiology or human social groups or the physical environment and many other things in terms of the combination or perhaps nexus that we were talking of earlier.

Now, the question arises "At what point and to what extent can man inject himself into this situation to give it some kind of conscious direction?" My belief is that we are, in a sense, reaching an epitome in the area of science. We now have at hand cognitive devices by which we can not only understand and describe what is going on, but actually set up processes by which we modify the conditions which affect man in his relationships to others and his view of the world. So that we are moving, for good or ill, in the direction of greater capacities to influence our environment and to handle ourselves. Does this help?

Dr. Cottrell: Yes, it says to me that the nature of cultural determinism is so pervasive that it even extends to an influence upon man which permits him to change the influences upon man.

Dr. Kimball: Correct.

Dr. Albee: I believe that man has relatively less, rather than relatively more, influence on his culture. For most of man's existence on earth he was a nomad; he was a food-gatherer before agriculture was discovered. Only in the last 6,000 years have men been able to store up food through the discovery of agriculture, and to have leisure to contemplate the universe around them. The culture of the food-gatherers is a strictly eye-for-an-eye, tooth-for-a-tooth kind of aggressive culture, to which man is basically well adapted in terms of his autonomic nervous system. And this is really the animal, or the natural man, underneath all of the cultural sophistication.

Dr. Kimball: There are primitive peoples who are not "eye-for-an-eye."

Dr. Albee: But are aggressive and peaceful groups different because they are somehow constitutionally different or are they both the same, basically and physiologically? Isn't it rather the cultural conditions which determine whether they are aggressive or peaceable? It seems to me that one group will be peaceable because there is plenty of food and no competing tribes are trying to seize the sources of supply; while another group will be competitive because there is not enough food to go around and because of the pressures of population. I guess what I'm really asking is this: Is not man fundamentally, physiologically, and basically the same wherever he lives? Doesn't his personality, if you will, depend almost entirely upon cultural or natural forces that surround him?

Dr. Kimball: I think the import of your original question was "If we see that our environment and culture are influencing us in directions in which we don't really want to go, can we change our direction?" I'm saying that we have less freedom than we wish we had.

Dr. Cottrell: I didn't mean to suggest that we were as free as God about all this, but we are tampering with God's business every day. We're not doing it with God's wisdom, but we're "messing around" in his territory.

Dr. Kimball: Certain kinds of changes occurred in the industrial life of England which created the industrial slums. Was not man, then, under certain circumstances, able to bring about desired changes and to assess the changes brought about?

Dr. Albee: But did he change these living conditions deliberately because he regarded the industrial slum as something undesirable, or did he build sufficiently productive machines so that it was no longer necessary to have an industrial slum? I think we sometimes take more credit than is due us.

Dr. Kimball: Aren't you saying that, irrespective of man's desires, the conditions must be such as to affect the capacities of man to do something?

Dr. Albee: Yes.

Dr. Kimball: And isn't it possible to make decisions about what kind of changes you're going to make and to move in this direction?

Dr. Albee: Well, I think that's why we're here, hopefully. We always hope that by intelligent examination of what is, we may point ourselves and society in directions that are more desirable in terms of some value system.

Moderator: Hasn't this issue been discussed at considerable length by B. F. Skinner in *Walden Two* and in some of his subsequent works on the design of a culture where man could consciously change his world and also, to some extent, certainly change man?

Dr. Kimball: Of course, there's always a problem here of who makes the decision of the direction in which one should go. I'm not certain that I would want to live in Skinner's world. He might try reinforcement on me of a kind that I wasn't particularly eager to have.

Dr. Albee: This is another problem.

Dr. Kimball: I think we might move on to the next concern of my position paper. I'll quote from the "Cultural Patterning and Learning" section:

> It would seem that this is an appropriate time to examine what we mean by the patterning of culture and its relation to the socialization of the child. . . .

> Although this proposal does not contradict our normal assumption that the infant is always prepared at birth to receive and organize stimuli, it does assert that the pattern of organization of experience is a variable and is external to the infant in origin.

Now if this is the case, then conscious man can change the organization of experience because it is a variable and in this way he can change the nature of the experiences which come to the child. I used the description of the Hopi Indians to illustrate the nature of the use of what Dorothy Eggan calls "affect" or the emotional aspects of indoctrination within a concept of the duality of the good and evil parts

Dr. Kimball asks, "Isn't it possible to make decisions about what kind of changes you're going to make and move in this direction?"

of the individual. I showed how the Hopi world view served to color all kinds of distinctions in their culture.

I then went on to talk about prepubertal and postpubertal learning. In this presentation, I pointed out that the learning which comes to an infant informally through his intimates—his family and his peers—is learning of a different kind than that to which the child is subject when society educates the child by transmitting that part of the culture which gives the world view about which I have been talking. The child has, of course, already been prepared, both cognitively and emotionally, to receive the kind of training which he gets in his initiation ceremonies. This preparation is of great relevance because any formal educational system is one in which the child is delivered to strangers. Although the teacher may be considered to stand in a substitute parent relationship, the school does represent a new kind of social situation for the child; and in our society the greater part of the child's formal educational experience is directed by strangers.

Dr. Ferree: You indicate in your paper that the stimulus-response paradigm appears to be adequate to explain affective and skill learning, but that we must look to some other mechanism to explain cognitive learning. Is the stimulus-response paradigm adequate to explain affective responses?

Dr. Kimball: I would like to refer that question to Dr. Albee.

Dr. Albee: The answer is yes.

Dr. Ferree: Well, then, a second question: Is it inadequate to explain cognitive learning?

Dr. Albee: No.

Dr. Ferree: Then you believe the stimulus-response paradigm adequate to explain both cognitive learning and affective learning?

Dr. Albee: It is generally agreed by learning theorists that affective learning is acquired through classical conditioning. Involuntary responses such as smooth muscle responses, endocrinological responses, and affective emotional responses are very easily demonstrated to be a consequence of classical conditioning. I would argue also that instrumental conditioning (or Skinnerian operant-type conditioning) can account not only for the acquisition of skills but for the acquisition of concepts. The stimulus-response paradigm is not limited to external stimulation but can include all sorts of internal cues.

Dr. Kimball: If we look at the variety of educational systems including the Hopi system we can say that there are three commonalities at the cognitive level which are important to us. These are: (1) the categories of knowledge; (2) the canons of discrimination, that is, the ability not only to identify an item but to evaluate it with respect to criteria; and (3) the process by which relationships are established between the separate variables with which one is concerned. A research study based upon this formulation of objectives could, hopefully, lead to the development of theoretical understandings of the learning process, and its relationship to the individual and to society, that would be beneficial to the enterprise of education.

Moderator: I'd like to move now to Dr. McMahon's paper.

Dr. McMahon: History, I'm happy to say, undergirds practically everything that has been said in this colloquy. I'm reminded of the graduate who met his economics professor at a class reunion twenty years after he had been his student, and said: "Well, Professor, I see you're still asking the same old questions." And the professor replied,"Yes, but remember, the answers have changed." And so we ask the same old questions over a period of time, but the answers do change.

In my paper, I first considered the nature of history and its function in the general education of man. Secondly, I considered what history, not only as a subject but also as a method of study, might offer education. Finally, I considered the approaches used today by historians of education and the ways in which they look at the past in order to shed some light on the present.

Over a long period of time, I have been particularly interested in the development of education as a body of knowledge. When teacher preparation first became a subject of study, it appeared at the university level where many critics today think it does not belong. As you know, the medieval university had primarily one purpose, that is, to train people to teach. In fact, one requirement for a degree was a two-year period of teaching, at the end of which the individual was given a license to teach anywhere he wished, provided he got the approval from his superior to start a school or to engage in some form of teaching in a locale not already too crowded.

The emergence of history as a discipline occurred at almost the same time that education was emerging in this country as a subject of study. Some of the criticisms made against the writing of the history of education could very well have been applied to the writing of history during the same period. The emergence of history as a separate study in our institutions of higher learning came almost as a direct result of their modeling their programs on those of the German universities, which were, of course, the prototype of our own institutions of higher learning. At that time the German historians were busily laying out some kind of content and research methodology which could be comparable, in some sense, to the work being done by the scientists of the day.

Most professional historians have shown little interest in the history of education. Only since 1957 or 1958 have historians recognized that the history of education is a neglected but fertile field of study, rich in materials to be gathered together and interpreted. Yet, as far back as 1908, Henry Suzzalo said that the trouble with most of the courses in the history of education and most of the monographs and textbooks then being produced was that a number of conditions affecting education which ought to have been included in the history of education had been neglected by those working and teaching in education—the economic, political, and cultural aspects of history, for example, so necessary for understanding the history of education.

History of education became very firmly entrenched in university departments of education primarily, I suppose, because it could lay some claim to having intellectual content. If history could be recognized and taught, you see, as a study in the great universities of the day, then the history of education ought to be acceptable as a university subject.

Dr. Kimball: What was it that you said began in 1957 or 1958?

Dr. McMahon: Some American historians became aware of the tremendous resources in history available for studying the history of education, and formed an association to facilitate research in a field that they believed had not been properly explored by educational historians.

Dr. Kimball: Have historians also become interested in the history of music or the history of other fields?

Dr. McMahon: I'm afraid not; little interest has been shown by historians in the history of music and art. Bernard Bailyn points out that there are other social agencies which influence education besides the school, but that not too much has been done on them. There has been more interest in the history of science, history of medicine, and history of theology. The informal agencies which have played a great part in the development of education really have *not* received as much attention as perhaps they should have.

It is easy to say that history of education has never been done properly by those people in schools of education, and that it requires the work of historians with a broader background to set us right. Historians complain that Ellwood Cubberley tried to write the picture as he wanted to see it, not as it really was, and they are now going to set Cubberley right, and also set the rest of us right. I suspect that fifty years from now someone will need to set them right, too, since more information is always gathered, as time goes on, which changes the picture.

Dr. Albee: Haven't I read somewhere recently that someone has been given a huge grant to study the history of education?

Dr. McMahon: Yes, Lawrence A. Cremin; he is writing a new interpretive history of American education.

Dr. Ferree: Cremin exhibits the techniques of the scholarly historian, but his training has been in education and his perspective is very sympathetic to education.

Dr. McMahon: In addition, he is director of the Philosophy, the Social Sciences, and Education Division at Teachers College.

Dr. Cottrell: There is much writing on the history of music, done mostly by professors in university departments of music. I wonder if you have the impression that I've had at times that this good work on the history of music is unintelligible to the general historian. He just doesn't know the terms that are being used.

Dr. McMahon: That's very true. I think, however, that the history of music has not been approached from the point of view of its effects on our educational system.

Dr. Cottrell: How it has affected music, that's all.

Dr. McMahon: This emphasizes some of the omissions in the historical study of education pointed out by both educators and historians.

This whole idea of what constitutes education beyond the organized form of schooling deserves more attention; for example, the newspapers, journals, lyceums, and the kinds of informal organizations that have existed. Although many of these agencies have had a direct influence on our patterns of thought concerning what should be taught in the schools, their historical development has not been properly analyzed. I now have a student who is analyzing the *Tatler* and the *Spectator* to find out exactly what opinions Joseph Addison and Richard Steele expressed about the education of their day. This student is pointing out that these sources should be examined by those interested in the history of education in the United States because many of the issues of the *Tatler* and the *Spectator* were current in this country, and many of the outstanding American leaders of the day were familiar with the writings of Addison and Steele; hence these writings in turn might have had some indirect influence on what was going on in American education.

The idea of teaching the history of education as part of the preservice preparation of teachers has been criticized by some educationists for many years. Even though history of education had intellectual content which was acceptable, at least in part, to other faculty members, the question has been raised: "Will studying the history of education produce a better teacher than he would have been had he not had this study?" I'm sure there is little or no connection between the skill of a teacher in the classroom and the fact that he has studied ancient, medieval, or modern history of education. However, if the teacher trainee has some realization of the problems that have occurred in education through the centuries and knows some of the attempts that have been made to solve them, he may be more sensitive to the fact that these problems are not unique with each individual teacher, or even with each generation.

I have frequently emphasized that "there is nothing human which should be foreign or is foreign to education." This is an old saying of Juvenal's from many centuries back. Adlai Stevenson once opened an address on Winston Churchill with this very quotation. I thought at the time that Churchill, with his tremendously varied interests, exemplified the breadth of interest which our teachers should have, and many do. While we want teachers to be specialists in certain areas, they must be generalists also. Each teacher is working with students who must have a general background in areas other than the particular subject which they are studying under that teacher. Probably there is nothing more useful or more valid for the general education of prospective teachers than the study of history since it is the study of man's past, not only of his activities but of his thoughts.

Dr. Kimball: You have spoken about the transmission of the heritage and I have talked about the transmission of culture; the concepts are quite similar. Now the question arises: "At what point and to what extent do professional educators make decisions about what part of the total cultural heritage is to be transmitted and how it is to be transmitted?" In your case, for example, a historian can make decisions that only this part is going to be taught, or is going to be taught with this bias.

Dr. McMahon: That's right, and this is one way of making history. Deciding what should be included and what should be emphasized is itself creating a kind of history, since those who come after will be influenced to such an extent that they may look at questions in education, and the history of education, from an entirely different point of view. I'm not sure, however, that educators decide, really, what should be taught. For example, do you think that the reason for teaching business education and business courses is that educators decided that these ought to be included in the school curriculum? I don't think so.

Moderator: How about driver education?

Dr. McMahon: A very good example. With the current emphasis on studying more intellectual content in the high school program, a county school system which I know decided to discontinue their driver education courses. A service club then decided to survey the parents, asking them what they thought about driver education. At least 90 per cent of the parents said that driver education ought to be in the curriculum; so the school superintendent put the course back in the program. He's torn, of course, by a number of pressures just as we have pressures exerted on us.

Dr. Albee: Could you not say the same thing with respect to the content of history textbooks? Their content is determined, in part at least, by external cultural pressures. For example, one textbook will use the word "evolution" and another will substitute another term so that the book can be sold in certain states. So educators are not solely responsible for determining the content of the curriculum.

Dr. Ferree: I'm glad you said "solely." It's not a disjunctive "either-or" matter. Educators have some role in determining curriculum building, though we must take into account the various forces that have been called to our attention. I think you raised the $64,000 question when you asked how one justifies one set of elements in the culture as over and against alternative sets to be communicated deliberately in school. This is a question of values, and one on which philosophers, as well as people who aren't philosophers, disagree considerably. Here's where we need much more inquiry and research. John Dewey's answer was that the substance of the curriculum should be relevant to the hard-pressing, inescapable human problems. This answer, of course, requires a definition of hard-pressing, inescapable human problems.

Dr. Albee: It has just been suggested that one of these inescapable problems is the sale of automobiles.

Dr. Ferree: Dewey might support driver education in the curriculum. He might well maintain that, since the world has highways like the one between here and Washington, D.C., and since there is a car or two in every family, this is jolly good knowledge to have.

Dr. McMahon: Think of the number of proposals about the licensing of teenage drivers. The newest proposal to be made in Maryland is that a person can be licensed to drive an auto at age sixteen if he can show that he has passed the driver education course at school. Otherwise he'll have to wait until he is eighteen. Now this ruling has a tremendous force in keeping adolescents in school.

Dr. Albee: This is a good example of changing the conditions of learning. Consequences of quite another kind, which were unanticipated, flow from this change in conditions.

Dr. McMahon: Many students will now stay in school beyond age sixteen if they can get the course in driver education.

Dr. Albee: And all the exhortation in the world couldn't keep some of them in school otherwise.

Dr. McMahon: No, but this is strong motivation.

Citizen advisory committees make many proposals that certain things be introduced in the schools which either are not being done or are being done in a way different from their wishes. Some teachers would say that such committees are causing more harm than good. Yet, in citizen advisory committee reports there is always the insistence that there be clear lines of communication between school and community. Maybe such communication can eventually result in a greater understanding of some of the pressures and a lessening of them, presumably leaving curriculum matters in the hands of educators.

We think of history as trying to determine what happened in the past and the presentation of these findings to the public. To paraphrase Louis Gottschalk, let us consider the tremendous number of people who have lived during the past 1,000 or 2,000 years and all the things that they said and did and thought; how little of this was observed by others, and of what was observed how little was recorded; how little of what was recorded has been preserved, and how little of what has been preserved is credible; how little of what is credible has come to the attention of the historians, and how little of what has come to the attention of the historians has been narrated. Thus, we can understand that what we know is an infinitesimal part of all of mankind's history, and how little we really know, despite the great advances we have made in accumulating knowledge and in producing theories of what went on in the past.

Dr. Albee: I shudder to think of all that has been recorded.

Dr. McMahon: And I shudder to think of what is being recorded right now.

Moderator: Next we will ask **Dr. Cottrell** to elaborate on some of the ideas he presented in his paper.

Dr. Cottrell: I started with the observation that education is a phenomenon; and since it is a phenomenon, it can be studied concretely. Education can be observed in process and in terms of its results. Theories can be propounded to explain it; and it is possible, in some measure, to control educational processes experimentally and to offer guidance. So I didn't have to argue with myself very long when it came to the question of whether there is a field of potential systematic scholarship in education. Every discipline has its cognate fields, its

Dr. Cottrell asks, "How can we improve the profession?"

supporting disciplines. Like every other human study, education is necessarily interdisciplinary. The more disciplines that are involved in the study of a human problem, the more opportunity there is of getting some glimpse of the truth about human beings.

Dr. Ferree has defined satisfactorily the sense in which education has a unique body of knowledge. But it doesn't greatly interest me whether or not a field is "unique." My concern is chiefly with what the professional practitioner needs to know, how he commands this knowledge, how he uses it, and what happens as a result of his knowing it. We teach prospective professionals a great many things, with the sublime faith that, having taught them, we've done the Lord's work, and in most cases we don't know at all that any good comes out of it.

The practitioner of education is obliged to know more than what is, in declaratory fashion, true; he has to have something in the way of dimensions of competence that lie back of his grasp of the truth.

Teaching is an art as well as a science. The insightfulness of the practitioner and his sense of the appropriateness of certain techniques, whether or not they are supported by research data, do not relieve education of the necessity for genuine concern for truth. The practitioner has to be a doer, and in order to be a doer he has to be a person with a conscience. It's not just knowing *how* to do what he's supposed to do; he has to know whether or not to do a certain thing at a certain time. And if he knows, or thinks he knows, whether or not to do it, he has to know why. He must have a concern for theory.

We have many people who are doing things in the classroom that they couldn't possibly explain intelligently. These people are craftsmen rather than professionals. Teacher education, in my judgment, needs to have a vast body of knowledge which must be shored up by a theoretical system in order to be knowledge.

It is not sufficient, however, for a teacher to know what can be done, whether it should be done, and why it should be done. He can't talk about being a professional unless he does his teaching with maximum skill. One cannot call himself a professional when he is actually just "getting by" as a routine performer. This is in contradiction to the professional ideal. The teacher must be self-critical and he must be constantly trying to do better, or he isn't a professional. Do we have enough of this kind of professional rigor in our ranks? Well, obviously, I don't think we have. This is one of the dimensions of teacher education which we need to learn about and improve.

How can we improve? Inquiry into successful practice is one means. A number of my colleagues have studied teaching intensively. Tapes have been used for recording the classroom behavior of the teacher. Such evidence is very partial and hard to understand because the tape gives us voices only—no gestures and no background information. I don't believe that you'll ever find a sensitive detector which will make possible a faithful and adequate recording of the teaching process. Teaching is a transaction between people, a relationship that develops between teacher and student.

Dr. Kimball stressed that it's not the individual nor is it the culture apart from the individual which is studied in anthropology. It's the individual in a cultural context. Similarly, it is the relationship between the learner and the teacher that we should be studying. I don't deny that the tapes will help us to understand that relationship, but I fear that we may be making very superficial, if not false, inferences from inadequate data. What is going on there? That is what we should be asking. And it isn't a simple question. It's extremely subtle.

We should be finding out what insights young people have gained, what values have become functional in their lives. I've rejected the idea that you can have teaching without learning. You cannot study teaching unless you also study learning. It's the *teaching-learning* situation with which we must be concerned.

Longitudinal development of teaching-learning situations must be studied. Only over a period of time can we obtain diagnostically relevant evidence. You don't just take a photograph of the teaching act. It's the change in teaching-learning situations that enables the teacher to know whether he is or isn't teaching and especially whether he's improving as he teaches. The teacher and the student together may open up whole new worlds. One never knows, and that's one of the things that makes it so exciting to be a teacher.

Dr. Ferree: I've been pondering a remark you made that there's no teaching unless learning occurs. This is the slogan which Israel Scheffler treats in his book *The Language of Education*. The term "teaching" is ambiguous. There's one sense of the term "teach," the success sense, to use Scheffler's language, which makes the claim that there's no teaching unless learning occurs. However, I wonder whether we shouldn't recognize that an alternative sense has some validity, at least in some contexts. Let me explain what I mean. If a physician uses the very best knowledge and techniques available in ministering to a patient but the patient dies, would you say that the doctor hasn't practiced medicine? If a lawyer uses the very best knowledge and skill in the defense of his client but loses the case, would you say he hasn't practiced law? If a swimming teacher uses the very best knowledge and techniques available to him but at the end of the summer his student still sinks, would you say that the teacher hasn't taught?

Dr. Cottrell: What was the purpose of this teacher?

Dr. Ferree: To teach the youngster to swim.

Dr. Cottrell: To swim, but the child didn't learn to swim, so the teacher didn't teach him to swim.

Dr. Ferree: Not in terms of the success usage of the verb; but if you recognize an intent usage, teaching is, by definition, using the very best knowledge and techniques available, regardless of outcome. There are many teachers who work their hearts out, use the very best knowledge available, meager as it is, in my estimation; but at the end of their effort they are not successful. Should we say they haven't taught?

Dr. Cottrell: You can define your problem away, but the problem is still there.

Dr. Ferree: There are various ways to define terms. I'm against absolutism. I'm against trying to define a term in one way, singularly, finally, for all purposes.

Dr. Cottrell: I like a lawyer who works at winning a case and I'm willing to pay him for working at winning the case, and I like the teacher who works at giving swimming lessons.

Dr. Ferree: You prefer to define "teaching" in terms of success?

Dr. Cottrell: I do. I think it's too dangerous to get into the habit of doing otherwise.

Dr. Ferree: On the other hand, it's dangerous to stress success to such an extent that teachers have strong guilt feelings, even though they've done their "dead level" best and lived up to the best knowledge available to them and haven't been successful. So I suppose it depends on the context in which you wish to define your terms.

Dr. Cottrell: That's right. There was some learning that went on even though the child didn't know how to swim at the end of the summer —some learning that was associated with the effort to learn to swim. Of course, that teacher may have taught the child something he never intended to teach, something which may cause other failures in the future, such as failure in the stock market.

I have emphasized that teaching is a matter of example rather than of didactic precept. Some of us have become too deeply involved in this business of issuing didactic precepts to prospective teachers on the assumption that this will do them some good. Recently it has been recommended to us that practical experience, with or without guidance, is all the teacher education that is necessary. I think this position is extremely dangerous; we cannot abrogate our responsibilities as teachers of teachers by saying, "Go out and learn," nor can we delegate our teacher education responsibilities to people who are much less competent. Field experience has its place, but it is no natural substitute for thorough-going intellectual inquiry and thorough-going sympathetic guidance by people who have engaged in the intellectual inquiry and understand its relevance to classroom practice. In order to save some money, many people are now trying to turn teachers out to pasture and say,"Learn it yourself and do it yourself." We're great people on "doing it yourself." We ask people to do things which they *can't* do themselves, and that's one of the reasons why we don't have more respect from the community. We have frequently failed to teach methods of teaching to prospective teachers. We might just as well recognize this and start over again; but I think we should be very careful how we start over again. The person who knows mathematics is not necessarily qualified to teach people to teach mathematics. The mathematician has some knowledge that is vital to the understanding of how to teach mathematics. His knowledge is necessary but not sufficient. In a sense, education is a program for masses of people, and this can be dangerous because it is possible for us to suppose that there is a consciousness to a group. It's dangerous, isn't it?

Dr. Kimball: It is, indeed. This is what is known as "reification."

Dr. Cottrell: I didn't want to get into that if I could help it. I didn't want to start reifying. I shall never forget to my dying day hearing outside the window of the hotel, "Heil, Sieg Heil!" It was the German youth corps going down the street. Did you ever hear it?

Dr. Kimball: I not only heard it, but I also saw school teachers herding little children down the street.

Dr. Cottrell: Isn't that the tragedy of it? They were using programmed education as an instrument of national policy, and this is dangerously close to being unethical and evil. It isn't inherently so; it depends upon national policy, doesn't it? Dewey emphasized that a criterion of morality is inherent in the democratic way of life. Inherent in the democratic action experiences are criteria of what is ethically good and what is not. Dewey contended that that which leads to more growth, more life, is good, and that which stultifies is evil. Well, let's pass that classic formulation of the problem of pragmatism. I think it is a problem.

But let's ask whether the use of programmed education for the accomplishment of some goal of society must necessarily be regarded as evil. I don't think so. We are going to have to use more carefully programmed education if for no other reason than the very worthy goal of self-defense. That's not good enough, but that is a reason. The system of technology will take over if one doesn't defend himself in a programmed plan. We read now that this country lacks purpose, lacks a sense of the meaning and significance of a day's work. Why is that? It's because people haven't planned the conversation that is necessary to illuminate the goals of their day's work.

I end my paper by stating five types of problems that require programmed attack by responsible educational leadership.

Moderator: If I have interpreted correctly the position papers and the statements made by panel members, we could answer affirmatively the question: "Is there a body of knowledge unique to the profession of education?" We haven't done much yet, however, in defining that body of knowledge. If we were going to publish this series of papers, how should we interpret to the reader the expression "body of knowledge unique to the profession of education"?

Dr. Kimball: It seems to me that we have been talking about the sources of understanding which pertain to the enterprise of education and the practice of education. In the sources of understanding we include the various disciplines from which knowledge can be taken; but one must keep in mind that all of these disciplines are in a process of continuous growth and reformulation themselves. So the body of knowledge is a growing thing; it's not static. It's not something which one attains and then has forever. New kinds of understanding are developed as new kinds of problems arise or as old problems are redefined.

Dr. Cottrell: Dr. McMahon has emphasized that we are influencing these other fields also, that the interest in education is becoming a fruitful influence upon other fields.

Dr. McMahon: It seems to me that much of this can be rephrased in the form of questions. What are the questions which we as educators want to have answered and where do we get the answers? It may be from one source or from a dozen sources. The questions change as time changes, as cultural conditions change; and even when we ask the same questions, we look for different kinds of answers. We go to psychology, philosophy, anthropology, sociology, biology; we go to every source we can find.

Dr. Albee: We must, however, be careful not to convey the impression that this is a constantly changing scene with new interests that come and go, that wax and wane. Although I don't believe in absolutes, I do think, and I tried to show this in my paper, that there are some very definite areas of knowledge, which have been explored and reexplored for the past seventy-five years, which are just as crucial to the field of education today as they were in Edward Thorndike's day.

As we do research in these areas, we get more and more sophisticated in our answers to some of these questions; but teachers will always need to know about motivation, individual differences, maturation, and other relevant topics. Cultural determinism and the influence of culture on our educational practices is a category of knowledge that will always be important to the field of education. Our level of understanding and our perceptiveness about the changing influences of culture certainly will have to be improved, but as an area it will continue to be important.

Dr. Ferree: If one defines the "body of knowledge unique to the profession of education" as I have attempted to define it, there are alternative ways of organizing the corpus of statements which comprise such a body of knowledge. There is what might be called the *parent disciplines approach* which uses the logic and organization of the parent discipline as a basis for organization of an educational discipline derivative from it; then, there is the *behaviors and activities approach,* which draws from diverse sources and organizes the statements around the activities or behaviors in which professional educators characteristically and recurrently engage; and the *outcomes approach,* which organizes statements around a given goal sought in the educational enterprise. These are three approaches. I don't claim that these are the only approaches.

Which mode of organization of the statements in the body of knowledge unique to the profession of education is most defensible for the purpose of an undergraduate program in teacher education? If our concern is to train graduate students, some of whom are not going to be practitioners, but researchers and theorists, should we employ the same mode of organization that we employ for the undergraduate? I'm raising rhetorical questions, in a way. I don't have answers to these questions. I think we need experimental programs with differing modes of organization of statements in the body of knowledge unique to the profession of education to serve different purposes.

If we offer courses organized around the parent disciplines at the same time that the student is acquiring other sorts of knowledge, for example, psychology as well as psychology of education, then doesn't it become especially crucial that the course in psychology of education not be just an attenuated, watered-down course in psychology with a few generalizations about education?

Moderator: Are all the disciplines represented here that should have been represented? Are there other disciplines which can contribute to the profession of education?

Dr. Ferree: I wonder if we would have all there is to know about education even if we got all the parent disciplines together and had a corresponding educational discipline for each one. Is there anything else? Is there a body of statements which *doesn't* come easily out of some parent discipline? We have been talking about the sociology of education, the psychology of education, the philosophy of education; but there are courses such as curriculum and techniques of instruction. Does one get all the knowledge that's in those courses from the parent discipline courses, or is there some corpus of statements, and some way of organizing it, not easily classified under the rubric of a related parent discipline?

Dr. Cottrell: I think that the major problem areas inherent in the practice of the profession provide the best basis for organization, rather than to take the existing disciplines as the initial focus. Of course, we must not be superficial in our treatment of these problems. If we take this approach and treat each of these problem areas in depth, we'll push ourselves back into the existing disciplines; we'll probably push ourselves into disciplines which we haven't even mentioned. Let's ask what we want a professional to prepare to do and let's set some standards concerning the level of competence we want him to have in doing those things. Then let us go wherever we have to go to get the materials and the techniques with which to help him attain that level of competence.

Dr. Ferree: Regardless of whether we have a disciplines approach or an activities approach, what are some of these disciplines, or fields, other than those represented here, which potentially can make a contribution?

Dr. Cottrell: Medicine is one. We know a great deal that we haven't used about the effect of nutrition upon the acuity of learning and upon the efficiency of learning. For example, every teacher faces the actual, practical problem of what to do with hungry children in school. Even in the best neighborhoods children are malnourished because they live on chocolate bars and hamburgers instead of a balanced diet. Then they go to medicine and ask, "How can you help us with this problem? What are the relevant facts about nutrition?" Teachers need to know those before they even start to teach the youngsters in these different kinds of communities.

Dr. Albee: I think that's a beautiful illustration, although I'm not sure that it's medicine that has this knowledge. There's a whole field of nutrition which is so highly specialized that most general practitioners and most medical students haven't heard one tenth of what is to be known in this field. I think this is a beautiful example of a field that can contribute very significantly to education.

Dr. Kimball: I want to associate myself with the activities or problem approach, which I believe to be more fruitful than the disciplines approach.

Moderator: Let us now attempt to identify some of the questions, problems, or behaviors that you consider pertinent to our problem in selecting the contributions from the various disciplines. Dr. Ferree, would you care to state some of the questions, behaviors, or problems as you see them?

Dr. Ferree: I would like to preface my response to that request with the observation that, although the problems, activities, or behaviors approach is a very fruitful one, it is only one of several ways to organize the body of knowledge unique to the profession of education. I tend to feel that this approach may have great promise right now, particularly in the education of preservice teachers. But I don't want to convey the impression that I am committed to this particular approach to the exclusion of the others. I think there are contexts in which all three of the approaches that I've specified, and perhaps a good many more, would be appropriate. But I would be happy to direct your attention to some of the behaviors of teachers toward which the statements in the body of knowledge unique to the profession of education could be oriented. I make no claim to originality here. I refer you to David Ryans' classification of what he calls five major classes of teacher behavior.

1. Motivating-reinforcing teacher behavior
2. Presenting-explaining-demonstrating teacher behavior
3. Organizing-planning-managing teacher behavior
4. Evaluating teacher behavior
5. Counseling-advising teacher behavior

Since all teachers engage in the business of motivating students, or reinforcing certain behaviors, let's get whatever knowledge we can get, from wherever we can get it, which is pertinent to that task.

Perhaps the work of B. O. Smith on the logic of explanation, to which I alluded earlier, may be pertinent and relevant to the second behavior mentioned. Also, if there is knowledge from diverse fields, as diverse as dramatics and logic, then let us bring such knowledge to bear and let us focus sharply on explaining, presenting, and demonstrating teacher behavior. Let's organize such knowledge under this rubric. This is one way to do it.

Even though Ryans did not propose these five categories as a basis for organizing the body of knowledge unique to the profession of education, these five categories could serve as a basis for bringing together and coordinating a great variety of statements, many of which have places in other bodies of knowledge with different bases for organization.

I'm wondering if teachers and those who know teaching think that Ryans' scheme is sufficiently inclusive and that his five categories really get at the major kinds of behaviors of teachers. That is to say, can we subsume all the key behaviors in which teachers recurrently engage under these five classes?

Dr. Kimball: May I ask, first, does this scheme take account of the reciprocal in this activity?

Dr. Albee: I was going to ask a similar question, going back to something which Dr. Cottrell said about the mysterious alchemy that goes on between teacher and student. Could we add "serving as a role model" as a sixth category? I think a good teacher finds that his students identify with him. You get a teacher whose enthusiasm for his subject is infectious and soon you find a number of his students also becoming interested in it because of their identification with the teacher. I don't know how you would prepare the teacher to do this, but the objective would be to serve as a role model.

Dr. Kimball: Should all the activities be teacher-focused, or must we consider, as Dr. Cottrell has indicated, a teacher-learner relationship? Does this system of classes include this or am I just injecting it? Rosalie and Murray Wax made a study of what went on in an Indian reservation school. I want to describe one aspect of this study. They discovered that, by the time the Indian students had reached the age of twelve or thirteen, they had become experts at sabotaging any efforts on the part of the teacher to teach anything. Now this is what I meant by the reciprocal, because there is a student body. There is a kind of subculture which exists among this group. There are common values which they hold and there are things they do as a result. What the teacher encounters in the classroom, in extreme cases of this kind, has a significant effect upon what the teacher can accomplish or how the teacher behaves. So, is this classification too one-sided?

Dr. Ferree: I don't know. Much depends on what these terms mean to you. If the term "motivate" suggests a one-sided thing to you, then maybe we ought to use a different term that brings into motivation recognition of the reciprocal relationship between students and teacher. These terms don't particularly bother me, and I, in some ways, assume the sort of thing that you're calling for. It certainly should be included either tacitly or explicitly.

Dr. Kimball: It might be very easily handled if it's needed. I'm just trying to find out. I'm putting a hyphen there, teacher-student behavior, but that might not be the focus that was intended.

Dr. Ferree: I think it is important to recognize the reciprocal influences between student and teacher and that teaching is a transaction. I wonder what we would have if we, by some magic, could bring under each of these rubrics, or some modified rubrics that interject your notion, all of the statements that are well confirmed as true or highly probable?

Dr. Albee: It would be a very interesting task.

Dr. Ferree: And an important task. This would be a good way to bring together the body of knowledge unique to the profession of education. I wish that someone would grant a goodly sum of money for persons to engage in this task of bringing together or promoting this "Diaspora in reverse," which is what I guess I would call it.

Dr. Kimball: My own sense of this is that I would make it broader than it is here and I would approach it from the point of view of the situation. A classroom situation consists of a person who is called a teacher, persons who are students, and the relationships between them. Within this situation all of these types of behaviors that you have just listed occur. But this situation also includes external conditions, that is, external conditions *within* the classroom and *to* the classroom. The external conditions *within* the classroom have to do with the kinds of chairs, their arrangement, other kinds of facilities. The conditions external *to* the classroom include whether or not you have an understanding principal, the other teachers with whom you work, auxiliary services available, and the nature of the community within which you're operating.

Dr. Ferree: I really think that Ryans was focusing more sharply on what we sometimes call instruction, and I did not mean to suggest that I was proposing these five categories as some all-inclusive scheme of classifying educational activities or doings. I think you're right that in order to get at what we might call a complete, or a more nearly complete, body of knowledge unique to the profession of education, we certainly have to go way beyond these five rubrics, although they do provide some focus and a plan or a scheme of organization. We need something like this as a beginning point, but certainly we need a larger frame of reference to which you're calling our attention.

Dr. Cottrell: It would seem to me that building models around which to hang and within which to place truth would have some value here. Take the very first concept, motivation. The instructor feels an obligation to try to generate a certain kind of motivation. Now, what is he doing? To start with, he is undertaking to find what's there already. He's trying to shape behavior, to modify it in response to the situation, and to take account of the frustrations that the student may experience in his drive to proceed with his work. This relationship of teacher and student is generating significant motivation for learning, and is a kind of model which we could describe. We could then ask ourselves, "What do we know on the basis of fairly well demonstrated evidence about what takes place, which elements of the situation are present, and when does the shaping of the motivation take a certain direction or form?" The model of motivation that I just sketched does not mean that we are dealing with a situation in which a bureaucracy decides on the imposition of a cultural design in advance. When we are building these models, we need to reflect upon what this implies with regard to a total systematic or schematic culture. There is a very sobering caution for educational theorists to remember what they're doing by way of influencing the development of a large cultural commitment on the part of the people.

Dr. McMahon: I can see this extending, however, to such a degree that it becomes too ponderous to handle. For example, if you took motivating-reinforcing teacher behavior, I can see this being examined in a nursery school, kindergarten, elementary, intermediate, junior high, and senior high school; then being examined in different kinds of communities in terms of subject matter, because all of these are important. I can see a model so inclusive that it would be almost impossible to complete.

Dr. Kimball: No, it depends on how you build your model. If you build your model on categories, then what you are describing here will happen. If you build your model on systems, then it doesn't happen.

Dr. Ferree: Would you elaborate on that? I don't quite understand.

Dr. Kimball: I'm speaking now of what has happened in the history of the development of anthropology. About thirty years ago there was the tendency to pay attention to traits. There was an attempt to create categories under which traits could be listed. For example, a general category was "technology," and under that was the general technical term "containers" and the more specific term "basketry." And so the anthropologist developed a picture of a culture by a listing of discrete items within a culture system without asking the question "What are the relationships among the items which are being examined?" When people began to ask this question, which is best represented in Ruth Benedict's *Patterns of Culture,* they began to look at the patterns of relationships, so that anthropologists now look at a system rather than at discrete items.

Dr. Ferree: The approach you've just described appeals to me. I think it's high time we had inventories of scientific findings. I don't think that's all that we should do. I think there's a place for the sort of thing you're demanding. If a student came to me about problems of motivation in education, I wish I could say, "Here's some knowledge. Look at it." I wish I had a place to direct him. I think we do have such knowledge. I think there are ways to classify such knowledge to make it available to students, and I think this approach has some merit though I'm not proposing it as the last word. It's a way of organizing.

Moderator: Does reexamination call for reorganization? Does the pattern which has been suggested have flexibility enough and framework enough to permit the analysis that we're talking about? Dr. Kimball, would you expand this concept of systems and indicate to us, if possible, some of the problems involved?

Dr. Kimball: In the evolution of field work analysis in anthropology, the methodology of the biologists has been the source from which we have drawn our greatest inspiration. This means that we look at the human body and its systems and its subsystems and the relation between these in the same way the biologist does. If we are studying a Navaho family, we wish to know the nature of the types of persons within a family, and the relationship between the kinds of activities in which these people engage and the types of persons. We are describing the system of a Navaho family. In the nature of our field work it is not necessary to determine how many Navaho families we have to examine. Theoretically, we examine only one, so that we have no problem of sampling. Rather, we have the problem of discovering the interrelationships between people operating in terms of events in the world in which they live.

Moderator: Do you have to determine some kind of dimensionality that you're going to investigate when you explore the family relationships?

Dr. Kimball: Not necessarily. It depends upon the focus with which you are dealing. You can look at the nature of the family in relation to the division of labor within the family and in relation to the utilization of land, to production, or whatever you want to, you see. Or you can define your problem in a more academic way, which is "What is the pattern of a Navaho family; and how does it contrast with the pattern of the Hopi family or some other families?" Then you're asking academic questions about the comparative nature of family systems. If you wish, you can also ask practical questions such as "What are the relationships of differences of family systems to economic systems, or political systems?" As you can see, it isn't that you don't need categories—your categories are systemic categories rather than trait or item categories.

Dr. McMahon: Could you compare that to selecting a school in a particular area and using that for your sample?

Dr. Kimball: That's correct.

Moderator: Were you suggesting that perhaps this analysis would be a team analysis rather than an analysis by an individual?

Dr. Kimball: Oh, yes, it could be, but it depends upon what you are looking for. You could bring into this type of analysis people from a variety of disciplines who would ask questions other than the ones you're asking. It depends on the problem. A major problem in Appalachia might be the man-land relationship.

Moderator: What about your idea of magnitude, or sample size, which you brought up in connection with your discussion?

Dr. Kimball: I think numbers have a tremendous contribution to make in the analysis of educational problems because, you see, it's not alone the number of persons and the characteristics of those persons in terms of age, sex, occupational characteristics, and so forth, but it is also the level of schooling which these kinds of people have; it is also the relation of this kind of schooling to the economic pattern, so that demography is certainly important.

Dr. Ferree: Demography is the discipline or area of knowledge or body of knowledge that you bring to bear on what large class of problems? I'm following your suggestion that the kind of knowledge depends upon the problem. Man-land relationship is a problematic area. Are you saying that, from your point of view, demography is relevant to that particular problem?

Dr. Kimball: Population is relevant to this problem. Demography is the process of the study of population.

Dr. Ferree: So at this point you're bringing demography to bear on the man-land relationship problem.

Dr. Kimball: Yes, and the education problem.

Dr. Ferree: Your approach to the problem is different, dramatically different in some ways, from Ryans' classification of teacher behaviors, but what you're doing now is listing a set of problems toward which knowledge pertinent to education can be oriented. Using your method instead of Ryans', and beginning with something like the problem of man-land relationship, what are some of the others that might follow in the same system of discussion?

Dr. Kimball: Well, I think they are not too numerous. There would be the relation between man and his physical environment; it would be concerned with the nature of the technical processes which man utilizes in exploiting his physical environment; it would be concerned with population, in relationship to the level of the technology to provide the livelihood for a people and, of course, migratory characteristics are a part of demography; it would include the nature of the traditional social institutions within this area.

Dr. McMahon: Perhaps including the set of values?

Dr. Kimball: I would include the set of values which I would call the cultural behavior and beliefs related to that behavior.

Dr. Ferree: I think all these terms you are using are very important and very pertinent and appropriate. I wonder whether it's not stretching the use of the term "problem" a little bit to call these problems; these are areas of inquiry that are pertinent to education.

Dr. Kimball: I'm working from a position which says that if you are going to engage in educational development, which means assessment of the educational situation and of the educational needs of a population, then you must also know the other facets to the problem and of the relationships among them.

Dr. Ferree: Then you're talking about the activity as a task of educational development, essentially, and the knowledge relevant to a specific geographic location.

Dr. Kimball: In terms of Ryans' five classes, the nature of the behavior of the teacher within the classroom in Appalachia would be of a different kind than that which would be found in another part of this country or in another country.

Dr. Ferree: Yes, and this is the point that Dr. Cottrell makes very well in his paper, namely, that it's very dangerous to suppose that there's some one single body of knowledge that all teacher education institutions should be offering all the time. It depends upon the student body and the sorts of problems that they may reasonably be expected to encounter as they go forth. I believe that's your point essentially.

Dr. Kimball: Yes.

Dr. Albee: Are we moving in the direction of more specialization here? I hope not. I think, to take social work as a comparable profession, there has been a tremendous drive in the past fifteen or twenty years to make social training more generic so that the social worker completing two years of post-baccalaureate study is indeed prepared to work in a slum area or in an upper-middle-class agency or in a public agency. The attempt is made to prepare the social worker, with supervision, to begin to work in almost any social work setting.

Dr. Ferree: I certainly didn't intend to advocate a moving into some kind of hyperspecialization.

Dr. Cottrell: I think we need to remember that we could make this problem very difficult by breaking the body of knowledge into so many fragments that we would then have to spend much time putting these fragments back together again. We could tease out all the areas and have a beautiful fan like a peacock's tail before we got through; then we'd have to take a brush and make major color areas in the picture. We'd have to focus it and organize it for a purpose.

Dr. McMahon: But isn't that what we're suggesting should be done? Not at this meeting, but by a high-level group who can attack this thing and then organize it for practical use. I think there is a definite need—there must be something like this.

Dr. Ferree: This may be one way to attack it, with some high-level scholars in national conferences or committees.

Dr. McMahon: I'm thinking not only of high-level conferences of scholars. I'm thinking of trying to find some people, and these are rare people, who will work on this kind of project without any commitment to anybody. They don't work on it because they know down here somebody is going to train a teacher to go into the classroom, but they work on it because they are interested in assembling this knowledge which appears to have relevance for education. Then people like us could come in and say, "Well, now, how can we use this and for what purpose?"

Moderator: Since this is the conclusion of the colloquy, are there any general statements of agreement or disagreement that you would like to make at this time?

Dr. McMahon: I think we can say that there is a body of knowledge unique to the profession of education.

Dr. Ferree: I think that there is evidence that the members of this group believe that there is a defensible conception of a body of knowledge unique to the profession of education, but we have treated that body of knowledge as one that does make use of some statements from a variety of other bodies of knowledge. I think we concur on that.

Dr. Cottrell: The only really substantive difference that I've heard mentioned between a body of knowledge for education and a body of knowledge for any other subject is that perhaps the body of knowledge in education is considerably more complex than that for other human or social processes or functions. That doesn't, it seems to me, make it substantively different in its method of derivation, in its range of sources, or in what can be done with it. I'd like to see us point out parallels between the evolution of our knowledge about education and the evolution of knowledge about the physical sciences or the social sciences or any other recognized field of academic inquiry. I think we could go at our work with no apology for pursuing it, in exactly the same way any other group of intellectuals pursues its work.

Dr. Ferree: I can wholeheartedly concur with you. At the same time, may I stress that, from my point of view, the statements in the body of knowledge unique to the profession of education must be uniquely formulated and ordered so that their relevance to the concerns of education is clear.

Dr. McMahon: This matter of concern may really be the key to the body of knowledge of every discipline. It's the kinds of questions with which that discipline is concerned which make it a subject for investigation.

Dr. Kimball: I have one question. Is the body of knowledge of a kind that is primarily concerned with realizing academic purposes, or is it also concerned with the purpose of improving the process of education?

Dr. Cottrell: I think it's both, Dr. Kimball. I believe that a good case has been made for the assertion that the field of education is a field of knowledge. It can be treated as such and, like the field of biology, for example, it can be pursued for quite a number of purposes. You may pursue the field of education simply to find out about it. Or you may pursue the field of education with the view to using that knowledge to influence professionally the education process.

Dr. Ferree: And it's precisely for this reason that I submit that there may very well be more than one logic of organization.

Dr. Kimball: Well, then, this would mean that the body of knowledge has two purposes, or two aspects: one in and for itself, and one in its relationship to the profession of education.

Moderator: In the profession of education can we separate them, or do we have to consider both aspects?

Dr. Cottrell: If the pursuit of the practice of the profession of education does not in and of itself lead us to examine the phenomena of education in their fullest depths, then we would be wise, I think, to adjure ourselves to do so.

Dr. McMahon: One can study the role of organized education in the formation of American society or the role of society in the formation of schools without having any motive to explain how we learn, for example. The two could be entirely unrelated and actually immaterial in such a study.

Dr. Cottrell: I think all of us have contributed to the development of the thought that anything we know about education in a culture is a function of what we know about that culture. We have not neglected in this discussion to observe that the culture setting provides a backdrop that is the ground on which the figure is to be found.

Dr. Ferree: I certainly can agree that education may fruitfully be regarded as the transmission of culture.

Dr. Kimball: But I would add to that that there is also a psychological dimension that is culturally related. You can make studies of cultural behavior without examining the psychological characteristics of the people who are behaving in this way. You can examine human behavior in terms of certain foci, one of which would be cultural, one psychological, and one biological.

Dr. Albee: There are psychological principles that occur universally. And while these may operate in different ways in different cultures, still they transcend cultural contexts in which they occur—the principle of reinforcement, for example. Those things which are rewarding may differ from one culture to another. It may be a piece of candy in one culture and it may be something else in a different culture, but the psychological principle of reinforcement is universal and, therefore, applies to all efforts to change behavior.

Dr. Cottrell: We have all relied very heavily, in our discussion of the phenomena of education, upon the necessity for historical understanding. In other words, we have treated the phenomena of education as occurring through time rather than as instantaneously recordable phenomena. Educational processes are understandable only as we see them in a dynamic condition of change and development.

Dr. Ferree: We seem to agree that there is a defensible notion of a body of knowledge unique to the profession of education. I take the position that, at least comparatively speaking, our body of knowledge is somewhat limited. I wonder how my fellow members of the colloquy feel on that point.

Dr. Cottrell: I'm afraid that I would have to agree that what you say is true. In one sense of the word I consider it extremely limited. But yet, isn't it miraculous how much we've learned about education?

Dr. Kimball: If you are saying the body of knowledge that has specific relevance to the process of education, I would also agree with you.

Dr. Ferree: I have, in my own treatment of the body of knowledge unique to the profession of education, stressed the importance of establishing the relevance of the knowledge to the educational context, and if one approaches it that way, I suppose you'd agree.

Dr. McMahon: But it's limited because we haven't really explored related disciplines sufficiently to see what does exist.

Dr. Ferree: Yes, which is a way of saying, I suppose, that we agree that there's a vast resource of knowledge that is out there ready to be tapped and that it's time for the "Diaspora in reverse."

Moderator: Do we see any other areas of agreement?

Dr. Ferree: There seems to be some agreement here on the view that there are several different ways to organize the body of knowledge. I don't find anyone who is pushing for just one and only one logic or organization.

Dr. Albee: We have just agreed to the statement that the body of knowledge is relatively limited, but from our earlier discussion when we contemplated the enormous task of codifying or organizing what is known around a particular logical structure, it seemed to be an overwhelming task. I can't quite reconcile these two points of view.

Dr. Ferree: I can, because I can envision that much of the knowledge out there is not yet formulated so that its relevance is clear; in that sense, it's not yet within the body of knowledge unique to the profession of education. There's an enormous resource out there that can be brought to bear on educational problems; it presumably has not been brought to bear in a manner which makes its relevance to an educational context very explicit.

Dr. Albee: I really can't speak for other disciplines, but for psychology it seems to me that there is a tremendous amount of fairly well-organized knowledge that is available and is being used extensively.

Dr. Ferree: Are you saying that the relevance of psychological knowledge to educational context has been made quite explicit so that it is useful to prospective teachers?

Dr. Albee: I'll have to ask the people from education, but I think there is considerable knowledge about the psychology of learning, and of individual differences, of maturation and growth, which is relevant to education. In one sense a considerable body of significant knowledge about psychological aspects of education is available, but it's still true that there is much more to know.

Dr. Ferree: I would hasten to say that many of the observations we're making about psychology could be made equally well about sociology, anthropology, or philosophy.

Moderator: Are there other areas of agreement, or are there some areas of disagreement on which we wish to focus?

Dr. Cottrell: I think we have an agreement in the relationship which we have endorsed between the field of knowledge called "education" and all of the other disciplines that contribute to the general and liberal education of the prospective professional person. We have said, all of us, that we must not isolate the process called "education" and suppose that it's unrelated to the rest of the cultivation of the person if we are going to have a sound concept of the professional.

Moderator: Any other observations, positive or negative? Do you mean to say that the impossible has happened here, that we have arrived at the end of the colloquy without disagreements?

Dr. Ferree: I think some of us have puzzlements, but not disagreements.

Dr. Kimball: I would like to make one general comment about the relation of Pi Lambda Theta to the colloquy. In the nature of the American society we have on the one hand the great operating institutions of education, business, and the like; we have associated with this form of organization voluntary associations, of which this is one example. In the way in which our society operates, we frequently go to voluntary associations and ask them to examine some problem related to the functioning of our institutional life. The Flexner report is an example of this. The Gardner report on international education, upon the relation of AID to the American university, is another example. So this device in our society is a common one. In the same sense, you are operating within a traditional and a completely legitimate range of activities, which is to bring to bear upon the enterprise of education your own direct interest to it as a voluntary association related to this enterprise.

Moderator: Since we must close, I want to take this opportunity, for myself as well as for Pi Lambda Theta, to thank all members of the panel for the excellent work they have done on the papers and for their contributions here. We all regard this topic as a very worthy one which we hope will have benefit far beyond this particular meeting.

Dr. Hayden and Dr. Albee review the discussions and ponder the dynamic implications.

III
IMPLICATIONS OF THE COLLOQUY

Implications of the Colloquy

THE CATENA on the topic "The Body of Knowledge Unique to the Profession of Education" was conceived as a way of simultaneously making a contribution to the profession of education and serving the membership of Pi Lambda Theta. A professional education association has a responsibility to attack problems and issues in its own field. Pi Lambda Theta is an organization whose base is scholarship and whose contribution in the last fifty years has been in providing professional leadership as a direct outgrowth of intellectual competence.

The responsibilities of leadership require the organization, and the people in it, to carefully investigate issues which seem to demand unbiased assessment. Once the assessment has been made, having used the tools of the researcher and the scholar, *action* is in order. Then, the daring aspects of deciding to attack the problem in the first place take on new dimensions. The members of Pi Lambda Theta, with the leadership of the National Board, must be willing to identify their concerns and to suggest a plan of action.

The idea of the Catena—to identify and then pursue a topic of major import in the profession of education through discussion, preparation of scholarly papers, and a "conversation of scholars"—is not in itself new. To ask scholars to carefully examine a topic will always be a time-consuming, expensive, yet entirely worthwhile undertaking. The responsibilities which accompany an idea of this sort are many. The questions which have been raised often—what responsibilities? why? by whom?—will continue to require cogitation. The answers to such questions are never simple, but there must be answers. Intellectual curiosity, research, and the development of new ways to look at things mean essentially that the findings, the results, the outcomes must be shared with the members of the profession, regardless of whether these outcomes delight and enhance the view of the sponsor of such activity or whether they dig away at the very heart of the sponsor's thesis.

The first important task is to share the information. The second equally important task is to suggest ways in which the membership of the sponsoring organization might profit from the pursuit, either individually or collectively. The third task, and without question, the one requiring the most strength and commitment, is the responsibility of identifying for one's professional colleagues the implications of such a pursuit as clearly and as thoughtfully as possible. The purpose of such identification is, quite properly, to establish the sponsor's eye-view of the outcomes, but it is also to suggest further development of the topic or a course of action which will permit full use of the new information. To this end, and with full knowledge of the responsibilities involved, members of the National Board of Pi Lambda Theta met in October, 1965, to examine the transcription of the colloquy meetings, to reflect on the colloquy itself which they attended as silent participants, and to direct their best thinking toward identifying the implications. The results of this meeting were left with the writer to analyze, reconsider, recast, or reorder.

The first important task, then, is to share the information. Pi Lambda Theta has done this with the publication of this book. Papers, colloquy proceedings, and the implications appear in one book for members of the profession to read and think about. But simply publishing a book is not sufficient. Every effort must be made to bring the results of the study to others who may not come upon a copy of the book or who may not have available the time which is required to read it.

That there is a body of knowledge unique to the profession of education has been established in the papers and the colloquy. That this body of knowledge is drawn and derived from a number of disciplines has been documented in the presentations of the scholars who examined the topic. The dynamic and changing quality of the body of knowledge unique to the profession of education will continue to be the strength of the education profession. As knowledge grows, so will the body of knowledge of the profession of education, because of its dependence upon other expanding disciplines. Educators and researchers must constantly examine the related disciplines for evidence of those pieces of information which have particular relevance to the profession of education.

What does all this mean for the teacher? for the researcher? for the college of education? for Pi Lambda Theta? What must a teacher know? The colloquy identified motivation, maturation, individual differences, learning theory, measurement, and transmission of culture

IMPLICATIONS OF THE COLLOQUY

as areas in which a teacher must have to function properly. In addition, the colloquy raised a number of fundamental questions. What do teachers know about the transmission of culture? What knowledge do they have about the manner in which the culture is transmitted and by whom? Do they recognize the power—and danger—of the mass media as educational tools? Do they realize how important it is for teachers to be competent in analyzing propaganda, to be skillful in using the mass media? Do they recognize their role as powerful communicators in the classroom—and is that enough? How much do teachers know—how much should they know—about the sociology of the community in which they teach? Are they willing to assume the responsibility of assessing the community and of combining their best thinking with that of those in the community similarly interested in the transmission of culture to produce a program of education for the youth of that community which will substantially alter, direct, or control their society's development? Should they do this? Dare they do this?

Does the teacher recognize his role as a diagnostician—as a selector of appropriate activities to further develop the knowledge and experience of the student in the light of his diagnosis? Does he recognize his role as a model, as a guide, as an agitator, as an insurgent? How shall he ever know enough to do even a smidgeon of the task assigned to him? How shall he be comfortable with the realization that his role is not to impart series of facts, bundles of historical information, barrels of grammatical rules, but rather to work with his colleagues to design a set of principles which seem to have lasting value and which, presented with the proper illustrations and experiences, may make a contribution toward developing a student who is a thoughtful and informed person capable of independent action? Does the classroom teacher realize that he is a formulator and tester of hypotheses? that he can add to and test the truth of the body of knowledge appropriate to the profession of education? that he, as the classroom teacher, is the final tester of the effectiveness of educational theory and method in the classroom? He is the one who finds out whether and how the theory works. He can be a most likely and valued source of fruitful suggestions for experimental research. How can a teacher acquire this information, or keep up with the continuous flow of information?

For the practicing and experienced teacher whose life is filled to overflowing with responsibility, detail, organization, background reading, and preparation for five and six classes per day, the time available for an in-depth study of the questions raised above simply does not exist. It is, therefore, important for the professional associations, local teachers' organizations, state teachers' associations, and chapters of Pi Lambda Theta to offer the leadership in arranging stimulating conferences at which some of the topics may be pursued with the aid and guidance of sociologists, anthropologists, philosophers, psychologists, historians, and educators.

A comprehensive program of in-service education to consider selected educational problems from the points of view of psychology, sociology, and other related disciplines would be fruitful, but to attempt a full-scale program during the school year is probably impractical. Teachers simply do not have that kind of time, however important the topic may be. Moreover, to merely bring information to anyone is seldom enough. True, the more interested and enthusiastic, and the philosophically oriented, may think a bit—even discuss among themselves some of the statements made, the implications, and the possible long-range effects—but there will be many who, because of many other thoughts competing for their share of the "thinking" time, will not have time to do much more than agree that the topics probably need further discussion. If this is the case, and it may well be, it is unlikely that any significant increase will be made in the teacher's knowledge of and interest in the body of knowledge unique to the profession of education.

The problem is, therefore: How are these statements from supporting disciplines to be made a part of the teacher's background information? How can these suggestions as to what ought to constitute the body of knowledge for educators have some meaning for those educators whose training and experience have not always provided an opportunity to know and to use information of this type? Shall we wait for those teachers who have had a collegiate experience in which these statements from supporting disciplines have been an essential part before we expect educators to base their daily performance and operation on the body of knowledge unique to the profession of education? Shall we wait until those who may have been exposed to a much richer and more extensive pursuit of the body of knowledge appear in the teaching ranks? Certainly not!

School administrators must find a way to bring these statements

IMPLICATIONS OF THE COLLOQUY

from supporting disciplines to their staffs *now*—a way to encourage further examination of other disciplines, a way to identify yet other statements with particular relevance to education—a way to help professional personnel recast their perspective of their own role in the light of the body of knowledge of their profession. The discussion of the information must be accorded the same support and professional prestige that accompany specialized meetings on linguistics, team teaching, merit salary, and similar popular topics which seem to demand the teacher's attention.

Perhaps, since the task is one of communication, and because it is a necessary and very important task, and a mammoth one, a similarly powerful tool of communication might be used to make this information available to a large number of teachers efficiently and quickly. The use of television could assist teachers to more quickly and surely make new information an integral part of their thinking and ultimately their behavior. Summer institutes, sponsored by universities whose staffs are committed to the exciting yet delicate role of making a three- or six-week period a stimulating professional experience for in-service teachers, ought to be encouraged. Certainly, the basic aspects of the colloquy—if not the entire information of the colloquy—could quite appropriately constitute part of the content of institutes in history, economics, reading, English, and disadvantaged youth already sponsored by the United States Office of Education.

Special short-term summer institutes ought to be sponsored by several school systems who can combine their resources and bring knowledgeable specialists in the various disciplines to their teachers. Week-long colloquies on selected educational problems, in which recent findings from such areas as learning theory, motivation, maturation, and measurement are studied, might well encourage some teachers to provide the nexus between theory and practice and to share their new skill and sensitivity with their colleagues in the ensuing year.

Professional associations in cooperation with textbook publishers might well explore the possibility of special two- and three-day sessions to which selected teachers could be invited for the purpose of examining the body of knowledge unique to the profession of education, and establishing guidelines for making this information available to others.

The most important implication for educators may well be that as individuals each might become familiar with the content of the colloquy and the position papers, each might examine the characteristics of a profession, and, finally, each might examine his own philosophy of education. Does it allow him to evaluate his performance? Is what he does in concert with his philosophy?

And what do the colloquy proceedings mean for teacher education? Several courses of action seem to be evident. Teachers of teachers could begin by examining their course offerings and the textbooks they select to ascertain whether adequate treatment is given to the components of the body of knowledge unique to the profession of education as presented in this book.

Faculty in education departments might well explore the hypotheses and conclusions in this book with their colleagues in other departments. Experimentation with course content—with a multidisciplined team approach to at least one course—might result. The content of the book ought to be brought also to the attention of deans and chairmen of departments of education. Perhaps members of the science, mathematics, political science, economics, and communication departments would consider engaging in a local colloquy to seek out "confirmed statements" in their fields of study which have immediate relevance to education.

It may be possible for education faculty members and other interested colleagues to join in regional groups to pursue the results of the colloquy. If this is not possible, it might be fruitful to encourage students to do so. But best of all—faculty members *and* students representing three or four institutions within a particular geographic area might meet regularly to conduct their own colloquies.

Students could be requested to examine this book and to use their creative powers to design at least a theoretical model of a sequence in teacher preparation which might embody those areas identified as pertinent to and part of the body of knowledge for education. Clear thinking, imagination, and freedom from limitations of experience are necessary to develop such a sequence. Prospective teachers and graduate students would find this a stimulating and scholarly enterprise.

Though some may think that the time may be long overdue for adjustments in teacher education programs, it must be remembered that sizeable funded projects are providing selected universities throughout the country with some opportunities for experimentation. The

IMPLICATIONS OF THE COLLOQUY

results of these studies will bring about change. Another source of change will be research leading to the development of statements in the body of knowledge of education formulated and ordered so that their relevance to education is clear. It is dangerous to suppose that there is or ever will be one single body of knowledge which should be offered in every teacher education institution. The problems the student is likely to encounter should provide guidelines for selecting the knowledge which should be most useful for a beginning teacher.

The third responsibility, that of identifying the sponsor's eye-view of the entire Catena project, is, of course, the one that requires the strongest commitment.

The National Board of Pi Lambda Theta has identified a sequence of events which should now occur.

1. Immediate plans should be made to arrange another colloquy on this topic with representation from those disciplines which were not represented in the first colloquy, so that the same scholarly treatment may be given to consideration of those statements having particular and unique relevance to education.

2. While the other disciplines are being examined, Pi Lambda Theta could assume the task of initiating a major project to gather in one place all confirmed statements (scattered throughout the literature of the parent disciplines) which have unique relevance to education. The "body of knowledge" can be formulated and ordered only by those scholars who have had sufficient background in education to perceive the relevance of the confirmed statements to problems in education as precisely as possible. The task is mammoth. Outside funding to support the task must be sought.

The gathering of confirmed statements in one place in itself could not determine the content of courses for teachers. The next step would be to select and order these statements to serve specific purposes. For example, the organization of statements for beginning students may be, quite appropriately, very much different from the organization of statements for advanced graduate students or teachers in service. But suggestions for course content and sequence and intensity must wait for the basic study to be completed. Before the study is begun, basic questions must be answered, such as:

What plan of organization is appropriate to the body of knowledge unique to the profession of education?

Should the *parent disciplines approach* be used? This approach would use the logic and organization of the parent disciplines for the ordering of statements derived from them.

Should the *behaviors and activities approach* be used which would draw from diverse sources and organize the statements around the activities or behaviors in which professional educators characteristically and recurrently engage?

Or should the *outcomes approach* be used which would organize statements around a given goal of the educational enterprise?

The decision must be made as to which mode of organization of the statements in the body of knowledge unique to the profession of education is most defensible for the purpose of programs in teacher education for undergraduate students, for graduate students, and for inservice teachers.

Any set of statements from the related disciplines selected as relevant to education must, regardless of the care and skill with which they are selected, be reexamined and reevaluated periodically by scholars in their respective disciplines and by educational researchers and practitioners as well. The age of perpetual discovery and change in which we find ourselves suggests that statements acceptable today may be disproved tomorrow.

If the body of knowledge unique to the profession of education is to be complete, reliable, and timely, there must be both immediate and permanent cooperation between the scholars in the related disciplines and researchers and practitioners in education. Each group has much to contribute to the other. A proper "meeting of the minds" can be achieved only if there is mutual concern for the body of knowledge unique to the profession of education and real appreciation of the contributions that can be made to its selection, organization, and utilization by the two groups.

Some formal organization is necessary to promote this meeting of the minds. Pi Lambda Theta should accept this responsibility and begin to arrange the steps in such a task.

Once the statements of the related disciplines to education have been reexamined, reevaluated, and, if necessary, reformulated, a thorough examination of the array of education courses can be undertaken by schools of education. The content of each course and of textbooks and other instructional materials can be examined. Less strategic courses which overlap more strategic courses should be dropped; the courses retained should be taught in depth that will allow the fullest treatment of pertinent statements from the past and from the present; and textbook authors should concentrate on statements which have been confirmed or are highly probable.

Professors who teach such courses as educational philosophy, educational psychology, educational sociology, and so forth, should have had thorough training in the parent disciplines. Scholars from the related disciplines might also be influenced to take staff assignments in schools of education.

Professors of education might be encouraged to undertake postdoctoral study in the related disciplines. Similarly, scholars in the related disciplines might be encouraged to do postdoctoral work in the field of education. Postdoctoral fellowships should be made available in increasingly large numbers, and more grants should be provided for cooperative research by educators and scholars on problems of significance educationally.

And finally special attention should be given to the kind and quality of practice teaching experience offered by schools of education. Student teachers ought to be assigned only to school situations in which daily supervision by master teachers thoroughly acquainted with the body of knowledge unique to the profession of education and sympathetic to new theories and developing concepts can be assured.

Never has education so basked in the spotlight of public concern and daily publicity. Concerted efforts should be made by all members of the profession of education to acquaint the public with the background of knowledge and the variety of techniques necessary for effective teaching today. There is no better way to increase the prestige of the profession than to let the public know what good teaching really requires in the way of knowledge and experience.

As the prestige of the profession and of its members increases, efforts of government and lay groups to concern themselves with the determination of educational policy and practice should decrease.

That the profession of education does indeed have a body of knowledge unique to its own practice has been established by this colloquy. That the body of knowledge is interdisciplinary has been agreed upon by the participants. The body of knowledge exists, it draws upon other disciplines for knowledge that is to be uniquely applied, and it is dynamic. It is clear that the implications of the colloquy are as challenging as the basic discussion of the topic itself. As a professional organization in education concerned with evaluation and improvement of the profession, Pi Lambda Theta should accept the responsibility of furthering these implications with the ultimate goal of improved instruction for children and teachers alike.

M. VIRGINIA BIGGY
Pi Lambda Theta Consultant

The final chapter in this volume, presenting the implications of the colloquy as seen by the National Board of Pi Lambda Theta, has been written by M. Virginia Biggy, during whose term as national President the colloquy was held.

PI LAMBDA THETA NATIONAL BOARD*
1963-64

President	M. VIRGINIA BIGGY
First Vice-President	MARY I. ELWOOD
Vice-President	GEORGIA SACHS ADAMS
Vice-President	MARION RHODES BROWN
Vice-President	LUCILE U. HOLLIS
Vice-President	LOUISE P. OWEN
Treasurer	JANE M. HILL
Editor	MIRIAM M. BRYAN
Consultant	SYLVIA VOPNI

1964-65

President	M. VIRGINIA BIGGY
First Vice-President	MARY I. ELWOOD
Vice-President	GEORGIA SACHS ADAMS
Vice-President	MARION RHODES BROWN
Vice-President	LUCILE U. HOLLIS
Vice-President	LOUISE P. OWEN
Treasurer	JESSIE L. MCGLON
Consultant	MIRIAM M. BRYAN
Consultant	SYLVIA VOPNI

1965-66

President	MIRIAM M. BRYAN
First Vice-President	MARY I. ELWOOD
Vice-President	GEORGIA SACHS ADAMS
Vice-President	LOUISE BELTRAMO
Vice-President	MARION RHODES BROWN
Vice-President	LOUISE P. OWEN
Treasurer	JESSIE L. MCGLON
Consultant	M. VIRGINIA BIGGY

* Board members are elected for two-year terms and are not permitted to succeed themselves in the same office more than once. Thus, some have been members of the Board for the continuous period during which the various steps of the Catena have been developed, and others have been members for a portion of that period.

Pi Lambda Theta National Office

Executive Director ....JANE M. HILL
Editor ....WILMA A. BAILEY

Suite 404, 815 Seventeenth Street, N.W., Washington, D.C. 20006